GERSHOM BULKELEY

Zealot for Truth

The conscience of Colonial
Connecticut

RICHARD G. TOMLINSON

CONTENTS

Gershom Bulkeley, Zealot for Truth

PREFACE

The December wind gusted from the north down the frozen river sweeping a thin blanket of snow off the ice and plastering it onto the side of the darkened, wooden house on the west bank. It rattled the shutters and ran away into the gloomy woods. Inside the house a frail man sat in his study lit by a single candle. He bent over the manuscript on the desk before him. The room around him was unadorned and featured a row of tall, locked cabinets which only he could open. Inside the cabinets rested his precious books written in English, Latin, Greek and Dutch. The silence of the room was broken only by the ticking of a grandfather clock in the hall, an occasional rattle of the shutters and the scratching of his pen. He wrote steadily pausing only to dip his pen in the inkwell. He was angry, and his anger increased as he wrote. He worked furiously in a white-hot passion over the long document that would make him the most hated and feared man in the Colony of Connecticut.

The Reverend, Dr. Gershom Bulkeley's life had traced a long arc from birth as a member of the Puritan elite, to brilliant scholar at Harvard, to honored minister, to trusted advisor, to celebrated physician and now, to an isolated and embittered outcast; the enemy of his old friends and a threat to bring down the government of Connecticut. The major object of his scorn was his former friend, neighbor and war-time commander, Governor Robert Treat. Bulkeley had been a key member of Treat's three-man war council during the bloody King Philip's War. Bulkeley entitled his treatise, *Will and Doom, or the Miseries of Connecticut by*

5

and under an Usurped and Arbitrary Power. The intended audience for his document was no less than the court of the King and Queen of England, William and Mary. In his treatise, Bulkeley railed against a self-appointed, illegal government that deprived the citizens of Connecticut of their natural rights and freedoms as loyal subjects of the crown. He implored the king that their lives and property be protected from this arbitrary and dictatorial rule and that the citizens of Connecticut be restored to their rights as Englishmen and loyal subjects of the Crown.

There was reason to fear that Bulkeley's arguments would carry weight. He was no outside rebel. He had been in positions of trust and confidence, including an appointment as Justice of the Peace for Hartford county, which, although now in question, he believed still made him an officer of the Crown. He was more than willing to carry his complaints all the way to King William and Queen Mary. The validity of Connecticut's charter was far from certain. Bulkeley's criticisms were most untimely and unwelcome. He was a dangerous man. His pen might bring down the government.

This *Will and Doom* treatise was not Bulkeley's first objection to Connecticut's government, but it was the most vitriolic. Enraged that Connecticut's leadership scorned his advice and counsel, he labored on, heedless to the consequences to his reputation … and possibly even to his life.

I. INTRODUCTION

*[Gershom Bulkeley author of] one of the ablest of
colonial political tracts prior to the American Revolution*

~Samuel Eliot Morison

He was always a discontented and troublesome person

~John Gorham Palfrey

*He was ... Universally acknowledged ...to be a Person of
Great Penetration, and a sound Judgment...having served
his Country many years successively as Minister, a Judge
and a Physician with great Honour.*

~ Boston News Letter, December 1713

WHETHER IT WAS A QUESTION OF POLITICS, RELIGION,
SCIENCE, MEDICINE, ALCHEMY OR LAW, Gershom Bulkeley
always had an opinion and stated it often and strongly. He
expected his advice and his opinions to be respected and to
be followed. To those who accepted his views, he was a
sage and wise counselor. To those who did not, he was an
irritating, obnoxious scold and a potentially dangerous
person.

To the extent that Gershom has been remembered in
Connecticut history, it has been because of his political
views. Connecticut long based its right to govern itself on

a charter granted by King Charles II in 1662. In1686, King James II revoked that charter, along with those of Massachusetts and Rhode Island. He established the "Dominion of New England" with Sir Edmund Andros in charge. When James II was ousted in the "Glorious Revolution" of 1688, Andros was overthrown. Connecticut again took up the government again under the old charter. Bulkeley argued that this government would not be legal until it obtained a new royal endorsement.

A furious battle of words ensued, and Bulkeley hardened his position. He came to believe that the 1662 charter had never really provided a right to erect a government over all the people of Connecticut. Instead, he believed, it was only a charter to establish a corporation, like many others in England, and to make rules or laws that applied only to its members. In any case, he asserted, that no Englishman could be deprived of his rights as a subject of the crown, and that Connecticut was using its charter to do so illegally. Bulkeley's best-known tirade against Connecticut, *Will and Doom, or the Miseries of Connecticut by and under an Usurped and Arbitrary Power*[1], has been called "a minor masterpiece" by historian Perry Miller[2], and "one of the ablest of colonial political tracts prior to the American Revolution" by historian Samuel Eliot Morison.[3]

Although Connecticut's right to govern was ultimately accepted by the English crown, there was a period of uncertainty, resistance and fierce local opposition led by Bulkeley. Only a few men supported Bulkeley's position. There was a public clamor in support of "our charter government", and Bulkeley was vilified. There was a great pretense that the charter had never been surrendered, and that leaders had only sworn allegiance to the Andros government under duress. The outcry was particularly loud because Bulkeley's objections were uncomfortably well-founded. Even into the nineteenth century Connecticut historians still felt the need to dismiss Bulkeley and his views. J. Hammond Trumbull, the editor of *The Public Records of the Colony of Connecticut,* was critical of what he called Bulkeley's "high Tory loyalty" and "passive obedience to the crown". In 1854 Trumbull wrote that Bulkeley's "overweening self-importance, adherence to his own opinions…and the peculiarities of his political creed…kept him almost continuously at strife with his parish, his neighbors, or the government of the colony."[4] John Gorham Palfrey, who published the *History of New England* in 1870, said of Bulkeley; "He was always a discontented and troublesome person…"[5]

Prior to the bruising fight over "charter government" Gershom Bulkeley had led a life of nearly universal approbation and honor. He was the accomplished scholar, the respected minister, the wise arbitrator and the cherished medical doctor. His roots went deep in Connecticut, and the list of his accomplishments on behalf of the colony was long.[6] He was no "outsider" in Connecticut. He was born and reared as one of the Puritan elite, who settled and ruled New England. His father, Reverend Peter Bulkeley, was one of the principal founding ministers of New England, and spent his personal fortune to establish the town of Concord, Massachusetts.[7] Gershom was sent to Harvard and was awarded two degrees, a Bachelor's degree in 1655

and a Masters in 1658. After graduation, he stayed at
Harvard as a tutor. In 1659, he married Sarah Chauncy, the
daughter of Charles Chauncy, the president of Harvard.[8]
Economic necessity caused Gershom to leave the academic
life at Harvard for which he was so well suited and take up
his service as a trained minister. He first served the church
in New London, Connecticut and then the church in
Wethersfield, Connecticut before he retired from the
ministry.

Like his father, Peter, who had nurtured the little town of
Concord, Massachusetts, Bulkeley took his duties as
minister to include being pastor to the whole community,
not just the members of his church. He did not support the
restriction of church membership to a small group of elites
but favored the extension of full church membership to any
citizen of good conduct. Deeply concerned about a
growing rift within their churches, Connecticut's leaders
convened a group of ministers, led by Bulkeley, to address
these divisive church issues. Bulkeley's group forged a
compromise between warring factions. This brought some
peace to the Connecticut churches in which both the
traditional Congregational "way" and the more liberal
Presbyterian practices were both acknowledged as
acceptable.[9]

In Wethersfield, Gershom assumed responsibility for both
the spiritual and economic welfare of the entire town. He
built and operated an economically important grist mill.[10]
By grinding the corn into meal, he enabled local farmers to
ship it to distant markets, even as distant as Boston. He
helped procure seeds for the farmers and experimented with

processes to speed germination. He studied agriculture and advocated the use of clover and the rotation of crops to renew worn out fields.

Bulkeley was a friend of Connecticut's famed governor, John Winthrop Jr., and a member of his informal network of alchemists.[11] It was to Bulkeley that Winthrop turned for help to prevent the execution of a woman convicted of witchcraft. In 1669 Catherine Harrison of Wethersfield, was tried and found guilty by a jury.[12] Governor Winthrop, reluctant to pronounce the expected sentence of death, enlisted Bulkeley's help. At Winthrop's request, Bulkeley presided over a group of ministers who reviewed the evidence. They found that the evidence was insufficient for conviction. The opinion issued by Bulkeley's group allowed Winthrop not only to overturn the conviction, but also to pardon and release Catherine. With this ruling, a precedent was set that narrowed the allowable evidence to the point that later convictions for witchcraft were nearly impossible.[13]

In 1676, the Narragansett Sachem known to the colonists as King Philip, mounted a nearly successful attempt to unite the various tribes and drive the white men out of New England. Gershom may have had some medical education, because he served as the surgeon to Connecticut's army during the King Philip's War. During that war, he was also the trusted advisor to Colonel Robert Treat, (later Governor Treat) the commander in chief of Connecticut's army, and he was a member of Treat's three-man War Council.[14]

At the opening of the war, Sir Edmund Andros, representing the New York interests of the Duke of York (later King James II), tried to lay claim to the western half of Connecticut, all the way from New York to the Connecticut River, under the guise of protecting Connecticut from Indian attacks. It was Bulkeley who was called on to represent Connecticut's interests in a face-to-face confrontation with Andros and to rebuff the Duke's claim.[15]

During King Philip's War, the combined armies of the United Colonies of New England made a daring, winter attack on a fortified camp of the Narragansett tribe in a frozen swamp in Rhode Island. The attack succeeded, but the Connecticut troops were shattered, with four of its five captains killed in the first assault. It was Bulkeley who administered to the badly mauled Connecticut soldiers. He tended the dying and wounded all through an arduous, night-long, march to safety as the withdrawing army wandered, lost in a heavy snowstorm.[16] Afterward Gershom resigned his post as minister at Wethersfield and devoted himself to medicine. But, he continued to care for the wounded soldiers long after the war had ended.

When Connecticut's charter was revoked by King James II, and the government was placed under the control of Sir Edmund Andros. Bulkeley, despite his earlier confrontation with Andros, accepted a position in the Andros government. He was appointed as one of the justices of the peace to administer the law in Hartford County.[17] Gershom had a keen sense of the law, and made a detailed study of and wrote a treatise about the traditional role of the justice of the peace in England. Connecticut had not previously adopted the office of justice of the peace, which was common in England.

Gershom had a sense of "the right order of things". For him, legal authority flowed from God to the King, to the courts and institutions of government.[18] When the King was driven from the throne of England, the Andros government in New England fell. Bulkeley first tried to convince Connecticut's leadership that it must obtain a new royal mandate to govern. When that failed, Bulkeley became the leading critic and enemy of Connecticut's newly self-established government. He agitated against it, even to the extent of petitioning the crown not to recognize it. In his opposition, he wrote his most famous treatise, *Will and Doom.* For Governor Robert Treat and Connecticut's leadership, Bulkeley's opposition could not have been more ill-timed as they struggled to get recognition of the legitimacy of their government.

In all his political activities Bulkeley saw himself as the spokesman for the rule of law and the rights of the common people. In his opposition to Connecticut's government, he began with objections to the renewal of charter, which had been revoked. His counsel to Connecticut leaders was to wait until a new royal charter was granted. When his advice was ignored, he became increasingly irate, with his objections to Connecticut's government growing more heated. He finally reached the conclusion that Connecticut, from its founding, had never had the right to govern the people at large. He was incensed by what he saw as an intrusion by a self-appointed government of elites into the natural rights of the people as subjects of England. He became convinced that Connecticut's government was fraudulent, raging against what he saw as the oppression of the common people. However, when the English crown finally seemed to accept the *de facto* reality of Connecticut's acting government, Gershom gave up the fight and withdrew from politics, devoting himself to medicine and science. Others, however, would continue to attempt to use *Will and Doom* to attack Connecticut's government for decades.

Because of his fight against charter government, Gershom found himself and his opinions scorned by most of the people of Connecticut. Only a minority resisted the assumed charter government and refused to pay their taxes. The majority stridently proclaimed their support for "charter government" and denounced any, like Bulkeley, who resisted or defamed it.

However, with the passage of time the furor died down and Gershom would eventually be restored to his place as respected counselor. For example, when a group of Connecticut's leaders sought to found a college in Connecticut, equivalent to Harvard, they now sought Gershom's advice on the project.[19] Not surprisingly, he told them they could not do it without first obtaining a royal charter from England. His advice was not heeded, but, at least, it was sought. The college was established and would become Yale University.

Bulkeley's help was sometimes solicited in controversies
involving important criminal cases, as well as religious
disputes. But he was always ready to deliver his opinion,
whether it was solicited or not. He incurred the wrath of the
authorities by arguing that it was not incestuous for a man
to marry the sister of his deceased wife.[20] He argued
against the death penalty in the case of Mercy (Tuttle)
Brown, a "distracted woman," who killed her son with an
axe.[21] He came to the defense of Abigail Thompson, who,
during a domestic fight, gave her husband a wound that
eventually proved fatal.[22] When Mercy Disborough, the
last woman convicted of witchcraft in Connecticut, was
reprieved, Bulkeley supported the reprieve. He defended
her against a later attempt to bring capital charges against
her for infanticide. Mercy had been a servant in Bulkeley's
household when he was the minister in New London. The
charge was that she moved to Wethersfield with Bulkeley,
and there had a baby out of wedlock and murdered it. The
strong implication was that Bulkeley was the father.
Bulkeley rebutted the allegations with a letter which was a
masterpiece of humor and sarcasm directed at the accuser.[23]

Bulkeley created a large library of books, primarily in
English and Latin.[24] The fraction of his library that
survives reveals him as an intellectual, a chemist, alchemist
and scientist. He read and made annotated copies of
important books that he did not own. He embraced the
teachings of alchemist physicians Paracelsus and Johannes
Baptist van Helmont, which firmly rejected the entrenched
medical theories of the Greek physician, Galen, which had
dominated western medicine for more than one thousand

years. He was a follower of contemporary authors, such as the German-Dutch chemist, Johann Rudolf Glauber, and England's leading scientist, Robert Boyle. His manuscripts and laboratory notes show his serious efforts to stay in contact with emerging scientific and medical progress both in England and elsewhere. In his well-equipped laboratory, he tested the medical recipes of others and worked to create new medical treatments of his own.[25]

LATE IN LIFE HE AUTHORED a medical treatise, *Vade Mecum*, comprising more than three hundred pages, which summarized his medical knowledge and presented a long list of medical preparations.[26] Many of these preparations were copied from the publications of English physicians, but were sprinkled with comments and critiques by Bulkeley. Some of his criticisms were biting. He not only refuted the ancient teaching of the long-honored Greek physician Galen but also rejected the medical appeal to astrology, endorsed by the famous alchemical physician, Paracelsus. Bulkeley's treatise was written for the instruction of his daughter, Dorothy Treat, and his grandson, Richard Treat, who, he hoped, would follow him in the medical profession. *Vade Mecum* may represent the best and most comprehensive presentation of the leading edge of medical knowledge in Connecticut at the end of the seventeenth century.

At the end of the manuscript Bulkeley appended a memorial to his youngest daughter, Catherine. Dropping all pretense of the solemn and arrogant sage, Gershom revealed himself as a grieving and anguished father. Catherine had been a high-spirited young woman, who had not taken religion or her father seriously. Injured by a midwife, she had not cooperated with Gershom's attempts to treat her. She had not always taken the medicines he prepared for her, and to his dismay and disapproval, she kept a cup of cold beer by her bedside. She would not permit her father to examine her injured womb. After her death a horrendous, gangrenous infection was uncovered.

When Catherine died, Gershom was wracked with grief and self-recrimination for not detecting the source of her affliction. He wrote, "O that I made known this but 3 or 4 days before she died! For if we had had but so much time to have scratched and scarified the part, to let out the virulent matter and by application of proper means to correct and stop the gangrene, I do not know but by God's help, she might have been recovered." "Poor heart, we little imagined the sore agonies that she underwent, did not feel what she felt, not knowing the cause of them, as aforesaid, which appeared not to us till after her death...." An aging Gershom also blamed his weakening faculties for his failure to detect Catherine's grave situation. "By reason of my deafness, I could not hear her, and so could not discourse with her and apply myself to her so aptly...." "...she took my hand and put it to her belly, to feel the strange commotion and fluttering there and presently died...."

Gershom Bulkeley died at the home of his daughter, Dorothy Treat, in the Nayaug section of Glastonbury on 2

December 1713. In his will Gershom called himself a "Practitioner in Physick". He wrote that for twenty years he had "walked upon ye very mouth of the grave and under so great infirmity that I can but wonder how I have all this while escaped falling into it."[27] .

At the time of his death, Gershom, had been fully accepted back into good standing in Connecticut society, and was eulogized as one of the wisest and most intellectually gifted citizens that Connecticut had ever produced. A contemporary account of his death in the *Boston News Letter* for December 28, 1713 declared

> *He was Eminent for his great Parts, both*
> *Natural and Acquired, being Universally*
> *acknowledged besides his good Religion and*
> *Vertue to be a Person of Great Penetration,*
> *and a sound Judgment, as well in Divinity as*
> *Politicks and Physick; having served his*
> *Country many years successively as Minister, a*
> *Judge and a Physician with great Honour to*
> *himself and advantage to others.* [28]

Gershom Bulkeley was a man who took it as his duty to mold the world around him. Whatever the subject, he labored energetically and passionately to sway others to accept the truth as he saw it. *Vade Mecum* meaning "Go With Me" could well serve as his credo.

II. ENGLAND TO NEW ENGLAND (1559 – 1660)

*My worldly estate…is now very little in comparison of what
is was when I first came to this place… [I have] little to
leave the children what God hath given me.*

*I have found as little [brotherly love] towards myself as
ever I did in any place God brought me unto.*

~Reverend Peter Bulkeley

GERSHOM BULKELEY WAS A MEMBER OF THE PURITAN
ELITE. His father Peter Bulkeley was one of New England's
most famous ministers. Reverend Peter Bulkeley was one
of those profiled[29] by Cotton Mather in 1702 in *Magnalia
Christi Americana*.[30] Peter was included in book three of
this seven volume work which was dedicated to "The Lives
of Sixty Famous Divines, by Whose Ministry the Churches
of New England have been Planted and Continued."

Gershom was born in Massachusetts to Reverend Peter
Bulkeley and Grace Chetwood Buckley in December 1635.
Both parents were descended from a long line of notable
English ancestors. The Bulkeley family lineage in England
claims to have been traced back as far the 13th century in
the reign of King John when Robert Bulkeley was lord of
the Manor of Bulkeley in the County of Palatine of Chester.

19

If this lineage is correct, Robert Bulkeley was the 11th great-grandfather of Gershom Bulkeley.[31]

Gershom's father Reverend Peter Bulkeley and his grandfather Reverend Edward Bulkeley were both ministers and highly educated. Reverend Edward Bulkeley matriculated from St. John's College, Cambridge with a Bachelor of Arts degree in 1559/60. He also received a Master of Arts degree in 1563, B.D.in 1569 and a Doctor of Divinity degree in 1578 and was a fellow of the college in 1560. He became the rector of the Church of Odell in the County of Bedfordshire in 1571. He was the prebend of Chester in 1574; of Westminster in1583; of Litchfield in 1594; and vicar of St. Mary, Shrewsbury between 1578 and 1582.[32]

The Bulkeley family in England enjoyed wealth as well as prestige. Reverend Edward Bulkeley had a large inheritance from his father Thomas[33]. He accumulated substantial wealth in his own right. As Rector, he received both the greater and lesser tithes, and as prebend he would have received generous stipends. He passed on his fortune to his son, Peter Bulkeley.

Peter Bulkeley was born at Odell in Bedfordshire on 31 January 1582. At sixteen he entered Saint John's College at Cambridge. He earned a Bachelor of Arts degree in 1604/5 and a Master of Arts degree in 1608. He was called "an excellent scholar, a very well-read person." He was ordained a deacon and a priest in June 1608; canon of Litchfield in 1609; and University preacher in 1610. Peter followed his father, Edward, as rector of the church at Odell 12 January 1609/10.[34]

Peter married Jane Allen, the daughter of Thomas Allen of Goldington, in Bedfordshire, on 12 April 1613. The Allen family was wealthy and well-connected politically.[35] Jane's nephew was the Lord Mayor of London. With his inheritance and his marriage Peter could reasonably anticipate a life of comfortable security.

Peter and Jane had at least nine children: Edward (1614), Mary (1615), Thomas (1617), Nathaniel (1618), John (1620), Mary (1621), Joseph (1623), Daniel (1625) and Jabez (1626).[36] Jane (Allen) Bulkeley died 8 December 1626 and was buried at Odell.

As a minister, Peter had a commanding style and a booming voice. People came from far away to hear him preach. He was not aloof and frequently walked about the town during the week, engaging those he met with conversation and encouragement. There are indications, however, that in these discussions he sometimes devoted more intensity to the religious implications of small matters than seemed warranted to others.

A few years into his ministry, Peter began to drift away from the elaborate ceremonies of the Anglican Church and into Puritanism. He adopted a great simplicity in his dress and wore his hair closely cropped. He did not wear the surplice and stopped using the cross in baptism[37]. His non-conformity was protected for a while by his high-placed connections and the bishop of Lincoln.

His strict Calvinistic theology was like that of the famous English theologian, William Ames. Ames railed against ceremony in worship and against debauchery at Christmas. Interestingly, Ames is the author of the largest number of surviving books inventoried in the library of Gershom Bulkeley. Based on their publication dates, these books almost certainly had belonged to Gershom's father, Peter. There are twelve books by Ames in Gershom's collection that were in Latin and published from 1615 to 1635, the year the Bulkeley family went to New England. There is one book in English, a reprint of Ames's manual for Calvinistic students, *The Marrow of Sacred Divinity*, and which was published posthumously in 1642.

Under increasing pressure to conform, Puritans began to leave the country in large numbers. More than 20,000 Puritans left for New England between 1620 and 1640, a period later termed "The Great Migration".[38]   When Reverend William Laud became archbishop of Canterbury in 1633, the drive to rid the Anglican Church of non-conformists increased sharply. An outspoken and popular preacher like Peter Bulkeley did not escape notice. Bulkeley was suspended in 1634 and was forbidden to preach. To continue his ministry, he decided to join the Puritan migration to New England.[39]

IT WAS NOT EASY for a prominent non-conformist minister like Bulkeley to leave England. There was a high probability that he would be intercepted and arrested if he tried. Plans to leave had to be carefully made. Peter quietly began to sell his vast property holdings. Peter's eldest son, Edward, and other relatives preceded him to America. Edward was there by 22 March 1634/5 when he became a member of First Church in Boston.

The major changes to Peter's life were not limited to leaving his congregation and his comfortable life in England. After having lived as a widower for eight years, he decided that it was time to remarry. In early April 1635, Peter, at the age of 52, married the much younger thirty-three-year-old Grace Chetwood, the daughter of Sir Richard Chetwood. The Chetwoods were also a landed family of long English pedigree, and could trace their ancestry back to the Plantagenet kings of England.

The plans to sail involved some subterfuge. On 13 April 1635, the name "Jo Backley" aged 15 was entered on the shipping list for those to sail on the *Susan & Ellen*. Five days later the names, "Ben. Buckley," aged 11, and "Daniell Buckley," aged 9, were entered. On 8 May 1635, the name "Grace Bulkley," aged "22" was entered on the shipping list of the *Elizabeth & Ann* a ship that was sailing about the same time. This was apparently a ruse involving two women swapping places. "Peter Bulkley," aged "50," was listed as a passenger on the *Susan & Ellen* the following day. To avoid detection, they probably entered their names at the last minute and must have sailed shortly after May 9. Bulkeley is known for certain to have left England before 22 May 1636.[40]

Peter did not leave his life in England empty-handed. In addition to his family of three of sons and a young wife, he brought his extensive library of books. Maintaining and treasuring a large private library was a distinguishing and continuing feature of the Bulkeley family. Having disposed of his lands and estates, Peter accumulated a fortune of several thousand English pounds. He carried this money (which may have been equivalent of $2 to $20 million dollars) with him to New England.

ACCORDING TO BULKELEY FAMILY TRADITION, Grace (Chetwood) Bulkeley fell into a coma during the voyage to America. Near the end of the voyage she appeared to be dead. Peter entreated the captain not to bury her at sea. After three days, she showed signs of life.[41] When the ship landed in Boston in midsummer, 1635, Grace was carried ashore an invalid, but later recovered. Gershom was born a few months later in late December or early January 1636.[42] His mother would have only been in the fourth month of her pregnancy when the *Susan & Ellen* landed in America and her pregnancy may have been unknown when the ship left England. In addition to the nine children born in England to Peter and his first wife, Peter fathered five more children in Massachusetts by his second wife, Grace.

Peter went almost immediately from Boston to Cambridge, Massachusetts. There he joined with Reverend John Jones and a group of planters who were planning a settlement. While still in Cambridge, they organized a church on 5 July 1636 with Reverend Jones as Pastor and Bulkeley as Teacher. Jones and the planters, followed by Bulkeley, "went into the woods" to settle in a new town[43] which they named, Concord.[44] Gershom's birth is not recorded in the town records of either Cambridge or Concord, but it is likely that he was born in Concord.[45]

Peter devoted himself and his fortune to the success of the little settlement of Concord. He did not disappear from the wider affairs of New England, even though he was far removed from the centers of New England life at Boston, Hartford and New Haven. He was almost immediately involved in the Antinomian Controversy which embroiled all New England.

Anne Hutchinson, a disciple of Reverend John Cotton, ignited the controversy in 1636 by claiming that most of the ministers of New England were false preachers. She said that Cotton preached a theology of justification by grace while the others erroneously preached justification by good works. The controversy split the Bulkeley clan and created conflict between Bulkeley and his good friend, John Cotton. Hutchinson continued to fan the flames by making increasingly disturbing statements and enraged the ministers of the standing order by charging that they were false ministers. Cotton seemed in sympathy with Anne at first but, as the debated waxed hotter, even he backed away from defending her views.

In 1637 Hutchinson was put on trial before the church, and Peter Bulkeley was one of the leading voices in condemning her. He even accused her of advocating free love, which she denied. She claimed that her views came from divine inspiration and prophesized ruin upon the colony of Massachusetts. Bulkeley went on to call her "that

Jezebel whom the Devil sent over thither to poison these American churches with her depths of Satan, which she learned in the schools of the Familists."[46] Anne was charged with contempt and sedition and was summarily excommunicated and banished from the Massachusetts Bay Colony. After her banishment, Anne, along with her supporters, went on to establish the settlement of Portsmouth in present day Rhode Island.

In the aftermath of the Hutchinson affair, a great Ecclesiastical Council was held in Boston to consider the "errors" that were creeping into theology in New England. Peter Bulkeley and Hartford Connecticut's founding minister, Thomas Hooker, were chosen to serve as moderators. This council was, in a sense, a challenge to the free grace theology of Reverend John Cotton. Cotton was in a great deal of trouble and found most of New England's ministers lined up against him. Cotton and Bulkeley debated a list of eighty-two "erroneous" theological concepts drawn up by the Ecclesiastical Council. Cotton conceded most points and convinced the group of his basic conformity to orthodoxy. While Cotton and Bulkeley never came to complete agreement, they remained friends and continued a life-long correspondence.

Peter Bulkeley saw himself as the guardian of the planters in Concord and lavished his fortune on them. He employed many of them as servants and presented them with gifts of land to settle on. However, despite his care, the Concord church experienced discord. The town did not prosper. In 1644, Reverend John Jones left, and took many settlers with him to Fairfield, Connecticut. Bulkeley's son, Thomas, who was married to Sarah Jones, went with them, as did Peter's son, Daniel. Only thirty families remained in Concord, but Peter Bulkeley continued as their pastor. A dispute between Reverend Bulkeley and the ruling elder required the convening of a council with other New England churches. The disagreement ended with the abdication of the elder.

Peter Bulkeley was not very content in his small, isolated community. He wrote to John Cotton, "I lose much in this retired wilderness in which I live, but the Lord will, at last, lighten my candle".[47] Yet, even from his somewhat remote residence, Peter Bulkeley had a wide influence. He was acknowledged as a leader by the ministers of New England. He wrote a book, *The Gospel Covenant,* which was considered the first religious book of importance written in New England, and one of the first American books printed in England. It was popular and went through many editions in England.[48]

When the Puritans prevailed in the English Civil War (1642-1651), Reverend Bulkeley could have returned to England, as many New England ministers did. Bulkeley, however, remained with his little congregation in Concord, but may have come to regret his decision. He had invested so much of his life and his fortune in Concord that he was not willing to abandon it even though he felt estranged from the community. He complained in a letter to Cotton, "...I have found as little [brotherly love] towards myself as ever I did in any place God brought me unto. It is a place I have desired to show love unto for His sake …yet I have found so many strangenesses, alienations and so much neglect from some who formerly have visited me, yet will they pass by my door as if I were a man they had not known…"[49] He also wrote, "I am persuaded that except there be some means used to change the course of things …our churches will grow more corrupt day by day, and tumult will arise hardly to be stilled.…I pray the Lord to heal the evil of the places and times we live in.…"[50]

GERSHOM BULKELEY WAS BORN INTO A FAMILY that considered itself destined to lead, but that also felt somewhat estranged, alienated and under-appreciated. The name, Gershom, occurs in Exodus in the Bible as the name given by Moses to his son. In the loose translation, it means "a stranger in the land." For Gershom Bulkeley that would turn out to be an appropriate name.[51]

Few children in New England were reared in a world as rich in books as those in the family of Reverend Peter Bulkeley. They were surrounded by their father's massive private library when few in New England owned a single book other than a Bible. It was expected that Gershom and his brothers would be scholars and go to college. The Bulkeleys were both early supporters of and students at Harvard College. Reverend Bulkeley donated many of his books to create a portion of the library at the college.[52]

John Bulkeley, Gershom's half-brother, was a member of the first class to graduate from Harvard in 1642.[53] John went on to receive the first master of arts degree granted by

Harvard.[54] He was considered brilliant and the most
intellectually gifted Bulkeley.[55] John Bulkeley and George
Downing, who had received bachelor degrees, were chosen
in 1643 to be "teachers" at Harvard and to "help the
President and read to the junior students." For these
services, they each received four pounds per year.[56]

John Bulkeley did not stay in New England but returned to
England to become a minister. There he was silenced for
preaching Puritan theology and turned to a career as a
medical doctor.[57] John retained great affection for Harvard
and showed his gratitude to the college by making a
bequest. On 20 December 1645, he gave the college his
portion of a one-acre garden adjoining the college. The land
in Cambridge on Harvard Street was designated for the use
of resident Fellows and was called "Fellows Orchard". It
eventually became the college yard.

Gershom also showed an early disposition to learning and
entered Harvard at the age of fifteen or sixteen. He received
a bachelor's degree in 1655 and a master's degree three
years later. The college steward's books contain a full
record of undergraduate charges from the time of his
admission (entrance charge one shilling) until 5 September
1656, the last quarter bill. His education was mostly paid in
goods such as rye, wheat, meal, butter, cheese, apples,
bacon, beef, turkeys, lambs, sheep, a cow, an ox, 430 feet
of boards, etc. His total undergraduate bill amounted to an
equivalent of just over 45 pounds.[58]

It is likely that Gershom's education included Latin, Greek,
Hebrew, physics, metaphysics, philosophy, history,

theology and, perhaps, medicine. The only surviving example of his academic work is a Latin poem composed 10 August 1658 as part of his master's degree. Gershom was comfortable in the academic life. He remained at Harvard after completing his second degree and served as a tutor and Fellow from 1658 to 1661.[59]

Gershom's younger brothers, Eleazer and Peter, also attended Harvard. Eleazer, who was born in 1638, was a member of the class of 1658, but did not receive a degree. He is named in his father's will of March 1658/9, but apparently died soon after.[60] Peter, who was born in 1643, was a member of the class of 1662 at Harvard. He also appears not to have received a degree, although he became a physician.[61]

The Bulkeley family's connection to Harvard continued through Peter, the son of Gershom's half-brother, Edward. This Peter is often confused with Gershom's brother, Peter. Edward Bulkeley was born in 1614, and his son, Peter, was born in Concord on 3 January 1640/1, and was older than Gershom's brother, Peter. Peter Bulkeley, the son of Edward, graduated from Harvard in 1660. For some unknown reason, he is referred to in the college records as "little Peter." In 1663, he received a second degree. In that same year, Peter was named a Fellow of the College.[62]

Gershom's son, John, would graduate from Harvard in 1669 with a degree in divinity. He was considered a genius by his classmates. He was to become one of the leading clergymen of New England.

Gershom's father, Reverend Peter Bulkeley, died at Concord on 9 March 1658/9.[63] In his will he complains that "my worldly estate...is now very little in comparison of what it was when I first came to this place...considering my wasted estate, which I have here consumed, [I have] little to leave to the children what God hath given me...."[64] Peter is thought to have brought a fortune of 6,000 pounds with him to New England.[65] (Comparisons English pounds of this era to contemporary US dollars vary widely, but by any measure this fortune would be well over one million dollars). Peter Bulkeley spent significant funds to support the settlement at Concord, Massachusetts and the inventory of his estate after his death came to only 1,302 pounds. He left a significant library of books valued at 123 pounds.[66] In Peter's will, Gershom was not bequeathed a financial legacy, but he did receive some of his father's precious books.

On 26 October 1659, while still at Harvard, Gershom married Sarah Chauncy, the daughter of the Reverend Dr. Charles Chauncy, the President of Harvard.[67] Sarah gave birth to a son, Peter, born on 7 Nov. 1660. Gershom fit comfortably into university life as a tutor and scholar. However, since he had inherited books rather than money or estate from his father, he had meager means. As a tutor, he probably received compensation like the four pounds per year that John had received. This would not be enough to support his growing family and at age 25 he made the decision to leave the sheltered university life and seek work.[68]

Sarah and Gershom had seven children:[69]

Peter, born 7 November 1660; died young.

(Dr.) Charles, born about 1662; died at New London, Connecticut in 1692.

Peter, born about 1664; died at sea about 22 November 1701.

Dorothy, born about 1667; died at Glastonbury, Connecticut 17 January 1712/3.

Catherine, born about 1675 in Wethersfield, Connecticut; died there before 1712.

(Capt.) Edward, born about 1677 in Wethersfield; Connecticut and died there 27 August1748.

(Reverend) John, born about 1679 in Wethersfield, Connecticut and died at Colchester, Connecticut 9 June 1731.

III. MINISTER (1661-1676)

The town [is]...willing to leave Mr. Bulkeley to the liberty of his conscience without compelling him or enforcing him to anything...contrary to his light

~Wethersfield town vote

*...a plurality of witnesses [must] testify to one and **ye same** individual fact; without such a plurality, there can be no legal evidence.*

~Gershom Bulkeley

IN 1661 AN OPPORTUNITY FOR GERSHOM BULKELEY AROSE in New London, Connecticut. The town had been without a settled minister since 1658 when the Reverend Richard Blinman left and returned to England.[70] Gershom was one of the ministers who preached occasionally at New London on an interim basis.[71] Finally, Gershom was invited to come and preach in the New London church on a trial basis. After serving several months, he was offered a contract to preach on a regular basis for three years, 1661 to 1664. This was merely a contractual engagement and contained no reference to settlement or ordination. However, the town did agree to pay Gershom to move his family from Boston to New London and to give him a home lot, house, orchard, garden, pasture, free firewood

33

and a salary of eighty pounds per year with the possibility of more at the end of the three-year term.[72] The town further agreed that, if he should die in office, his wife and children would receive sixty pounds sterling in exchange for the house and lot. The town also agreed to supply a servant and a maid, but with the costs to be paid by Bulkeley. It was also agreed that any silver offered by strangers attending church services would be given to Bulkeley to allow him to purchase books for his library.[73]

There was some delay in building his house and the agreement was modified. The town gave Gershom eighty pounds and told him to obtain his own house. Gershom purchased the homestead of Samuel Lothrop. Gershom released the town from its obligation to pay his family sixty pounds in the event of his death. However, the town stipulated that he must remain for seven years or else return the eighty pounds. Furthermore, it was stipulated that if he should die within the seven years, the eighty pounds did not have to be repaid by the family.[74]

Gershom's widowed mother Grace Bulkeley also moved to New London to live with him. Gershom and Sarah settled into their new community and had a second son, Charles. Charles would eventually follow Gershom's footsteps to become a doctor and surgeon.[75]

In 1661, New London was not a peaceful place. Caulkins in the *History of New London* said: "The years 1661 and 1662 were noted for strife and turbulence among the inhabitants. Cases of calumny and riot were common. The disorderly elements of society were in motion...."[76] In 1662, the town magistrate, John Tinker, was accused of treason by the town constable because he had refused to prosecute people who slandered King Charles II. Tinker, in turn, sued many of the accusers for slander. The cases advanced to the court in Hartford where Magistrate Matthew Allyn, sympathized with Tinker and threatened to hang half a dozen of his accusers. The court ruled for Tinker. While still in Hartford, Tinker died suddenly and was buried with great ceremony. The widow Tinker would later become an important player in the desertion of Lieutenant Samuel Smith which Gershom struggled to resolve.

After a successful trial period, Bulkeley was approved to become New London's settled pastor. A committee was appointed on 15 January 1663/4 to negotiate with Bulkeley for his settlement. It was agreed on 25 February 1663/4 that his annual salary would be raised to 120 pounds. In turn, Gershom was required to free the town of all the other obligations.[77] The four leading church and town leaders appointed to arrange for Bulkeley's settlement included Lieutenant Samuel Smith.[78]

SMITH MYSTERIOUSLY DISAPPEARED shortly after the committee was formed to negotiate with Bulkeley. It was rumored that he had abandoned his wife and fled to Roanoke. His wife, Rebecca Smith,[79] the daughter of the former pastor of Wethersfield, Reverend Henry Smith, received a letter from Lieutenant Smith explaining his sudden departure. He said that he had an urge to travel, but also wanted to escape from her jealousy.[80]

Caulkins said: "Lieutenant Samuel Smith, from his first settlement in the town was much trusted in public affairs, nor is it manifest that in any instance he performed his duties of office otherwise than with discretion and honor." [81] Caulkins identifies Samuel as Samuel Smith Jr. son of Samuel Smith of Hadley, but *The History of Ancient Wethersfield* casts some doubt on this lineage. [82] If Caulkins is correct, Samuel was born in England around 1625, and so he was only about 39. Smith was granted a land in New London in February 1652 and occupied a home lot on mill brook and owned farm land. [83]

On 15 February 1663/4, shortly after Smith disappeared, Alice Tinker was brought before the court "upon suspicion of being with childe". There were rumors that Lieutenant Smith was the father. Alice Tinker was the widow of John Tinker, a very prominent New London citizen who had managed many of John Winthrop's business affairs in New London. [84] Tinker had died in October 1662. [85] Alice was fined five pounds, but she did not name Samuel Smith as the father. She said that the father was Jeremiah, the 21-year-old son of Reverend Richard Blinman. Jeremiah was also fined five pounds. (Jeremiah did not leave the country with his father but remained in New London.)

Gershom and the citizens of New London were shocked by Smith's desertion of his wife. Gershom's response was in keeping with the tradition of his father, Peter. When Peter served as the minister in Concord, he considered all the citizens of the town to be under his pastoral care and guidance in every aspect of their lives. Gershom now took it as his pastoral duty to win the erring member's repentance and gain his return into the New London community.

On 18 March 1663/4Bulkeley wrote to Lieutenant Smith. In the letter, he showed great regard and respect and addressed Smith as "Good Lieut." He employed all his considerable skills of diplomacy and persuasion. He assured Samuel that his wife, Rebecca, continued to have affection for him and that she implores her husband to return. He referred to the land that the town had given Smith and offered that his lands could yet be recovered. In fact, he assured Samuel that his good standing and honor in the community could all yet be restored.

Gershom urged Samuel to do what was right and to return. He warned that all men must ultimately stand before God and justify their actions. Gershom signed the letter, "Your unworthy though distressed [Pastor] and your faithful friend, Gershom Bulkeley". He added, "If these lines find you, let it not be long before...you find us."

On 28 March 1664, Rebecca, tired of waiting for his return, sold Samuel's farm on Upper Alewife Cove, to Robert Loveland to pay Smith's debts.[86] She sold the home lot to Daniel Comstock.[87]

Information began to emerge indicating that Lieutenant Smith was not the man that the community had thought he was. It was alleged that he frequently spent time drinking at the home of Katherine and Humphrey Clay who kept an inn of sorts.[88] On 30 June 1664, Katherine Clay was presented to court for "selling liquors at her house, selling lead to the Indians, profaning the Sabbath, card-playing and entertaining strange men, etc." The Clays were convicted of keeping a disorderly house and ordered to leave the colony or pay a fine of forty pounds. Humphrey sold his land and two houses. For some reason Gershom purchased the houses, possibly to end their undesirable usage. The purchase was made under the condition that the Clays vacate the houses by Michaelmas [Christmas].[89]

Rebecca received a letter from Samuel on 24 September 1664.[90] He addressed her as "most loving wife" and ends the letter by saying, "Dear hart pray for me and forget me not and I hope that we shall see many happy days together before we die." He also wrote that he lived in Carolina. He said that any claims of intimacy with others were false and accused Rebecca of seeking a divorce so that she could remarry.[91] Rebecca responded with a letter of her own in October leveling many charges against him.[92]

Gershom tried once more, sending a second letter to Lieutenant Smith on 11 October 1664. The letter is addressed to "Mr. Samuel Smith at Roanoke or elsewhere," since it was uncertain whether he had gone to Virginia or to Carolina. Gershom retained his respectful attitude and began with the salutation: "Admired Sir." Gershom wrote that he has been "much solicited by your wife, whose conjugal affections cease not to offer out after you." However, Gershom's best efforts still failed to induce Smith to return. Rebecca Smith moved back to her home town of Wethersfield.

Rebecca filed for divorce and testimony was taken in May 1665. The testimony painted a much darker picture of

Lieut. Smith. [93] Witnesses testified that Mrs. Clay said that Smith was in the habit of taking his axe and going into the woods to make his wife believe he was working. But he would often come to her house and stay even into the night. On one occasion, when Rebecca Smith went to the Clay home looking for her husband, they said he hid from her. Mary Beckwith testified that several years earlier, Sarah Clay, Mrs. Clay's daughter, had said to her that she "could not abide to be in the house alone when Lieutenant Smith was there." When asked why, Sarah had said it was because "if ever there was a whoremaster in New London, he was one." However, Sarah would change her opinion and become his drinking companion, run away with him and, apparently, become his wife.

Smith was quoted as bragging that he had got the widow Alice Tinker pregnant and that the fact would soon be obvious, as she would deliver in nine weeks and hence he must flee. Sarah Clay had become his drinking companion and Samuel advised her to leave with him or she would be punished too. Samuel told her that he would never live with his wife again. Mrs. Clay said that she feared that, if her daughter Sarah went to Roanoke, she would never come back.

Attempts were made to reach Samuel Smith in Roanoke, but he was evasive. Joseph Calley testified that when Smith saw him on the ship with a white cap and a waistcoat he thought it was his wife and would not come on board until he knew she was not there. It was reported that Samuel had a young wife in Virginia. Samuel Wyllys and the magistrates of the General Court in Hartford sent a letter to

Samuel Smith on 17 August 1665 saying that his actions
tended to support the reports about him, which they were
previously not willing to believe. They recommended that
Rebecca proceed with a divorce.

Samuel wrote to Rebecca at Wethersfield on 1April 1666.
He repeated his love for her and his relatives but did not
offer to return. The court awarded Rebecca a divorce on 11
May 1667. They declared that the manner of Smith's
departure from his wife his "pertinacious continuance" of it
for more than three years and after "much direct & indirect
means used for his inducement" ...declare sayd Rebeckah
Smith...free from her conjugal bond to the sayd Samuel
Smith."[94] In 1669, Rebecca married Nathaniel Bowman of
Wethersfield.[95]

Some early historians, perhaps not having access to all the
records, speculated that Samuel had made a heroic
sacrifice.[96] They suggested that Samuel, believing that
Rebecca cared more for Nathaniel Bowman, a mutual
friend, than for himself, had left so that she could obtain a
divorce rather than embitter their lives and happiness. The
complete record, given here, shows this romantic
interpretation of events highly unlikely. It also shows why
Gershom Bulkeley's formidable diplomatic skills were in
vain.

THE BULKELEYS WERE NOT COMFORTABLE in
New London. Gershom continued to serve the parish and in
1664 his third son, Peter was born, but there was tension.

Throughout New England there was conflict in the churches over two issues: (1) requirements for full membership and (2) church governance. By the mid-1660s there was increasing pressure for the churches to adopt less strict standards for membership. Many people in the Connecticut colony, desiring membership in the churches, petitioned the General Court to address the issue. In October 1664, the General Court passed a resolution requesting the churches to embrace more liberal membership practices. The position of the General Court gave support to Gershom's position and probably was the cause of a town vote on 15 February 1664/5.[97]

> The town being desired to declare their minds concerning Mr. Bulkeley, it was propounded whether they were willing to leave Mr. Bulkeley to the liberty of his conscience without compelling him or enforcing him to anything in the execution of his place and office contrary to his light according to the laws of the commonwealth.[98]

Early settlers tended to favor strict membership that required a candidate must have experienced a conversion event and a "Congregational" church order where the local congregation was dominant, rather than more relaxed admission standards and a "Presbyterian" form of governance where the ministers of the region influenced church decisions.[99] Gershom favored a more open policy for church membership and was associated with "Presbyterian" ideas. Gershom was classified as a

41

Presbyterian minister by a fellow Connecticut Presbyterian minister in 1671.[100]

The New London historian Caulkins said that this was the first indication of uneasiness between Gershom and his New London congregation.[101] However, Gershom remained a popular preacher despite the policy differences. In June 1665 when rumors spread that he might be planning to move to the Massachusetts Bay Colony, the town voted to ask him to stay awhile and continue to preach to them. Gershom agreed to remain in New London and preached while the town sought a new minister. For this the town voted that he be paid thirty pounds for his service.

Since Gershom was no longer serving as the settled pastor of the New London church, and he had not served the required seven years of his contract, the town requested the return of the eighty pounds that had been advanced to him. The thirty pounds voted by the town for his interim service was applied as part payment. The remaining fifty pounds was not paid until 1668. Bulkeley left New London in 1667 and the house he vacated was leased for the use of the new minister, Reverend Simon Bradstreet.[102] In 1688, Gershom gave his son, Charles, by gift of deed, the new London house and lot he had purchased from Samuel Lathrop, another piece of land he had purchased from Jacob Waterhouse, and a strip of land by the mill that the town had given him.[103]

It has been suggested by some historians that Gershom left New London under duress and ill-will. This seems to be based on the town's demand that Bulkeley pay back the fifty pounds and Gershom's slow response. However, there is no actual evidence of any ill will. Even after Gershom left to become the minister at Wethersfield, he was invited back to preside at the ordination of the new minister. Bradstreet left autobiographical notes entitled, "Remembrances of the greatest changes in my Life: or a Record of the Chief of God's Providences and dealings with me." In which he wrote: "Octob. 5, 1670, I was ordained by Mr. Bulkeley and Mr. Haynes and established Pastor of the church of Christ at New London."[104]

THE WETHERSFIELD CHURCH had been in an unsettled state for its entire history.[105] The pioneers who first arrived had been church members in Massachusetts. They requested dismissal from their Massachusetts churches and formed a new church. They had no settled pastor among them but were served by several visiting preachers. The church, with only seven members, split in a controversy (the cause is uncertain). The riff could not be healed and most of the settlers of Wethersfield removed to Stamford, Connecticut.

The tiny Wethersfield church did not have a settled pastor until Reverend Henry Smith was installed in 1641. He did not have a happy ministry. Constant battles with the wealthy ruling elder, Clement Chaplin, produced civil suits and conflict that only ended when Reverend Smith died in 1648. The second installed pastor, Reverend John Russell, took office in 1650.

A great dispute arose in the Hartford church between Reverend Samuel Stone, who had been the Teacher under Reverend Thomas Hooker, and the church elders over the authority of clergy versus laity. This argument grew to encompass other churches, including Wethersfield's. The Wethersfield church took sides in the dispute which grew so contentious that Reverend Russell and most of the Wethersfield church moved to Hadley, Massachusetts, in 1659. This was the second time a controversy over religion fractured the Wethersfield community and demonstrates how explosive these issues could be.

The third pastor of the Wethersfield Church was John Cotton Jr., son of the famous Boston minister. After three years in Wethersfield, he left to preach to the Indians on Martha's Vineyard. The fourth pastor was Joseph Haynes, the son of Governor Haynes. He lasted one year before moving on to accept a call from the Hartford church.

This historically turbulent church then turned to Gershom Bulkeley as its prospective fifth settled minister. It took some time to persuade Gershom to come to Wethersfield. As early as June 1664, Wethersfield began seeking to attract Gershom as their minister. A town meeting voted to offer him an annual salary of eighty pounds if he would come. They sent elders, Josiah Willard and Samuel Hale, to New London to present the offer to Gershom. He refused. They renewed the offer in July. John Chester and Samuel Boardman were sent to New London to convey the offer. The new proposal raised the salary to 100 pounds and included a house, use of the commons and the transportation of his goods from New London to Wethersfield.

Bulkeley said that he would accept if they could provide an assistant or colleague to support him in the ministry.[106] In response to Bulkeley's request for an assistant, the town hired Samuel Stone Jr., son of Hartford's famous minister, in April 1666. The salary was divided, with Bulkeley receiving seventy pounds and Stone forty pounds.[107]

For all the Wethersfield church's desire to secure the services of Reverend Bulkeley, he was not immediately "settled" as pastor. On 4 November 1667, the town voted to give Reverend Stone, Jr. the use of "three acres of grass ground in the parsonage lot" and Reverend Bulkeley the use of the house in which he was then living and the use of the parsonage land, as long as they continued in the work of the ministry. The town also voted that Bulkeley should have 120 acres and Stone 100 acres at the mouth of Dividend Brook, for themselves and their heirs upon condition that they settle as officers to the church in Wethersfield during their lives.[108] That the deal was not immediately accepted is shown by the fact that the town again voted on 5 May of 1668, to give Bulkeley "six score" acres of land at Dividend Brook, "if he take the office in the Church". He was finally "ordained" on 27 October 1669. Reverend Joseph Rowlandson and Mr. Samuel Willard conducted the ceremony.[109] Rowlandson would later succeed Bulkeley as the pastor of Wethersfield.[110]

The town found the ministry of Gershom to their liking and moved to solidify his continuance.[111] The parsonage was rebuilt in 1669 and his salary was raised to 100 pounds in that year. The town added twenty acres to his holdings at Dividend Brook, making it 140 acres in one tract so that he could build a mill. Water power was a critical component in the economic well-being of New England settlements and the site at Dividend Brook was well suited for a mill. In addition to providing a source of income, it was not unusual for a pastor to take concern for the economic as well as the spiritual welfare of the members of his community. Indeed, Gershom's father, Peter, had operated his town's corn mill in the early days of Concord, Massachusetts.[112]

The controversy over church membership continued to trouble Connecticut after Gershom left New London. What were the requirements for church membership? Who could partake of the sacraments of baptism and of the Lord's Supper? On 16 May 1668, the General Court appointed four prominent ministers to meet in June to promote and establish peace in the churches and plantations by "searching out the rule and thereby clearing up how far the churches and people may walk together…notwithstanding some various apprehensions among them in matters of discipline respecting membership and baptism, etc."[113]

Gershom, probably appointed for his diplomatic skills, was made a member of this committee along with leading ministers from several Connecticut towns: Reverend James Fitch of Norwich, Reverend Joseph Elliot of Guilford, and Reverend Samuel Wakeman of Fairfield. They delivered their report to the General Court one year later on 16 May 1669 with a compromise that led to acceptance of both the

Congregational way and the Presbyterian way.[114] Although the adoption of this compromise was voluntary, it did bring a measure of peace to Connecticut's churches.[115] This committee was also given the specific charge in October to bring peace to the church and town of Windsor.[116]

IN HIS SELF-APPOINTED ROLE AS CARETAKER of the whole community, Gershom collected home recipes for medicines and cures and recorded local remedies in his notebooks,[117] but it is not certain to what extent he embraced them. One such notebook entry is from a fellow Wethersfield resident, Enoch Buck.[118]

> It is reported of ye juice of nightshade, that is
> an absolute remedy for all galls, swellings and
> wounds (as ye galled backs of horses,
> goaring, &c.) whether new or old though
> worn to the bone, as hath proved by
> experience. This I had from Enoch Bucke.[119]

A recipe for curing a sore nose came from the Dutch settlers at Hartford and was passed down from "Mrs. Willard" (probably wife of Josiah Willard who was sent to New London in 1666 to bring Gershom to Wethersfield to be the minister there). Several Dutch families that settled the site of Hartford remained after the English arrived.

> [Take] cream and chalk. Boil them to an oil in
> an eggshell. This is to cure ye nose inwardly
> and [is] ever so done when all other means
> availed nothing. [This from the] Dutch

gentlewoman, Mrs. Varlet[120] that sometimes lived at Hartford, as Mrs. Willard affirms. Probatum [something proved].

Bulkeley also recorded several local remedies for snake bite;[121]

> Some say of Mr. Pell[122], that he was wont to say the best & speediest cure was to stun (not kill) the rattlesnake that had bitten any & with a forked stick, fasten him to the ground, and cut off a piece of him, and apply warm to ye wound, & so (ye snake being yet alive) piece after piece as fast as need should be, till it had drawn out all ye poison.

> If a person be bitten with a Rattlesnake, take Carduus Benedictus, stamp it & strain it out the juice & let ye person drink as much of it as he can, & lay ye stamped and strained Carduus to ye wound. This will cure him alone as Mr. Eely[123] of Saybrooke hath experienced both in his son & Negro servant as Mr. James Fitch[124] of Norwich told me July 8, 1670.

> But it will be good, in ye first place, if ye person bitten be capable, to bind it hard and well above ye wound to stop ye leakage of ye poison to ye vitals; & also afterward to use some hot towels to ye wound to draw out ye poison, which will much facilitate & forward the cure by ye Carduus. Thus, they did to

Hugh Calkin[125] [son of John Calkin[126] of
Norwich] & by God's blessing cured him
quickly.

Carduus Benedictus or the Blessed Thistle had been noted
for its medicinal qualities for centuries and was often
recommended as a cure for the plague. It is mentioned by
Shakespeare in his play, *Much Ado About Nothing*, and is
still used today in homeopathic medicine.

Some of the medical recipes in Bulkeley's notebooks had
been handed down within the family. He recorded one that
had been given to his father, Peter Bulkeley, by his now
father-in-law, Charles Chauncy.

> A recipe against ye wind colic sent by (my
> now father-in-law), Mr. Charles Chauncy,
> then of Scituate, May 3, 1648, to my own
> father, Mr. Peter Bulkeley of Concord, for my
> mother who was wont to be much troubled
> with ye wind colic. The recipe is this when
> she hath the fits in any extremity. Take a thick
> toast of white bread. Toast it thoroughly and
> leisurely on both sides [until] brown. In the
> meantime, heat half a pint of muscadine
> [wine] or somewhat more (or want thereof of
> sacke) in a pewter dish upon a chafing dish of
> water, very hot, and put ye dry toast into it
> and let it drink up as much of ye muscadine
> (or sacke) over the coals as it will receive, and
> let this toast be applied as hot to her navel as
> she can possibly endure it, and let it lie on till

it be cold. Muscadine (if it can be gotten) is more effectual than sacke, and never failing in ye disease, that I could find, but ye other (viz. sacke) gives speedy ease, through God's blessing. [127]

Gershom recorded two recipes from his friend, Edward Palmes, who claimed that he "knew ye patients cured at Milford for ye flux, both white and red."

[Take] a nutmeg. Roast it in the flame of candlewood, and then bruise it to powder, and with some rye meal and white of an egg make it into pills.

[Take] eggshells. Dry them in an oven after ye bread is drawn or ye like and powder them and thicken some milk with them and let ye patient drink it.

Mixed among the medical recipes, Gershom gave recipes of a non-medical nature.

To make very good vinegar of peaches: Peaches, if you take & bruise them, & hang them up in a bag, that ye juice may drain out of them & set this juice in ye sun as you do with other liquids for that end, will afford you very admirable vinegar, next to wine vinegar. Mr. Simon Bradstreet told me this, July 7, 1670.

He recorded a recipe which, he said, was handed down from "Mr. Thomas Hooker (sometime minister at Hartford in Connecticut), his Rx of making Indian malt." "The only time to make it is in ye spring and so continue in ye summer, rather than at ye approach of winter."[128] Gershom also presented a long exposition on making candles, "An Rx of making waxe candles sent from Mr. Wilson of Boston to my father." "This Rx I found in an old paper among my father's writings, and I know ye writing to be old William Wilson's."[129]

DURING HIS MINISTRY IN WETHERSFIELD, Gershom was also involved in the witchcraft trials in Connecticut. There had been earlier prosecutions for witchcraft in Wethersfield. In 1648, Katherine Palmer had been warned and Mary Johnson had been executed[130]. Katherine, the wife of Henry Palmer of Wethersfield, was accused by his neighbor, Gentleman John Robins, of tormenting his wife by witchcraft. Henry was required to post bond for his wife's "good behavior". Mary Johnson, under the prompting of Reverend Samuel Stone, had confessed herself guilty. Stone labored to obtain her repentance and Cotton Mather wrote that Stone reported that "she died in a frame [of mind] extremely to the satisfaction of them that were spectators of it."[131]

In 1651, John and Joan Carrington of Wethersfield were tried for witchcraft and convicted of "familiarity with Satan" and "works above the course of nature." Both were hanged in Hartford. Other executions for witchcraft in Connecticut were Goody Bassett of Stratford who was hanged in 1651, Goody Knapp of Fairfield hanged in 1653, and Lydia Gilbert of Winsor in 1654.[132]

After John Winthrop Jr. became Governor of Connecticut in 1657, there were no fatal outcomes in witch trials, except for the Hartford Witch Panic of 1662-3 when he was away in England negotiating a new charter for Connecticut from the court of King Charles II. Winthrop's philosophy in addressing witchcraft cases assumed that witchcraft accusations were a result of a tear in the social fabric of the community. His approach was to acknowledge that the accusers had cause for concern, but to find ways to avoid executing the accused. Winthrop followed a consistent strategy in every witchcraft case with which he was involved. Recognizing that formal public witchcraft accusations reflected communitywide social pathology, his priority was always reintegrating the community and restoring social cohesion. Winthrop refused to let a witch die, but he was not at all averse to coercing a witch to conform to social conventions. Often, from Winthrop's perspective, this meant that it was useful for witch suspects to be found, not completely innocent, but, rather not exactly guilty.[133]

During the Hartford Witch Panic, four of the eleven total witchcraft executions in Connecticut's history occurred. Winthrop left for England in 1661 to negotiate and secure a charter from the court of King Charles II, recognizing the right of colonial Connecticut to conduct its own government. He had only been gone a few months when in June 1662 Andrew Sanford and his wife, Mary, were indicted for witchcraft in Hartford. Only Mary was convicted and hanged. By December 1662, Rebecca and Nathaniel Greensmith and Mary Barnes of Farmington were on trial for their lives.

Rebecca gave a colorful confession in court that included a claim that she had had sex with the Devil in the form of a fawn. She claimed that there were many witches in the area who met in the woods near Hartford to revel, dance and drink. Reverend Samuel Stone took an interest in the proceedings. Rebecca mentioned that she had been scheduled to sign the Devil's book at a merry meeting in the woods to be held on Christmas and Stone responded. He asked the court to note the Devil's love of merry making at Christmas; a practice which Stone opposed.[134] These trials concluded with the simultaneous hanging of Rebecca and Nathaniel and Mary Barnes in January 1663.

THE EXECUTIONS IN 1663, following the Hartford Witch Panic, were the last executions for witchcraft in Connecticut and were followed by a period of calm. Then in 1668, Katherine Harrison of Wethersfield was charged with witchcraft. Katherine, the enterprising widow of John Harrison, often quarreled with her neighbors. They may have resented her rise from servant to proprietor of a thriving farm. They may also have been stung by her sharp tongue. The neighbors began a campaign of harassment against her and ultimately in the summer of 1668 accused her of being a witch.

Katherine Harrison came as a single woman directly from England to Connecticut in 1651[135] and worked as a servant in the home of Captain John Cullick of Hartford. Katherine was a lively and apparently outspoken girl and she was dismissed by Cullick for fortune telling and "evil conversation." Soon after, she married John Harrison, the Wethersfield town crier. The couple prospered, creating a substantial farm at Wethersfield and conducting a business of trading merchandise along the Connecticut River. When John died in August 1666, leaving an estate of nearly 1,000 pounds, Katherine was left with three young girls, ages 11, 13 and 14, to rear and a large farm to manage.[136]

Unlike most colonial widows, Katherine did not remarry. She continued to operate the farm with success. Her success, her marriage above her station as a servant, her defiance of convention and her sharp tongue apparently incensed her neighbors. They began to hurl accusations against her and to attack her livestock and crops.[137]

Throughout the fall of 1668, Katherine's neighbors gathered depositions about her activities that produced suspicions of witchcraft. Numerous depositions to court were submitted in 1668. In one of these, Thomas Whaples of Hartford asserted that Katherine was named by Rebecca Greensmith in the Hartford Witch Panic of 1662-1663 as a member of her witch band.[138] It is claimed that there was a trial in 1668 and that it resulted in a hung jury.[139] There is no official record of this trial but, if one occurred, it did not result in her being imprisoned.

In the spring of 1669, Katherine was officially summoned to the Court of Assistants in Hartford. She was examined on suspicion on 11 May 1669 and committed to jail to await trial. On 25 May 1669, the following indictment was brought against her:

> Katheran Harrison, thou standest here, indicted by ye name, Katheran Harrison of Wethersfield, as being guilty of witchcraft for that thou, not having the fear of God before thine eyes, hast had familiarity with Satan, the grand enemy of god and mankind, and by his help hast acted things beyond and besides the ordinary course of nature and has thereby hurt the bodyes of diuers of the subjects of or sovereign Lord the King for which by the law of god and of this Corporation thou oughtest to dye. [140]

Katherine entered a plea of not guilty and requested trial by the jury present. The jury could not agree on a verdict and the matter was held over until the October session of the court. Katherine was ordered to be held in prison until then.[141]

Katherine did not remain in custody long. The jailer, Daniel Garrett, somehow managed to return her to her Wethersfield farm. (This was almost certainly at the order of Governor Winthrop.) Thirty-eight of Katherine's Wethersfield neighbors submitted an angry petition demanding to know why she was at liberty. They noted that most of the jury had thought her guilty.[142] On 12 October

1669, Katherine appeared at the Court of Assistants in Hartford with her attorney. The jury was summoned and finally brought in their verdict. They declared her guilty.[143]

The jury was dismissed, and the court proceeded to wrap up business. Governor Winthrop took no immediate action to pronounce sentence. The witnesses who had come from Wethersfield were given compensation and the jailer, Daniel Garrett, was allowed his charges for keeping Katherine. The court accepted a motion from the marshal and from Kate's attorney to collect various debts that were owed to her.

Winthrop clearly did not want to impose the death sentence. He questioned Katherine privately and then created a panel of ministers to advise the court on four points of law. The involvement of ministers was logical since all the capital laws were based on the biblical "laws of Moses". Each of these laws cited scriptures from the bible for their authority. The panel was led by Winthrop's good friend and the leader of the Wethersfield church, the Reverend Gershom Bulkeley.[144]

Many of the events that had historically been seen as producing a suspicion of witchcraft had lost their force, but the two things that could be relied upon for conviction were: 1) the testimony of two witnesses to an act that could only have been accomplished by the help of the Devil and 2) a confession by the accused.

Winthrop asked Bulkeley and the ministers to address four
legal points

> 1.) Was it necessary that more than one
> witness testify to the same event or would
> uncorroborated witnesses testifying to several
> similar events count as legal proof?

> 2.) Was the appearance of a specter or
> apparition in the form of a person, legal
> evidence against that person?

> 3,) Was fortune telling evidence of familiarity
> with Satan?

> 4,) Was the knowledge of things that were
> secret evidence of familiarity with Satan?

The panel of ministers reviewed the evidence in the trial
and considered the points of law in question. Bulkeley
prepared the report of the ministers and submitted the
following to the court.[145]

> ...a plurality of witnesses [must] testify to one
> and ye same individual fact; and without such
> a plurality there can be no legal evidence of it.

> It is not the pleasure of the Most High to
> suffer the Wicked One to make an
> undistinguishable representation of any
> innocent person in a way of doing mischief
> before a plurality of witnesses...This would
> evacuate all human [legal] testimony. No man
> could testify that he saw this person do this or

that thing, for it might be said that it was ye
Devil in his shape.

Those things, whither past, present or to
come, which are indeed secret, that is, cannot
be known by human skill in arts or strength of
reason, arguing from the course of nature
or...by divine revelation...nor by information
from man, must needs be known (if at all) by
information from ye Devil...the person
pretending the certain knowledge of them
seems to us to argue familiarity with ye Devil.

A special session of the Court of Assistants was held in
Hartford on 20 May 1670 to review the trial and the report
of the ministers. The court ruled that "having considered
the verdict of the jury respecting Katherine Harrison...
[we]...cannot concur with them so as to sentence her to
death". She was advised to pay her fees and remove from
Wethersfield for her own safety and the contentment of her
neighbors.[146]

IN FASHIONING THEIR OPINION, Gershom and the ministers
had struck a strong blow against the ability to convict
anyone of being a witch. Most allegations of witchcraft
included "spectral apparition" evidence. The plaintiffs
would allege that the accused had appeared to them as a
specter or ghostly figure or in a dream and had tormented
and afflicted them. The question was, since others usually
could not see the apparition, even if multiple plaintiffs had

a similar experience, did their testimony satisfy the "two-witness" rule or should their testimony be counted only as one witness and hence not provide sufficient grounds for capital conviction?

No two witnesses in the Harrison trial had testified that they saw exactly the same thing although many gave witness of actions which they believed could only have been done with the help of the devil. Bulkeley and the rest of the ministers of the panel, charged with how the "two-witness" rule should be applied, opted for a strict interpretation of the rule, namely that the two witnesses must have seen exactly the same event not just two (or more) similar events.

The "two-witness" rule had a long tradition as a requirement for conviction in a capital case. The tradition was so strong among the English that even in situations not explicitly covered by law, it was assumed to apply. Ample biblical authority could be found for this law.

> Whoso killeth any person, the murderer shall
> be put to death by the mouth of witnesses: but
> one witness shall not testify against any
> person to cause him to die. [Numbers 35:30];
> At the mouth of two witnesses, or three
> witnesses, shall be that is worthy of death be
> put to death, but at the mouth of one witness
> he shall be not be put to death. [Deuteronomy
> 17:6]; One witness shall not rise up against a
> man for any iniquity, or for any sin, in sin that

he sinneth: at the mouth of two witnesses, or
at the mouth of three witnesses, shall the
matter be established. [Deuteronomy 19:15];
"…in the mouth of two or three witnesses
every word may be established." [Matthew
18:16]; "It is also written in your law, that the
testimony of two men is true." [John 8:17].

The interpretation of the rule, however, had been subject to
controversy dating back to the very first adoption of laws in
the New England colonies. In 1641, the elders of the
colonies of Connecticut, New Haven, Plymouth and
Massachusetts conferred for several months on several
difficult issues of law including whether there were
exceptions the "two-witness" rule.[147]

THE TWO-WITNESS RULE BECAME AN ISSUE in 1649 when
Ezekiel Cheever, the schoolmaster in New Haven was put
on trial by the New Haven church for his offensive carriage
toward the elders and was also accused of "other offences
of a very high nature" which had aggrieved both church
members and other members of the town. Although it had
not been one of the original charges, the trial turned to
Cheever's comments in public meetings about the two-
witness rule.

Cheever asserted that comments made in private to
different individuals could not be taken together as an
offense under the two-witness rule. Disliking his opinion,
his interrogators put a hypothetical case to Cheever.
"Suppose three women testify, each for herself against one

man, that he hath abused her (and so each of them) by an adulterous fellowship,[148] whether three such testimonies of one and the same act, committed by one and the same man, would not prove him an adulterer." Cheever said this was a gross act but refused to give his opinion about it. When told that failure to state an opinion might encourage dangerous behavior, he said, "We must attend the rule and not the consequences". Cheever argued that every sin occurs at a time and place and therefore witnesses must have observed both to be credited as more than one witness.

Reverend John Davenport, leader of the New Haven church, ruled against Cheever, and the two-witness rule in the laws of the New Haven Colony left no doubt about its interpretation:

> That no man shall be put to death, for any
> offense, or misdemeanor in any case, without
> the testimony of two witnesses at least or that
> which is Equivalent thereunto, provided, and
> to prevent or suppresse much inconvenience,
> which may grow, either to the publick, or to
> particular Persons, by a mistake herein, it is
> Ordered, and declared, by the Authority
> aforesaid, that two, or three single witnesses,
> being of competent age, of sound
> understanding, and of good Reputation, and
> witnessing to the case in question (whither it
> concerne the publick peace, and welfare, or
> any one , and the same particular person) shall
> be accounted (the party concerned, having no

just exception against them) sufficient proofe,
though they did not together see, or heare, and
so witness to the same individual, and
particular Act, in reference to those
circumstances of time, and place.[149]

When the Hartford and New Haven Colonies were united
in 1665, the laws of the Connecticut Colony took
precedence.[150] The explicit description of how the two-
witness law should be applied did not appear in either the
Connecticut or Massachusetts law. However, among the
Wyllys Papers there is a document entitled, "Grounds for
Examination of the Witch" which articulates the following
concepts. After a litany of activities or "signs" that support
suspicion, this paper concludes that conviction requires:

But ye truer proofs, sufficient for conviction,
are ye voluntary confession of ye party
suspected, adjudged sufficient proof by both
divines and lawyers. Or second, testimony of
two witnesses of good and honest report
avouching things in their knowledge before
ye magistrate; first whether that party accused
hath made a league with ye devil or second
hath done some known practices of
witchcraft. And ye authors warn jurors, etc.
not to condemn suspected persons on bare
presumptions without good and sufficient
proofs. [151]

This paper is clearly based on *A Discourse of the Damned
Art of Witchcraft*, by William Perkins which was printed in

1618 in England.[152] After a discussion of the presumptions that lead to suspicion, the Perkins document says:

> Now follows the true proofes, and sufficient
> meanes of conviction, all which may be
> reduced to two heads. The first is the free and
> voluntary confession of the crime…a second
> sufficient means of conviction…is the
> testimony of two witnesses of good and
> honest report avouching before a magistrate
> that upon their own knowledge, these two
> things: Either that the party accused hath
> made a league with the Devil; or hath done
> some known practice of Witchcraft. And all
> arguments do necessarily prove either of
> these, being brought by two sufficient
> witnesses, are of the force fully to convict the
> party suspected.[153]

With the opinions set out by Gershom Bulkeley and the ministers, the Connecticut colony had come full circle back to Cheever's interpretation of the two-witness rule. While this did not absolutely prevent future convictions for witchcraft, it raised the bar. Under a narrow definition of the two-witness rule most of the evidence presented in past trials would now be inadmissible. Specifically, the validity of specter evidence was now in doubt. Two or more people were unlikely to have seen the same specter at the same time. Even in the case of "bewitched" children writhing on the ground while crying out that they were being attacked by specters, the question was in doubt because the specters were not visible to on lookers.

After the precedence established by the Harrison case, no one in Connecticut was successfully prosecuted for witchcraft with the sole exception of one conviction (followed by a reprieve) during the Salem Witch Panic in 1692-1693.

BULKELEY BECAME INVOLVED IN THE INCEST CASE of Thomas Rhood in 1672. Connecticut had to deal with a unique and sensational case, when, for the first time, a charge of incest came before the court. Thomas Rhood of Norwich was accused of getting his daughter, Sarah, with child.[154] Connecticut law had not envisioned a case of incest and there was no explicit statute to deal with the issue. In June of 1672, the court submitted the case to a group of ministers, including Gershom Bulkeley, for guidance on the proper punishment. Bulkeley along with Reverends Whiting, Haynes and Collins delivered their opinion that the law of God required the death penalty.[155]

Thomas and Sarah were brought before the Court of Assistants in Hartford on 8 October 1672. Both pled guilty to their indictments and were convicted by juries. The court met on October 14th and sentenced Thomas Rhood to be executed on October 18th. The court met the next day to consider the case of Sarah Rhood. The Assistants were not fully satisfied to impose the death penalty on Sarah and deferred the sentence to the next court.[156]

Sarah did not appear in court again until 19 May 1673, by which time she had presumably delivered the baby. The court ruled that her guilt was mitigated by her father's forcing himself on her, but that she bore responsibility afterward for concealing the fact and cause of her pregnancy. Therefore, the court did not sentence her to death, but ordered that "she be severely whipped upon her naked body once at Hartford and once at Norwich that others may hear and fear and do no more such abominable wickedness."[157]

To correct the defect of the law, the General Court ordered that Assistants should insert in the law that incest should be punished by death.[158] Gershom's actions in this case would later be used against him when he argued that residents of Connecticut should be judged only by English law. There was no law in England punishing incest.

Bulkeley would become involved in yet another case of alleged incest in 1694. This time, he argued in defense of the accused. The case arose when Samuel Hemmenway claimed that the marriage of his daughter, Elizabeth, to Nathaniel Finch of East Haven was unlawful because Elizabeth was the sister of Samuel's first wife, Mary. Mary had died about 1692. Nathaniel engaged an attorney (which may have been Bulkeley) to argue his case before the Court of Assistants. The court found the marriage to be unlawful and incestuous and declared it null and void. They found the arguments in defense not only insufficient, but also offensive.[159]

The reason for suspecting that Gershom was the attorney in the case is because his opinions about the case were later denounced by Governor Treat and Secretary Allyn. Bulkeley was assailed by them saying, "…however high his credit hath run abroad and formerly, we will here tell him that it is no good principle for any to hold that a man may lawfully marry with his deceased wife's natural sister, nor good practice to write a book to justify one that hath so done; which is said will be printed...."[160]

IV. ARMY SURGEON (1676)

[Dr. Bulkeley can go provided he is given] an easy and able horse.

~Israel Chauncy

THE SPRING OF THE YEAR 1675 opened with two grave concerns for the Connecticut Colony. The first was the threat of losing half its territory to New York and the second was the growing unrest spreading from the eastern Indians. The more serious of these threats seemed to be the one from New York. The Dutch had surrendered New York to the English in 1674. Sir Edmund Andros had taken New York in the name of the Duke of York, the brother of King Charles II. In May 1675, Andros informed the Connecticut Colony that the Duke's patent included all of Connecticut's land west of the Connecticut River.[161] This caused great alarm in Connecticut. Why would King Charles give a charter to his brother granting him all of Connecticut's land west of the Connecticut River, shortly after granting the charter won by Winthrop? It was suspected that the true intent of the king might be to consolidate all the New England colonies, revoke their charters and govern them directly.

Then in July came word of an Indian uprising that posed a more immediate threat. The trouble arose among the eastern tribes in Rhode Island. For several decades relations between the settlers of New England and the native population had been relatively peaceful. Suddenly, Metacomet, sachem of the Wampanoags, called King Philip by the English, led an uprising at Swansey in the Plymouth Colony. The uprising would grow to become New England's deadliest war. Other tribes joined King Philip's War, which eventually imperiled all the English settlements of New England.[162]

There was concern that the Narragansetts, a much larger and more powerful tribe than the Wampanoags, would join Philip. The Narragansetts exercised power within a vast area west of the Plymouth Colony including Rhode Island, Massachusetts and eastern Connecticut. News of the fighting reached Hartford on 1 July 1675. Fearing that the Narragansetts might join the uprising and attack the nearby Connecticut settlements, troops were sent to protect the eastern Connecticut towns of Stonington and New London. The coastal militias were put on alert.[163]

Gershom Bulkeley played a major role, both in diplomatically countering Andros and in the King Philip's war. He saw service in various roles during this war: as diplomat, minister, doctor and surgeon. When Connecticut learned of the uprising they immediately sent word to Andros in New York. Andros wasted no time in responding to the dispatch from Hartford. On July 4th, he personally sailed from New York with three sloops carrying a small force. He sent word to Hartford that he was coming to help with the defense against a possible Indian attack. It was suspected that Andros was using the excuse of defending against the Indians to assert his control of Saybrook at the mouth of the Connecticut River. In fact, that was his intention.[164]

The Andros dispatch reached Hartford on July 7th. Captain Thomas Bull, who had earlier been charged to see to the defense of the coastal towns from Indian attack, was ordered to go immediately to Saybrook and take command of the forces there.[165] Gershom Bulkeley accompanied Bull. Bulkeley may have been selected to be a negotiator to represent the interests of the Connecticut Colony.[166]

The Andros fleet entered Saybrook harbor early Thursday morning, July 8, before Captain Bull and Gershom arrived. To his surprise, Andros found two companies of local militia waiting. They had been assembled in response to the alert against the Indians. Robert Chapman, the leader of the local train band, was uncertain how to respond to Andros. He was without instructions from Hartford.[167] Chapman decided on his own to defend the town against a military takeover by Andros.[168]

 Bull and Gershom arrived. Gershom sent a dispatch to Hartford on Friday July 9th seeking instruction.[169] When he had had no response by Monday, July 12, an impatient Bulkeley sent another letter asking for supplies, "some meet agents" and documents to defend Connecticut's rights. He signed it "Haste, Haste." The General Court's answer to the first dispatch arrived the same day, but they sent no new negotiators. It was up to Gershom to parlay with Andros and to assert Connecticut's legal rights.[170]

On the morning of Tuesday, July 13, Andros and a few of his officers came ashore and asked to speak with the ministers and chief officers. While they were meeting, a second dispatch arrived from the General Court in Hartford. It contained a detailed protest of the Duke's claim and more explicit instructions for Bull and Bulkeley. As directed, they offered Andros an opportunity for a meeting at a place of his choosing to negotiate a formal treaty. He refused the offer and proceeded to read the Duke's charter and his commission. Bulkeley, Bull and the Connecticut group refused to listen.

Bulkeley presented the protest from Hartford, Connecticut. Their claim was based both on a charter from the King and that they had purchased the land from the Indians and defended it against the Dutch and hostile Indians. They rejected the Duke's claim to western Connecticut land but offered a negotiation. Andros declared the protest a slander. Frustrated, Andros said that he personally would return to New York, but would send some of his forces on to Martha's Vineyard to protect against the Indians.[171] Bulkeley was credited for diplomatically and adroitly managing the affair to defeat Andros's real purposes.[172]

THE TROUBLE WITH THE INDIANS signaled the beginning of the King Philip War. Philip, who the settlers called King Philip, was the second son of Massasoit, the famous sachem of the Wampanoags. Massasoit had befriended

Pilgrims at Plymouth and saved them from starvation in the early days of that plantation. Massasoit maintained cordial relationships with the settlers during his lifetime. However, he was insistent that they should not try to convert his people to Christianity.

Massasoit was succeeded by his eldest son, Alexander, and then his second son, Philip. Both sons became increasingly bitter about the conversion of tribal members to Christianity, the loss of tribal lands and the loss of their culture as their members became assimilated by the English. In 1670 there were troubling rumors that Philip might cause the local tribes to rise and destroy the towns of the Plymouth Colony. The English tried to avoid war through negotiations. On 12 April 1671, Philip signed a treaty at Taunton, Massachusetts, and agreed to give up the guns he had accumulated. However, Philip continued to plan an uprising and to conspire with the other tribes.[173]

One of Philip's chief counselors, John Sassamon, converted to Christianity and told the governor of the Plymouth Colony that Philip was planning for war. Sassamon was murdered, probably on orders from Philip, in June 1675. Three members of the Wampanoag tribe were convicted and executed by the English. Philip was enraged and began to harass the town of Swansey in the Plymouth Colony by killing livestock and burning barns. Finally, hostilities led to outright fighting. On 24 June 1675, the Indians killed several of the men of Swansey.[174] Despite the earlier signs of trouble, the English were dismayed to find that they were at war with the very tribe that had saved settlement. They were shocked at the depth of Philip's rage. He cut off the heads of some of the English slain at Swansey. He sent the heads[175] and clothing to neighboring tribes as trophies and as encouragement to join the uprising.[176]

As feared, the war spread beyond the Plymouth Colony. On July 14, the Nipmuck Indians attacked the town of Mendham, killing settlers in the Massachusetts Bay Colony for the first time.[177] Gershom Bulkeley and Reverend Haynes arrived back in Hartford from Saybrook on 16 July 1675. Captain Bull was ordered to take his men towards Stonington, New London and Norwich to guard the eastern frontiers of the colony against possible attack by the Narragansetts. He was cautioned to leave a small force in Saybrook against the threat that Andros might return.[178]

Meanwhile, Captain Wait Winthrop, in command of a company of Connecticut troops, had marched to Narragansett country. There he joined with Captain Hutchinson who led the Massachusetts forces from Boston. They negotiated a treaty with the Indians on July 15, which they hoped would keep the Narragansetts from joining King Philip's uprising.[179] It was uncertain whether the treaty would hold.

In the first week of August 1675, the Indians living along the Connecticut River near the Massachusetts towns of Hadley, Hatfield and Deerfield began assaults on isolated settlers in the area. The first actual town to be attacked was the Quaboag Plantation (now Brookfield). Forces from Springfield, Boston and Hartford came to the relief of the area. Captain Watts was sent from Hartford with twenty-five to thirty soldiers and many Indians. Both the

Mohegans under Uncas and the Pequots under Robin Cassicinamon offered their services to the English. Bulkeley, who was acquainted with both sachems, was encouraged by the General Court to negotiate with them for their support.

Gershom, in characteristic fashion, inserted himself into strategic considerations. On August 10th, he wrote from Wethersfield to Secretary John Allyn reporting the need for stricter measures for watchmen. He complained that, when young men had this duty, they did not stay awake all night, but fell asleep.[180] He recommended that older men should be assigned to watch with them. Two days later he and Samuel Talcott sent a letter asking that the town watches should be changed to military assignments and that needless gunfire should be stopped. He also offered advice on how the scattered farmers should be instructed on how to act in the event of an alarm.[181]

By the end of August all of Massachusetts was under a siege of terror of Indian attacks. Deerfield was burned on September 1st and a new plantation called Squakcag fifteen miles further up the river was attacked and devastated. Captain Beers, leading a force from the Massachusetts colony, was sent from Hadley to bring supplies to Squakeag. They were unaware of what had happened there and were ambushed by several hundred Indians. Beers and twenty of the thirty-six men with him were slain. The survivors fled back to Hadley.

Major Treat with a force of 100 from Connecticut, including Pequots and Mohegans, arrived two days later and came upon a ghastly scene. Some of the slain soldiers had had their heads cut off and fixed on poles along the road. One man had been hanged from a tree by a chain through his jaw, apparently while still alive. The Connecticut men buried the dead. Bulkeley may have been present since he served with Treat for much of the war.[182]

The commissioners of the United Colonies met in Boston and declared war on the Indians on September 9.[183] The war did not go well. On September 18, troops from Boston led by Captain Lothrop were ambushed while escorting a convoy of carts bringing grain from Deerfield to Hadley. Lothrop, along with most of the soldiers and teamsters, was killed. Only seven or eight of the nincty men escaped. September 18 was called "that most fatal day, the saddest that ever befell New England." This second disaster, following closely on that of Captain Beers, encouraged the Indians to bolder efforts and caused the English to reassess their tactics.[184]

Critics said that Beers and Lothrop were wrong to disperse their men and fight "Indian style" when they were attacked. The conventional English tactic was to form up into a cluster and march through the enemy. This had the advantage of concentrated and continuous fire and suited the relative lack of accuracy of muskets. Conversely, dispersing troops against a numerically superior enemy and fighting in their style resulted in men being cut off and surrounded.

The Indians were emboldened by their successes to attack a larger town. Springfield was alerted but did not believe the local Indians would rise against them. On October 5th, the leader of the Springfield militia rode out to speak to the Indians and they suddenly fired on and wounded him. The town's residents fled to a fortified house while the Indians burned the town. Major Treat and the Connecticut forces arrived in time to save them, but not the town.[185]

Alarmed by the destruction of Springfield, the General Court sent a force of Indians to support the Massachusetts forces, but ordered Treat to return to Hartford on October 7. They also requested that Massachusetts send 500 men to help to root out the Indians in Connecticut.[186]

There was another major battle in October. On the 19th the Indians attempted to burn Hatfield as they had Springfield. By now, diverse Massachusetts forces had assembled to meet them, and they were driven off with significant losses. This was the last assault before the body of Indian forces returned to Narragansett territory for the winter.[187]

Massachusetts questioned the withdrawal of the Connecticut forces and Treat offered to resign. The General Court reaffirmed their confidence in him and asked him to take charge of an army to go against the Indians.[188] It was customary to send a minister with the army to serve as an important advisor to the commander. Reverend Israel Chauncy, Gershom Bulkeley's brother-in-law,[189] was appointed minister to the army and Gershom was "improved" to be surgeon to the army. This may mean that Bulkeley served earlier, but not as surgeon. Both Chauncy and Bulkeley were designated to function as key members of the Council of War.[190]

The expedition marched up the Connecticut River to join Bay Colony forces searching for Indians around the Massachusetts towns. Finding none, they concluded that the hostile Indians had left the area. Treat brought the army back to Hartford on Nov. 17th.[191]

Although there was a treaty between the Narragansetts and the English, it had clearly been violated and the Narragansetts were giving support and aid to King Philip. The commissioners of the United Colonies in Boston declared war on the powerful Narragansett tribe. The United Colonies decided that the Narragansetts would be stronger by Spring and that despite the difficulty of military operations during the harsh winter, they needed to attack the Narragansetts and their allies in their winter quarters. The Indian raids during the fall of 1675 had lacked coordination but had still been devastating in destroying New England settlements. If the Indians were left alone to consolidate their forces and plan unified attacks over the winter, they might overwhelm the English the next Spring.

The commissioners ordered the Massachusetts, Connecticut and Plymouth Colonies to raise a combined army of 1,000 men by December 10th and to launch an attack.[192] Major Josiah Winslow of the Massachusetts Bay Colony was chosen as commander-in-chief with Major Treat as second in command.[193] The word of the Commissioners' actions reached Hartford and the Council acted to raise their share of the forces...110 from Hartford County, sixty-three from New Haven County, seventy-two from Fairfield County and seventy from New London County. Major Treat was commissioned to act as commander-in-chief of the

Connecticut forces until the united armies joined. Treat was ordered to assemble his forces in New London, Connecticut by December 10th.[194]

The army of the United Colonies assembled to attack the Indians in their winter quarters. The Connecticut army was organized into five companies. Captain John Gallop of Stonington led the First Company. Captain Samuel Marshall of Windsor led the Second Company. Captain Nathaniel Seely of Stratford led the Third Company. Captain Thomas Watts of Hartford led the Fourth Company. Captain John Mason of Norwich led the Fifth Company. Treat's staff consisted of Gershom as surgeon, Reverend Nicholas Noyes as chaplain, and Stephan Barrett as commissary.[195] The Council requested that Treat take special care for the safety of Bulkeley and Noyes.[196] The army, consisting of approximately 315 soldiers and 150 Mohegan and Pequot warriors left New London for the Narragansett territory. The weather was severely cold, and the march was through deep snow. They arrived at the place of rendezvous, Pettisquamscot (now Tower Hill) in South Kingstown, Rhode Island, on Friday, December 17th. All the United Colonies' army joined them there the next day. [197] There was no shelter, they spent the night in the open in a storm.[198]

The Narragansetts were known to have built a fortified village in a nearby swamp, but the exact location was uncertain. The army of nearly 1,000 men, with Governor Josiah Winslow of Plymouth as commander-in-chief, moved at daybreak led by an Indian guide. They marched until one o'clock without pausing to light fires or take food.

The Massachusetts forces, six companies of foot soldiers, numbering 465, and seventy-five cavalry were in the forefront. They were followed by the five companies of Connecticut soldiers numbering 300 with an additional 150 Pequot and Mohegan Indians. Half the Indians were attached to the First company led by Captain John Gallop of Stonington and half to the Fifth company led by Captain John Mason of Norwich. This order of march may have been intended to prevent confusing the Indians allies with the enemy.[199] General Winslow and his staff brought up the rear along with the Plymouth force of 158 men who were held in reserve.[200]

The fort was built on a raised piece of land of five or six acres like an island in the midst of a dense cedar swamp. The fort was unusually impregnable, being surrounded by a palisade which was protected by a thick brush hedge.[201] Within this fort were 400 to 500 wigwams whose walls were lined with baskets of food and tubs of grain, making the walls almost impenetrable by musket fire.[202]

The English soldiers came to the edge of the swamp where they were fired on by some Indians who then fled back toward the fort.[203] The leading soldiers rushed forward without waiting for orders or organization. An entry was found where a break in the fort's wall was blocked only by a large log. However, a blockhouse opposite the break in the wall poured deadly fire on soldiers scrambling over the log. By the time the Connecticut forces arrived, many soldiers had forced their way into the fort. The Connecticut men apparently were not aware that the blockhouse was still dangerous and as they crossed the log their ranks were devastated by a withering fire.[204] Connecticut lost four of its five captains. Gallop, Seely and Marshall fell dead at the log[205] and John Mason was mortally wounded.[206]

As the Indian warriors were driven out of the fort and fled into the swamp through concealed exits in the walls of the fort, some of the soldiers began to set fire to the wigwams. Colonel Benjamin Church tried to intervene. Church was used to working with Indian allies and did not want to see a massacre of the Indian women and children. Hatred of all Indians was so great among some of the men from the Bay and Plymouth Colonies that they spread rumors that the Mohegans and Pequots with the Connecticut force conspired to fire over the heads of the Narragansetts. [207]

Church was an advocate of including Indian allies. He would eventually be recognized as the "father of the rangers," forming a very effective mixed force of English and Indians that tracked down and ambushed Indian enemies. Church claimed that the fort was taken and begged that the wigwams be spared and used to settle the wounded men. Others insisted that they had orders from the General to burn everything. As they argued, one of the doctors (perhaps Bulkeley)[208] rushed up and insisted that Church was wrong. He said that, if Church's advice was followed: "it would kill more men than the enemy had killed for (he said) by tomorrow the wounded men will be so stiff that there will be no moving them." Noticing that Church himself was bleeding from wounds he had suffered, he said that if Church continued the argument, "he should bleed to death like a dog before he would endeavor to stanch his blood". Church relented, and his wounds were treated. [209]

The battle lasted three hours. After the fort was burned, the United Colonies army began a miserable retreat through the night in a heavy snowstorm. They carried the dead and wounded, leaving only eight bodies in the fort. Twenty-two died on the march from the fort to Richard Smith's garrison house at Wickford, Rhode Island. Gershom and the other surgeons must have had a desperate time caring for the wounded during the night-long struggle through the snowstorm. The general and the ministers (probably including Gershom) and forty troops with him became lost in the storm, marched nearly thirty miles and did not reach the Wickford camp until morning.[210]

The English suffered 170 killed or wounded. Many of the wounded soldiers died and were buried at Wickford. Most of wounded were evacuated from Rhode Island by sail. Estimates of the losses by the Narragansetts varied widely. Hubbard claimed that 700 warriors were killed that day, 300 more died from wounds, starvation and exposure along with an unknown number of old men, women and children.[211] The Narragansetts asserted that they lost only forty warriors and that their losses were mostly of old men, women and children.

Major Treat and his shattered army arrived in Stonington three days after Christmas.[212] Of the three hundred soldiers, seventy were killed and wounded. Treat was later criticized for withdrawing to Connecticut without permission, but he may have had little choice. With their officers dead, some of the untrained Connecticut soldiers simply headed home.[213] Gershom eventually moved the surviving Connecticut soldiers to New London. In addition to being a base of operations, New London had traditionally served as a "hospital town." This is a role it had played since early in the medical practice of Governor John Winthrop Jr.

Colonel Treat was directed to reassemble an army at New London and take to the field again. On 14 January 1675, the council appointed John Brackett of Wallingford "to go forthwith to New London to take care of and assist in the dressing of wounded men, in absence of Mr. Bulkeley whilst he goeth out with the army." They also dispatched Sergeant William Ward to New London to help with the care of the wounded.[214]

Gershom accompanied Treat's army on new expeditions in January and in February. Bulkeley served not only as surgeon to the army, but also procured supplies. He also used his good standing with the Pequots and Mohegans to enlist warriors to go with the army. Between expeditions, Bulkeley returned to New London to attend the wounded.[215]

Many of the Narragansetts were reported to have retreated to a strong camp at Wachusett Hill (near Princeton, Massachusetts) for the winter.[216] Massachusetts sent a force of 300 soldiers and a troop of horse under Major Thomas Savage to attack this camp.[217] Savage requested help from Connecticut and Gershom rode out with Major Treat and the Connecticut soldiers. On March 4, they found some of the Indian towns deserted. Fearing that the

Indians had gone to attack the settlements on the upper Connecticut River, they abandoned the attempt to attack Wachusett Hill and marched west toward the river. As the expedition ranged through the woods, they were suddenly fired upon from ambush by small party of Indians. Gershom was shot and wounded in the thigh, but the wound was not life-threatening.[218]

On 11 March 1676, the council appointed Gershom's brother-in-law, Israel Chauncy, to go with the army as surgeon.[219] However, on 27 March 1676 Mr. Chauncy, being informed that his wife was dying and his child was dangerously ill, wrote from Stratford and asked if Gershom could replace him. He requested that Gershom be provided with "an easy and able horse."[220]

March was the most successful month of the war for the Indians. Town after town was wholly or partially destroyed and many were abandoned as indefensible. Soon settlers were fleeing from Springfield, Deerfield, Northfield, Brookfield, Lancaster, Groton, Mendon, Wrentham, Swansey, Rehoboth, Dartmouth, Marlboro, Simsbury, Warwick and Providence.[221]

Adding to the depressing news, Gershom's good friend, the revered Governor John Winthrop Jr., suddenly died in Boston on 5 April 1676 while attending a meeting of the United Colonies' leadership. Winthrop's death removed a key force for mediation and diplomacy, both in the current conflict and in the struggles to come with England over the right of the colonies to govern themselves. Winthrop's sons, Wait-Still and Fitz-John, would eventually become important leaders for Connecticut, but they were not of the caliber of John Winthrop and years away from taking any significant roles.

Food had become so scarce that shipments out of the Connecticut Colony, even to Massachusetts, were prohibited. In April, Gershom sought and was granted the liberty to ship sixty bushels of corn to Boston. This was to purchase medicine and other supplies.[222]

Gershom returned to Wethersfield and continued to care for wounded soldiers there. On 11 May 1676, the General Court noted that many wounded men were coming to Bulkeley and expressed its desire that Gershom should take the care and dressing of the wounded soldiers "til God bless his endeavors with a cure." They also asked that Reverend Stone assist Bulkeley and, in his absence, relieve him in the work of the ministry at Wethersfield.[223]

On 19 May 1676, Bulkeley wrote the council urging that payment be sent for the drugs that had already been purchased so that there would not be trouble in getting more. He also requested that the commissary be instructed to obtain certain articles from Boston. He apparently went to Boston himself because he asked that corn be sent to Mr. Bradstreet (Simon Bradstreet, commissioner of the United Colonies and later governor of the Massachusetts Colony) for his entertainment of Captain Mason and Gershom. In this letter, he refers to his orders to go out again with the army. He asks that, if he goes, better provision be made for the town of Wethersfield, care of his family and care of the wounded.[224] Reverend Samuel Stone Jr. asked the council to provide some stated allowance for his labors at Wethersfield in Gershom's absence. The council replied that due to costs of the present troubles, they could provide only twenty shillings per week for Stone's work.[225]

Gershom went out in May with an army led by Major John Talcott. This force marched to Norwich on May 26th with Gershom and the chaplain, the Reverend Mr. Fitch, serving as Talcott's Council of War.[226] The army was detained at Norwich while it awaited supplies from New London. The Mohegans and Pequots were not disposed to go with the army because they had been poorly rewarded for past efforts. After some debate, they were convinced, and Talcott left Norwich with 240 English and 200 Indians.[227] Talcott marched north on June 2nd into the same area targeted earlier by Savage. From there they went to the towns on the upper Connecticut River including Hadley which they may have saved from total destruction. Talcott wrote the council from Northhampton on June 8, complaining the bread had not been properly prepared. It was infested with blue mold even though it had been kept dry. The soldiers suffered on this long march from the want of provisions and it became known in Connecticut as the "hungry" march.[228]

They fought several small battles but met with few of the enemy. The army returned to Connecticut on June 10th.[229] The Council of War ordered a coat be given to every Indian who served on this expedition, since "the service was tedious and little or no plunder gained."[230]

Talcott's army went out again after a few days rest, marching east toward Providence and wreaking havoc on the Narragansetts. Desperate and starving Indians surrendered in large numbers. The army returned briefly and then went out again on the 20th of July. Gershom was probably present on these expeditions. Talcott's army marched east to the very heart of the Plymouth Colony and then pursued a large group of Indians fleeing west toward Albany.[231] A fight with this group on August 15th was the last action of the war involving Connecticut troops.[232] The army returned to Connecticut on August 18th and was disbanded.

King Philip had been killed on 12 August 1676. Colonel Benjamin Church of the Plymouth Colony had formed a very effective mobile ranger force of English and Indian fighters which could strike without warning and then disappear into the forest. They hunted down King Philip's band and one of Church's Indian warriors ambushed Philip as he fled and killed him with a shot to the heart.[233]

In October 1676, Bulkeley asked to step down from his duties as minister of the Wethersfield church on a plea of impaired health. He cited particularly, "the weakness of my voice" arising from his exposures in the Indian campaigns. Bulkeley's voice may not have been all that weak, but he may have judged himself relative to his father, Peter Bulkeley, who had been famous for preaching in a booming voice.

The war continued for some time in northern New England, but not in Connecticut. On 2 January 1677, the Council voted to return a hearty thanks to the Reverend Gershom Bulkeley for his service during the war. They ordered the treasurer to pay him the sum of thirty pounds as an acknowledgement of his good service to his country, besides the satisfying of those that supplied his place in the ministry.[234]

V. MILLER, DOCTOR, LAWYER, FARMER (1676 -1684)

*In ye morning when I rose, a little giddy, but it went off...
but these two days of milling, etc. very hard [for me]*

~Gershom Bulkeley diary

GOVERNOR JOHN WINTHROP JR. had always maintained a broad interest in Connecticut's economic and industrial development. An important component of such development was the harnessing of water power from favorable stream sites. Winthrop had originally proposed to build a mill on the Dividend Brook site in Wethersfield, even though he was living in New London. The town had responded by offering him a gift of land for mills and dams, provided he built them.[235]

The Dividend Brook flowed into the Connecticut River near Wethersfield's southern boundary with Middletown. It passed over and through a ledge of rocks in a natural waterfall before entering the river. It was an ideal spot for a mill. John Winthrop's proposal to the town had been for a "corne-mill" or grist mill there. This would allow local farmers to grind their corn into meal for their own consumption and for trade.

Dividend Brook had never been mentioned in the records of Wethersfield until the 5 June 1661 grant to Winthrop.

The grant of 140 acres was described as including "Dividend Brook and sufficient land to build upon both mills and dams."[236] When other matters took Winthrop's attention, delaying construction of a mill, he released the land back to the town in 1668. The town gave it to Bulkeley.

For colonial settlers, the most dependable source of power, other than their own strength or that of farm animals, was waterpower. Almost every sizeable brook, stream and river was eventually harnessed with water wheels to drive gristmills, sawmills and, later, miscellaneous manufacturing. By necessity towns were dependent mostly on food and goods produced locally. Until the corn was ground into meal, it could not be baked into bread. Without a mill, the grinding was a laborious process. Furthermore, grinding by hand did not produce a sufficiently large quantity of meal to be sent out in trade.

A grist mill was a boon to the local economy. Leaders like Bulkeley and Winthrop, who had the means, saw economic development as part of their larger community responsibility. One of the first investments that Gershom's father, Peter Bulkeley, had made in the founding of Concord, Massachusetts was the erection of a mill. Of course, ownership of a mill also provided the owner with an assured source of income.

The town granted the site to Gershom under the same conditional requirement as Winthrop, namely that he build a mill.[237] Gershom did not immediately proceed with the development of his grist mill at Dividend Brook.[238] In

February of 1676, in the middle of King Philip's War, Gershom was reminded by the town of his promise to build a mill.[239] He must have acted quickly in response. By 10 April 1676 he was asking the permission of the General Council to ship sixty bushels of corn to Boston. He may have meant corn meal from his grist mill. As the war progressed, food had become an increasingly strategic issue for both the English and the Indians, and Gershom could have had help from the colony to expedite the construction of his mill in such a short time. The official records, however, make no mention of this.

Gershom's land holdings at the mill site were extensive. The town had originally granted 120 acres to Gershom and 100 acres to Samuel Stone Jr. at the mouth of Dividend Brook in November 1667 on the condition that they settle as officers of the church for life.[240] The town added twenty acres to Gershom's holdings in 1670. In November 1678, to expand operations at the mill, Gershom was given 150 acres more, making his total holdings 490 acres. After dams on the brook created two mill ponds, and grist mills were constructed at the lower end of each, the town decided to extend a highway to the mill to facilitate traffic to and from it.[241] There were complaints that this town expenditure unfairly enriched Bulkeley.

What became of the share that Reverend Samuel Stone, Jr. had in the land holding at Dividend Brook or whether he ever held any interest in the mill is unclear. Stone did not succeed Gershom as minister of the Wethersfield church. By April 1677, the church was in the hands of Reverend Joseph Rowlandson.[242] On 5 December 1678 Stone was in court in Hartford charged with drunkenness[243] and his life went downhill from there. He preached at Simsbury, but quarreled with the selectmen over his pay.[244] He was brought to court on two more occasions for drunkenness. The court declared that "he is not fit to be left to himself" and put him under the care of Nathaniel Ruscoe, the constable of Hartford.[245] On 9 October 1683 Stone fell down the bank trying to cross the bridge over the little river in Hartford after a night of drinking and was drowned.[246]

Corn meal was a valuable commodity. On 13 June 1685, John Hale of Wethersfield was committed to jail for stealing a bag of meal from Gershom's mill and also from Mr. Woodbridge and Thomas Williams.[247] Hale was fined and whipped.[248]

Despite failing health Gershom continued to operate the mill. His diary for 21 July 1699 contained the following entry. "In ye morning when I rose, a little giddy, but it went off and so next morning. But these two days I wrought at milling, etc. very hard [for me]". In November, he gave up trying to run the mill himself. On Friday 27 November 1699 he wrote, "Samuel Smith began to keep my mill."[249] Shortly before Gershom died in 1713, he conveyed the mill and some of the land to his son, Edward. The mill remained in succeeding generations of the Bulkeley family until 1830.[250]

The mill area is preserved as the Dividend Pond Trails and Archaeological District in present-day Rocky Hill, Connecticut. It is considered the first "industrial park" in Connecticut. There are two mill ponds. The site of

Gershom's original mill on the lower pond was obliterated by the construction of a railroad in 1871. His second mill site on the upper pond contains remnants of subsequent mills.[251]

In ADDITION TO BEING A MILLER, Gershom was also a farmer. Nearly all colonists, even those with a profession such as minister, doctor or lawyer, were usually to some extent engaged in some farming to produce their own food. Gershom was no exception. In farming, as in other matters, Bulkeley took an analytic and scholarly approach. He read the literature from England on the latest ideas about agriculture. Among his manuscripts are his notes on a publication by the English engineer and agriculturist, Andrew Yarranton.[252] Yarranton was one of the first to recognize the value of growing clover in fallow fields to enrich the soil. Yarranton's most famous book was, *The great improvement of lands by clover, or, The wonderful advantage by, and right management of clover.* This was probably not the book Gershom read because it was published in London in 1663. However, earlier Yarranton had printed two small pamphlets promoting his business as an agent selling clover seeds. Gershom had most likely read one of these. Even when he was the minister in New London, Gershom wrote to the English seed producers in December 1662, seeking better quality and less expensive seeds.[253] He suggested that many towns and cities in Massachusetts and Connecticut would provide a ready market for these seeds.

Bulkeley sowed wheat, barley and peas on land in Wethersfield that he referred to as Bats's. But he did not simply sow his crops; he experimented with soaking the seeds in various liquids to speed up their germination rates. One of these experiments was interrupted by a turn in the weather. Gershom noted that the ground was dry when the first parcel was set, but soon there was a thundershower and "wind and rain much like a hurricane wherein poured down abundance of water which, I think, was a great means to bringing up those seeds so soon."

Gershom also raised medicinal herbs. In his notebook in 1683 he recorded that he had planted senna seeds both at Bats's and in his house garden. He had received the senna seeds from the island of Antigua in the Caribbean. Gershom had visited Antigua in the spring of 1681 with his son, Charles.[254] Senna had been used for folk medicine for millennia and was usually used as a laxative. He carefully noted how many plants had grown and experimented by planting both seeds that had been soaked and seeds that had not been soaked.

Gershom also raised livestock, including pigs. In his 1683 notebook he commented that "May 8, the black sow pigged 10 pigs. May 10, another white sow pigged 6 pigs, whereof one died. Ye red spotted sow pigged 9 pigs."

He also noted when the first blossoms appeared on the quince trees. "June 8, 9, 10, one blossom upon one quince tree and 2 upon another at Bats's. June 15, one blossom and one bud more upon this last quince tree."

AFTER HE HAD RESIGNED FROM THE MINISTRY of the Wethersfield church in 1677, Gershom had turned his attention more fully to the practice of medicine. After that date, his name frequently appears in written records with the prefix of "Doct."[255] His responsibilities for the care of soldiers wounded in the King Philip's War continued for some time after the war. One of his most famous patients was Jonathan Wells, who was wounded in the "Falls Fight" of 19 May 1676. The "Falls Fight" occurred when residents of several towns near Springfield, Massachusetts, tired of fighting a defensive battle, decided to go on the offensive. Upon hearing that a large group of Indians were resupplying their food provisions by fishing at the falls on the Connecticut River, they planned an attack. Captain William Turner of Boston led a mixed force of 140 soldiers and volunteers, mostly from Springfield, Hadley, Northhampton and Hatfield, on an attack. The initial surprise assault was very successful and almost without casualties, but the Indians regrouped and counterattacked the retreating Englishmen. Captain Turner and forty of his men were killed.

Sixteen-year-old Jonathan Wells was wounded in this fight and made a miraculous escape. Jonathan's leg was shattered by a bullet and his horse was wounded. He escaped only to ride back into the battle to rescue another young soldier. He then fled the fight, pursued by Indian warriors. He turned his wounded horse loose and continued to flee on foot. He evaded his Indian pursuers in a series of escapes that would do credit to a tale by James Fennimore Cooper. At one point, he hid in a stream under a partially fallen tree with his head barely above water. He finally arrived in Hatfield several days later. His harrowing experiences are detailed in a manuscript he wrote, which was published in an appendix to a book on the captivity and deliverance of Reverend John Williams.[256] Wells was later known as the "Boy Hero of the Connecticut Valley." In 1901 a stone monument in his honor was erected by the children of Deerfield.

Wells was sent to Hartford and put under the care of Bulkeley and Mrs. Allyn for medical treatment.[257] His leg was not just broken; the bone was shattered, and he probably suffered massive infections. He was under their care for four years and two months. He lay in bed for the first six months without being turned and all the skin came off his back as a result.[258] Wells complained that this constituted poor medical treatment.

Gershom applied to the Massachusetts government for payment for treating Wells. In June 1680, the Massachusetts Court granted Bulkeley twenty-five pounds money or forty pounds in country pay (barter) in full payment for treating Jonathan Wells. Gershom refused the settlement. He sued in County Court in Hartford on 3 March 1680/1 against Major John Pynchon of Springfield.[259] Bulkeley claimed that in his public capacity of a senior officer in Springfield, Pynchon had requested that all due care should be given to his wounded soldiers and he had sent them to Bulkeley to cure their wounds. Gershom was suing for medications and physical care of Jonathan Wells and John Honeywell. He sued for sixty-three pounds for debt with damage. Only the case of Jonathan Wells went to trial. The jury found for Gershom and awarded him forty-nine pounds, eleven shillings and cost of court.

Massachusetts objected that the government of Connecticut should never have allowed this suit. They claimed that it was a breach of an early agreement among the commissioners of the United Colonies meeting in Plymouth that each colony would discharge all existing debts to their own inhabitants for charges incurred by the war. The matter came before a meeting of the commissioners of the United Colonies on 6 September 1681. They agreed to pay the forty-nine pounds awarded by the Hartford County Court. In exchange, it was agreed that all legal judgments against Major Pynchon were to be dropped.[260]

Although Gershom developed an active medical practice, he did not have official recognition as a doctor. In 1686, he applied to the General Court for such official recognition. The General Court in Hartford passed the following resolution on 14 October 1686. "The Court being well acquainted with the ability, skill and knowledge of Mr. Gershom Bulkeley in the arts of phissick and chirurgery, do grant him full and free liberty and license to practice in the administration of phissick and chirurgery as there shall be occasion and he shall be capable to attend."[261]

95

After the war, Gershom expanded his medical practice. His daybook shows that in1688 he treated patients throughout Connecticut. [262] There are charges for patients from Fairfield, Farmington, Hartford, Lyme, Middletown, New London, Simsbury, Wallingford, Wethersfield and Windsor.

GERSHOM ALSO PURSUED THE ACQUISITION OF LAND. Land holdings, as the core means of wealth, had always been an important goal of New England settlers. Litigation over land ownership was the major issue filling most of the court records. Gershom Bulkeley was noted for his knowledge of the law and was often involved in such legal cases. Expeditions to fight the Indians in the area north of Norwich during the King Philip's War had made the settlers aware of the attractiveness of this land. In May 1682, some of the inhabitants of Wethersfield petitioned the General Court for liberty to raise a new plantation in what was called the "Wabaquassit" country. The petition was in the handwriting of Gershom Bulkeley. It asked for a grant of ten square miles with the usual privileges and encouragements. The tract was so far north that the petitioners were uncertain whether it might fall partially within the jurisdiction of Massachusetts. Since the petitioners were not willing to move outside the Connecticut Colony, they requested that the location of the Massachusetts line be settled.[263]

Uncas also claimed this land by right of conquest ever since 1637 in the Pequot War.[264] Despite Gershom's efforts, the

Wethersfield group eventually gave up their attempts to obtain title to this land. Captain James Fitch of Norwich purchased the Indian rights from Oweneco, son of Uncas, on 24 June 1684.[265]

In 1672, the Connecticut General Court had moved to encourage settlement in some of the then unsettled lands. One of these actions was very important to the residents of Wethersfield since it extended the bounds of the town five miles to the east. On 15 January 1673, the town assessed the residents a tax of one half penny on the pound of their estate to pay for purchase of the land from the Indians. Gershom was one of the 114 who paid the tax. He paid one shilling and ten and a half pence. He received a grant of nearly 68 acres

Rather than extend its boundary, the town elected to allow the Wethersfield residents to hold the land as individual proprietors.[266] This land became known as the "Great Indian Purchase of 1673".[267] The proprietors were slow to take up their new holdings and others began to settle there. In 1701, Gershom was a member of a committee, established by the proprietors, to take legal action to recover the land from unauthorized occupants.[268] The matter was still unsettled by 1714 after Gershom had died, his son, Edward, joined the committee and continued to prosecute the lawsuits.[269]

In 1684, Gershom entered into a famous legal battle with John Hollister which eventually caused the boundaries of all the Wethersfield lots of Naubuc (now Glastonbury) on the east side of the Connecticut River to be resurveyed. The

Naubuc lots had first been laid out in 1640. Each lot was a horizontal strip bounded by the Connecticut River on the west and extending three miles east into the "wilderness." Beginning at the Wethersfield-Hartford boundary on the north the lots were laid out for six miles along the Connecticut River. The north and south boundaries of each lot were extended in straight lines except for the southern-most lot, which had been granted to Matthew Mitchell. Its southern boundary began at the mouth of the Sturgeon River (also called Roaring Brook) and ran east along the brook until it reached a marked tree near the "cow pens" and then went due east. This unusual boundary led to the lawsuit between Bulkeley and Hollister.

After Mitchell moved from Wethersfield, his large, 900-acre tract was divided into four lots of 225 acres each. One of these lots was acquired by Gershom Bulkeley and John Belden. An adjoining lot belonged to Lieutenant John Hollister. In addition, Hollister also acquired land south of the Mitchell lot which had not been laid out in 1640.

Bulkeley sued John Hollister on 4 September 1684, in County Court in Hartford on behalf of himself and John Belden, deceased, as well as his sons, Jonathan Belden and Joseph Belden. Bulkeley accused Hollister of detaining a portion of their land. Bulkeley sought return of the land and ten pounds in damages. The jury found in favor of Hollister and Gershom had to pay him two pounds and six shillings in court costs. Gershom appealed to the next Court of Assistants.[270]

The case was taken up in the Court of Assistants in October 1684. This time the jury found in favor of the plaintiffs, Gershom and Belden. Hollister was ordered to surrender the land and to pay costs of twenty-four shillings for witnesses. Hollister entered an appeal to the next General Court.[271]

The case came before the General Court on 9 October 1684.[272] The Court appointed a committee to view and measure the land in controversy, including all the Naubuc lots along the river from the Hartford line south. They were charged to attempt to compose the difference between Bulkeley and Hollister and to report to the General Court next May.[273]

The dispute hinged on the location of the southern boundary of the old Matthew Mitchell tract. The rather vague description in the land records said the line ran from mouth of the Sturgeon River (Roaring Brook) to a tree near the cow pens and then due east. The cow pens no longer existed, and tree claimed as the marker was in doubt. Bulkeley claimed that the cow pens and the marker tree lay to the southeast of the mouth of the brook. Hollister claimed that another tree, very near the mouth of the Sturgeon River, was the marker. The controversy was heard by a jury and the testimony grew voluminous.[274] Although Bulkeley was very able as a lawyer, he hired the famous Richard Edwards (later, in 1705, named the first Queen's Attorney in the colonies[275]) to plead his case. The equally regarded William Pitkin appeared for Hollister.

Many witnesses appeared to try to establish the location of the now the ancient "cow pens," but its exact location remained uncertain. The court decided that it would be necessary to re-survey all the Naubuc lots along the river. The surveyors began at the mouth of Pewter Pot Brook, which had been designated in 1636 as the boundary marker on the east side of the river between Hartford and Wethersfield. They measured all the thirty-eight lots along the river as they had been recorded in 1640 and arrived at Bulkeley's tree which was eighty-five and a half rods south of Hollister's marker tree. Furthermore, upon examination the marks on Hollister's tree were judged to be merely blotches, while Bulkeley's tree had clearly been marked with an axe.

Hollister suggested that the surveyors had erred because they had not correctly established the starting point at the Wethersfield-Hartford boundary line. In 1636, the demarcation for this line had been the point at which a small brook, called Pewter Pot Brook, flowed into the Connecticut River. Hollister contended that over time the river channel had moved so that the mouth of Pewter Pot brook was now eighty-five and a half rods south of its 1636 location.[276] Hollister insisted that his lot line, the southern boundary of the Matthew Mitchell tract, began at the mouth of the Sturgeon River and that any deficiency this caused in size of the other lots along the river should be made up by placing the Wethersfield-Hartford boundary line further north. The Court ruled otherwise. They declared the southern boundary of the Mitchell lot to be as Gershom asserted, giving him a clear victory.

It is interesting that, when the first history of Glastonbury was produced in 1853,[277] the author, Reverend Alonzo Chapin, wrote as though Hollister had been right about the location of the Wethersfield-Hartford boundary, now the Glastonbury-East Hartford boundary. The implication was that Bulkeley was to blame for Glastonbury losing some of its land. This argument was made explicit by the author of a 1970 history, *Glastonbury from Settlement to Suburb,* who wrote, "The long-term result of the proceedings was to deprive Glastonbury of rods of land now belonging to East Hartford." [278],[279]

Richard G. Tomlinson

VI. JUSTICE OF THE PEACE (1685-1689)

If I were to condemn ye Devil...I would give him a hearing

If we have an election before...orders come [from England] ...it will be a wonderful thing if you be not looked upon and dealt with as criminals

~Gershom Bulkeley

THE DEATH OF KING CHARLES II IN 1685 carried broad implications for Connecticut and for all New England. The king had initially ruled New England with a light hand but had begun to assert more control over the New England colonies toward the end of his reign. Connecticut considered its government well-established under the charter that Charles had granted in 1662 but was wary of attempts to weaken it. They soon had cause for concern.

When, on the eve of the King Philip's War, the Duke of York, sent Sir Edmund Andros to enforce his claim to all of Connecticut's land west of the Connecticut River, it was Gershom Bulkeley who faced him down at Saybrook. Bulkeley represented Connecticut's superior claims based on the charter of 1662 as well as the labor and sacrifice that the settlers had expended to settle, subdue and cultivate the land since the days of the Warwick Patent.

This was not the only assault on the government of Connecticut. Edward Randolph, who arrived in Boston in 1676, made annual complaints that New England was not properly governed. He sent regular reports to the Lords of Trade and insisted that the colonies needed to be more directly controlled by the crown. In 1680 Andros asserted control over Fisher's Island in Long Island Sound over the objections of Connecticut. Also, in 1680, Connecticut Governor William Leete was pressured by Randolph into taking an oath respecting English law on trade and navigation. Randolph's reports were presumably one of the causes of King Charles II's beginning actions in 1684 to revoke the charter of the Massachusetts Bay Colony and move to unify the government of the Massachusetts Bay Colony, the Plymouth Colony, New Hampshire and Maine under a single dominion.

At the request of the Lords of Trade, Randolph also drew up "articles of high misdemeanor" in July 1685. These were used to obtain writs of *Quo Warranto* against the colonies of Connecticut and Rhode Island with the intent that "their Charters being vacated they also may thereby be united under his Majesty's laws and government." The first in the list of misdemeanors by the colonies was that "They have made laws contrary to the laws of England."[280]

King Charles II died on 6 February 1685, before his appointed governor took control of the Dominion of New England. However, his successor, James II, quickly continued the effort to unite the New England colonies. King James allowed a temporary provisional government to

be established in Boston under Joseph Dudley, the
President of the Council of New England.

Rhode Island yielded its charter, but Connecticut resisted.
However, the handwriting was on the wall that King James
II intended to complete the consolidation of New England.
Dudley urged Connecticut to join with his dominion and
avoid the possibility of being forcibly joined to New York.
Dudley wrote to Governor Robert Treat and argued that
Connecticut should act before the *Quo Warrantos* were
actually served on them. He emphasized that the shared
religious and political ties of Connecticut and
Massachusetts made them a more congenial match than a
union with New York or any other entity. Treat also
received letters from Governor Donegan of New York,
urging that Connecticut join with his New York Colony.

Connecticut appealed to England to remain independent of
the other colonies.[281] On 24 August 1686, Governor Robert
Treat drew up a petition in the name of the "Governor and
Company," and sent it to Connecticut's agent in England,
William Whiting. Whiting was instructed to see that the
petition, seeking suspension of the *Quo Warrantos*, was
presented to the King. He was also asked to determine
whether, if no suspension could be obtained, his Majesty
intended to have Connecticut annexed to Massachusetts or
New York or divided between them.

Two other petitions were also prepared which were,
apparently, for Whiting to use as might be required. One
presented the reasons why Connecticut should be continued

as a single, distinct colony. The other asked that if the Charter were voided, certain religious and commercial rights be retained.

In December Treat received a letter from Randolph saying that a third *Quo Warranto* had been issued against Connecticut. This was accompanied by a letter from Andros to Treat. Andros wrote that the King had commanded him to "receive in his name the surrender of your Charter…and to take you into my present care and charge.…"

Many of Connecticut's men of influence, including Governor Treat, Secretary Allyn and Fitz John Winthrop, were in favor of ending the threat of the *Quo Warranto* by submitting to the King's will. Three of the principal magistrates, John Talcott, John Allyn and Samuel Talcott, addressed a message to the General Assembly on 30 March 1687 saying, "…we are for answering his majesty's expectation by a present submission, and are against all further prosecutions or engagements by lawsuits in opposition to his majesty's known pleasure for our submission."[282]

The General Court was not willing to follow this advice and Governor Treat was ordered by the General Court to send a new appeal to England in January 1686/7. This letter was sent to the Earl of Sunderland, the secretary of state. This letter indicated that, if Connecticut were to be conjoined with another colony, they preferred that of Andros. Gershom Bulkeley later construed this as the first surrender of the Charter. There was also an exchange of letters between Treat and Andros in which the Connecticut Governor insisted that any action must wait upon an official reply to the appeals to England. An increasingly irritated Andros accused the Connecticut government of obstinate delay.

Sir Edmund Andros decided to deal directly with Connecticut.[283] When Andros had first arrived in Boston in December of 1686 to take charge as the governor of the Dominion of New England, a decision had already been made to add Rhode Island and Connecticut to the Dominion. Rhode Island had readily yielded its charter, but Connecticut still resisted. Andros went to Hartford to meet with Governor Robert Treat and the General Court. Andros and his entourage arrived in Hartford in 31 October 1687 to receive the charter and assume control of the government of Connecticut.

Gershom Bulkeley was not present when Andros met with the General Court, but he wrote extensively about the event in his treatise, *Will and Doom*. According to Bulkeley's account, Andros and his entourage were "received with all respect and welcome congratulation that Connecticut was capable of." The Andros party was ceremoniously escorted from Wethersfield on the Connecticut River where it landed, to Hartford by a troop of horse. There the train bands of several towns were waiting to pay their respects. Bulkeley said that, "Being arrived at Hartford, he is greeted and caressed by the Governor and Assistants...."

The records of the General Court held at Hartford on 31 October 1687 state:[284]

> His Excellency Sir Edmund Andros, Knight, Captain General and Governor of his Majesties' Territory and Dominion in New England, by order of his Majesty James, the second, King of England, Scotland, France and Ireland, the 31 of October 1687, took into his hands the Government of this Colony of Connecticut, it being by his Majesty annexed to the Massachusetts and other Colonies under his Excellency's Government.

Secretary John Allyn concluded the record by writing the word, FINIS, indicating the end of the autonomous Connecticut government.

According to Bulkeley, Andros met with the governor, deputy governor, assistants and deputies in the Court Chamber. The chamber filled with people. Andros read his commission. Secretary Allyn turned over the seal of the Colony of Connecticut Andros moved carefully to establish a framework of government and law that would be recognized as legitimate and sound. He made Treat and Allyn and the General Court officers of his government and administered the oath of office. Only one man is said to have objected that he would prefer the government remain as it was.

AN ENDURING LEGEND IN CONNECTICUT HISTORY is the story of the hiding of the charter in the Charter Oak tree. According to this legend, the charter was laid on the table and Governor Treat argued until well into the evening for Connecticut to retain its charter. Candles were lighted as darkness fell. Suddenly, the candles were extinguished and when they were re-lighted, the charter had disappeared. John Wadsworth was said to have taken the Charter and hidden it inside a hollow tree in the nearby front yard of Magistrate Samuel Wyllys. The story of the candles being blown out first appeared in "A Memoir for the History of Connecticut" by Governor Roger Wolcott.[285] The full story of hiding the charter in a hollow oak tree, in all its detail first appeared 131 years after the event in Dr. Benjamin Trumbull's *Complete History of Connecticut* published in 1818.[286]

Bulkeley's almost contemporaneous account did not make any reference to a hiding of the charter nor did Andros in his report to Lords of Trade nor was it recorded in the Connecticut Council Records. Neither Lord Randolph nor any other contemporary reporter of the events made any mention of this supposed event. It is probable that it never happened. Perhaps regretting that Connecticut had not more firmly resisted Andros, it seems likely that the story was created later and intended to assert that Connecticut never yielded its charter government, even though it had.

ANDROS DEPARTED from one New England custom by creating the office of justice of the peace, as in England.[287] These legal officers were ostensibly to hear and dispense with minor cases that would not justify the expense of a full trial. However, it was also their duty to deal with any matter that might disturb the peace of the country. In this sense, they served as a network of influence, binding the community to a sense of unity and cohesion with the established practices and customs of England.

The justices of the peace were charged to deal with small legal matters not exceeding the value of forty shillings. It was argued that "many inconveniences may arise unto the inhabitants of this territory by being vexed and troubled with suits of law for small and trivial injuries, debts and trespasses wherein the customary fees and charges may exceed the original debt and damages." These "shall and may be heard and judged by any of his Majesties Justices of the Peace." Dates were set for a quarterly Court of Sessions to be held by the justices of the peace to "hear and determine all matters relating to the conservation of peace and punishment of offenders and whatsoever else." There were courts in Hartford, New London, New Haven and Fairfield County. Fines were payable to the King.

Andros was careful to appoint only men of high reputation as justices of the peace. For Hartford County, he appointed several of the existing magistrates - John Wadsworth, Benjamin Newberry, Samuel Talcott and Giles Hamlin - as justices of the peace to these he added John Chester and Reverend Gershom Bulkeley, both prominent Wethersfield citizens, and Humphrey Davie, a highly-regarded Bostonian who had recently moved to Connecticut. All these men had acknowledged experience in the law as indicated by the term "Esq." appended to their names in the court records. Bulkeley and the others may have been added as men who would base their judgments firmly on the precedents in English law.

Immediately following the closing of each meeting of a Court of Sessions held by the justices of the peace, a meeting of the Inferior Court of Common Pleas was held at the same time and place. In Connecticut John Allyn was the judge of the Inferior Court of Common Pleas and was aided by two or more of the justices of the peace. This court had jurisdiction on matters of less than ten pounds value. The judge and two justices could also probate estates of less than fifty pounds.[288] There are records of forty-two estates probated between March 1687/8 and March 1688/9.[289]

In all courts where a matter of fact arose, a jury of twelve men could be empaneled to hear the case. A representative case of this type occurred at the Court of Sessions of 1 March 1688 in Hartford. The litigants had appeared earlier before Justices of the Peace, Gershom Bulkeley and Captain Samuel Talcott. Mr. Stephan Chester of Wethersfield accused Joseph Mallison of beating him and sought forty shillings damages.[290] Mallison pleaded self-defense. Bulkeley and Talcott had ruled that the case rested in judgments and referred it to jury trial. The jury found Mallison guilty and the judge ordered him to pay twenty shillings to the King plus court costs and costs for the marshal.[291]

The work of the justices of the peace in the Court of Sessions included a variety of activities. It appeared sometimes to have reviewed indictments and sentences of other courts. For example, in December of 1699, Gershom was part of a special session of the court which reviewed the finding of a grand jury of the previous September. Joseph Scott of Farmington had been pressed to go with the militia to Northfield, Massachusetts, during an Indian uprising. He refused and was presented to court for saying that he would shoot himself in the heart if forced to go into the King's service. The case was reviewed, and Scott was admonished and ordered to pay court costs.[292]

Gershom sat on the case of John Dike on 4 September 1688. Dike, a husbandman in the county of Hartford, had been indicted the previous July. He was accused of using many lascivious and lewd words and gestures to "Invade the chastity of his own daughter." He pled not guilty and asked for a trial by the bench in the Court of Sessions. This again raised for Bulkeley the difficult issue of incest, and the court appeared reluctant to impose a sentence. The court ordered that a bond of twenty pounds be posted to ensure Dike's appearance at the March court and that in the meantime Dike should pay two shillings and two pence for his good behavior.[293]

It is not clear how justices of the peace were compensated. In an undated manuscript, Gershom wrote a treatise on the office of justice of the peace. He wrote that the office would offer "daily employment without any profit or pleasure, other than the public good." He said that justices should look for their real reward in the other world "for they are like to have little or none in this."[294]

Bulkeley studied English laws and wrote a treatise on the role of the justice of the peace. His treatise contains references to Dalton and Bond. There are two books by Dalton in the inventory of Bulkeley's books.[295] One is identified as "probably: Michael Dalton's *The Country Justice, Containing the Practice of Justice of the Peace Out of Their Sessions,* London, 1618, and "perhaps" Dalton's *Officium Vicecomitum, The Office and Authority of Sherifs,* London, 1623. The book by Bond would be one of the three editions of A *Compleat Guide for Justices of the Peace* by J[ohn] Bonds, Esq. The first edition was printed in London in 1685 and it seems unlikely that Gershom would have seen this. The second edition was printed in London in 1696 and the third in 1706. In any event, it is likely that Gershom wrote his treatise well after 1688 when his service as justice of the peace for Hartford County had ended with the demise of the Andros administration.

Bulkeley warned that "ill will and bad words from those with whom they have to do and after all be discountenanced and disgraced rather than encouraged by those in higher places," Gershom expected very high standards from those entrusted with the office of justice. He counseled that a justice must not prejudge a case but must be guided only by the testimony before him. Bulkeley asserted that if the Devil himself appeared before him, he would give him an impartial hearing. He wrote that "If I were to condemn ye Devil...I would give him a hearing."[296]

Bulkeley said that he never wanted to serve as a justice of the peace. He claimed that he was not at all ambitious to retain his position in this office. He wrote, "It is a burthen and no benefit to me; an orderly discharge will be very welcome, and the sooner the better; if I could absolve myself of my oath...." There is reason to question Bulkeley's candor in this remark as well as the assertion that he was not a freeman of the colony.

As to his having been a freeman, the General Court of the Connecticut Colony had requested that Gershom be given the freeman's oath in May 1666,[297] but he was not nominated to stand for acceptance until 1669.[298] He was elected deputy to the legislature in 1679. Deputies were usually required to be freeman to serve[299]. It is difficult to imagine that the citizens of Wethersfield would have elected him to represent them while knowing he might not be able to take his seat.

As to being a justice of the peace being a burden, it is hard to imagine a role more suited to Gershom's personality. Despite its drawbacks, the office of justice of the peace must have been highly satisfying to Gershom because he had always sought to play a similar role in civil life as counselor, arbiter, adjudicator and advisor, long before he became a justice. He was accustomed to being asked for his opinions and judgments, and he was accustomed to having his word respected. He often proactively sought to express his opinions in controversial criminal cases and was often appealed to as an impartial arbitrator. As he grew to believe that Connecticut law had drifted away from English law to the detriment of the general population, he became more insistent that justices had a duty to assert the preeminence of English law and tradition.

Richard G. Tomlinson

VII. OPPONENT OF GOVERNMENT (1689-1694)

...the country is in daily expectation of orders from the Crown of England for settling and regulating the government...If we have an election before these orders come ...it will be a wonderful thing if you be not looked upon and dealt with as criminals

~Gershom Bulkeley

...draw forth the sword of justice to defend... [the] privileges of the colony according to the charter; screw up the ink-horns, still the tongues, empty the purses and confine the persons of our objectors

~James Fitch

Due form of law is that alone wherein the validity of verdicts ... stands, and if a real and apparent murderer be condemned and executed outside of due form of law, it is indictable against them that do it. ... Spectral evidence, ill events after quarrels...and the like...are all discarded as being convictive of witchcraft and the miserable toil they are in in the Bay is warning enough. Those that will make witchcraft of such things will make hanging work apace

~Hartford Magistrates, Samuel Wyllys, William Pitkin, Nathaniel Stanley

----

IN 1688, THE REIGN OF KING JAMES II CAME TO AN END in the bloodless "Glorious Revolution." Never totally secure as a Catholic in a fiercely Protestant England, James was forced into exile in France. The Parliament invited William of Orange, who was married to James' daughter, Mary, to rule in place of James.

News of the events in England arrived in Boston in April 1688.[300] Wild rumors circulated, including that there was a plot to burn Boston and massacre the people. This was communicated in a letter to Bulkeley from "a friend in the Bay."[301] At the insistence of an enraged mob in Boston, Sir Andros was put under arrest for his own protection and a "committee of safety" (which included Wait-Still Winthrop) took control of the government in Massachusetts in the name of their majesties William and Mary.

In Connecticut, Governor Treat viewed the news of the revolution in Boston and the seizing of Andros with stunned amazement. But in Connecticut as in Massachusetts, the rage of the common people against the government seemed over powering and intimidating. While it was primarily directed toward Andros and his close associates; the position of colonists who served in the government was precarious. Bulkeley was not completely convinced that the revolt was a surprise. He believed that in the previous winter there had been a "plot on afoot in Connecticut, as well as other parts of the country, to make insurrection and subvert the government."[302]

There was a movement in Connecticut to resume government under the old charter. However, there was great uncertainty in Connecticut on how to proceed. No orders had been received from England. Some argued, that without confirmation of a new king in England, and with the administration of Andros ended with his imprisonment, there was no longer a government. Bulkeley said that, "There was a government yesterday, how came it to pass that there was none today?" He noted that Governor Treat and Secretary Allyn and the members of the Connecticut General Assembly who had served as justices of the peace under Andros are still in place."[303]

Captain James Fitch led a group that clamored to take up the government under the old charter. Bulkeley wrote that "a few fractious men…run to and fro in the colony of Connecticut, and by their false and fraudulent stories excite some of the old freemen to hold an election on the 9th of May ensuing… [1689]." Bulkeley identified Fitch as "a prime ringleader in the late motions." Fitch had served as a justice of the peace in the Andros administration, but he had strong incentives to see that government ended. His purchase of the Wabaquassit country and other Indian lands had made him one of the largest land holders in New England. Andros questioned the validity of such acquisitions, saying that Indian deeds were of no more value than "the scratch of a bear's claw."[304] Bulkeley said that, "… if we have the king's government they are afraid they shall lose the land that this and that man hath unjustly gotten…."[305]

BULKELEY ATTEMPTED TO ADVISE his old friend, Governor Robert Treat, and the leaders meeting in Hartford against holding an election to select new officers and restart the government under the old charter. Bulkeley sent Treat a letter.[306] Bulkeley was incredulous at a suggestion that an election could be held and the old charter government recommenced. Although he was not well at this time, he composed a long letter. His letter was addressed to Governor Robert Treat and to Justices, James Bishop, William Jones and James Fitch and "to any other whom it may concern, assembling at Hartford: to advise concerning holding a Court of Election by virtue of and according to the late Patent." (The letter was eventually published as: *The People's Right to Election or Alteration of Government in Connecticut Argued in a Letter*.) The letter is dated 8 May 1689, the day before the General Court was summoned to meet to address the issues. [307]

Gershom could reasonably expect his argument to carry weight with Governor Treat. He had been a trusted advisor to Treat and served on Treat's War Counsel during the King Philip War. At the opening of the war, Gershom had represented Connecticut's interests with great diplomacy in defeating the attempt by Andros to take Connecticut's western lands for the Duke of York. Furthermore, the Treat and Bulkeley families were close neighbors and friends. Gershom's daughters, Dorothy and Catherine, would eventually marry nephews of Governor Treat.[308] Bulkeley thought that his letter would carry weight and would induce the leaders in Hartford to postpone any attempt at establishing a new government and electing leaders, until their right to govern had been officially restored by King William.

Bulkeley marshalled multiple arguments against resuming charter government.[309] He deemed the motion to resume government under the charter to be, "illegal, needless and unprofitable" as well as criminally dangerous. Gershom pointed out that "private persons" outside the government, cannot set up and exercise a government, because that would be direct rebellion and treason. He told Treat and the others that, although they were personally in charge of the government when Andros arrived, they were no longer in those offices. Andros dissolved their government and made them officers in his administration. Even under the old charter, Bulkeley said, they cannot claim their old offices since that charter required that they be annually elected every May and there was no election in May 1688.

Gershom reminded them that they gave up the government voluntarily; it was not taken from them by illegal force. "[You feared] you should be annexed to Yorke [New York]; and hereupon you submit to the King...begging that you may be annexed to the Bay, he [Andros] performs this … [he] demands the government and you yield it up to him; if now you find it prejudicial, you must lay your hand upon your own mouth, and not take it [the government] again by force."

Connecticut petitioned the crown that it might be joined to the Bay Colony rather than the New York Colony. The King granted their request and they were joined with

Andros's administration in Boston. Bulkeley wrote that the King's government did not end with the imprisonment of Andros. "Andros was the King's minister and not the head of government. The King is still the supreme power. Some of the hot charter men...say that there was no King in England, and that there was no government. The supreme power has passed from King James to William and the KING never dies. There is always a king."

Gershom asserted that the oaths of allegiance and commissions which they took (including his own), although granted by Andros as governor, were sworn to the King and "...they do continue in force, notwithstanding the imprisonment or surrender of the governor...." Therefore, Bulkeley advised, "That instead of moving towards an election, the judges and justices [should] maintain and exercise the government according to their commissions...." He noted: "...the country is in daily expectation of orders from the Crown of England for settling and regulating the government...If we have an election before these orders come ...it will be a wonderful thing if you be not looked upon and dealt with as criminals."

For a detailed account of what happened in Hartford in May 1689, we have only Bulkeley's account in *Will and Doom*. He indicates that the "hot-heads" were eager to oust all those who had co-operated in surrendering the government to Andros. The freemen assembled on the green on May 9th. Three propositions were drawn up: 1) for those in charge of the government when Andros took it, to resume their place and power [but under the charter]; 2) for the present government [according to royal commissions] to continue; and 3) for a Committee of Safety to be formed to take over the government. Bulkeley reported that there was a great uproar about the first of these propositions, which would, it was charged, put back in power those who had betrayed the people and placed the government in the hands of Andros. Treat, Allyn and others who had surrendered the government and accepted offices in the Andros administration were in danger of being thrown out. Only the first proposition was put to a vote by the raising of hands. Bulkeley said that it was defeated. Then the meeting was moved inside, and a second vote was taken by ballot, and it passed. Thus, Treat and the existing leaders were restored to power.[310] Bulkeley commented that "It would be tedious to relate all the dirty tricks and abominable falsehood that have been used in these proceedings...."[311]

The General Court declared that by their actions on May 9th the freemen had voted to re-establish the government as it was before Sir Andros took the government. They declared that all laws previously made under the charter and the courts as they were constituted before for the administration of justice, were now in full force. Bulkeley declared that Treat and the others had destroyed the legal government and then replaced it with a new one. "Why, forsooth, they destroyed the government themselves and laid down their commissions...at the feet of a faction of their freemen, of which themselves also were the leading and commanding part. ...And so, they are in office and out of office, and exchange one for another when please."[312]

The newly declared government of Connecticut retained one vestige of the Andros government, by appointing justices of the peace, something that was not provided for in the charter.[313] New justices were appointed by town rather than by county. These did not include Bulkeley. But Bulkeley insisted that his commission as justice of the peace of Hartford County was still in force even though no courts were held.

Gershom's tone in the *"The People's Right"* was relatively restrained and reasoned compared to his more heated contributions to follow. He began by stating: "That though I was no freeman of the Colony, yet I never was an Enemy to our ancient Charter privileges, and could they now be regularly recovered, I should rejoice in it." However, he argued that he knows no way it can be done. He said that it is only the trust that was placed on him as a justice of the peace, the oath he took to discharge that office, and the desire for the common good that caused him to break his silence and speak out. He knows, he said, "that nothing but ill-will is like to be my reward." He said that he nevertheless, having taken the oath of Supremacy and Obedience and that of a justice for keeping the law, he felt compelled to speak.[314]

When his efforts to prevent an election were not successful, Gershom tried to retrieve the letter. He heard that Fitz-John Winthrop had seen a manuscript copy of *The People's Right* and he wrote to Fitz-John Winthrop on 11 October 1689 that "[I have heard] that you have somewhat reflected upon my sending or suffering of it to be so to go abroad…And now I hear that some do intend to print it. I assure you sir, that it is no desire of mine, and if your Honor can do anything to hinder that, I shall take it your kindness: for in my opinion, the season of doing good by that paper is now past."[315]

When the newly chosen officers, who were really the previously existing officers, took their oaths of office on 9 May 1689, they did so, according to Bulkeley's account, in the name of the Prince of Orange, since he had not yet been proclaimed king. When they received word from England in June 1689 that William and Mary were proclaimed king and queen, they called a general convention to proclaim allegiance to their majesties and to prepare an address to them asking that Connecticut's right to self-government under the charter be recognized. The petition asserted that the "… choice of ours [to be annexed to Massachusetts rather than New York] was taken for a resignation of our government, though that was never intended by us as such….Sir Edmund Andros…came to Hartford …and declared our government to be dissolved…The good people of the colony…chose…to be silent and patient (rather) than to oppose, being surprised into an involuntary submission to an arbitrary power."

With the arrest of Andros in Boston and the fall of his government, [the leaders in Connecticut] argued that it had been necessary to adopt some form of interim government until orders came from the king. "… there being none so familiar to us as that of our charter…and having never received information…which was interpreted a resignation of our charter, we have presumed, by the consent of the major part of the freemen…to resume our government according to the rules of our charter, and to continue till further order. Yet, as we have thus presumed to dispose ourselves, not waiting for orders from your majesty, we humbly…[entreat] your majesty's most gracious pardon…that you would be pleased to grant us…ratifications and confirmations of our charter…."[316]

Bulkeley was incensed by this petition which he called "… a strange piece of contrived fraud[317] … they speak one thing to the king…but they speak another to the people. [They tell the people] that their authority is good by virtue of their charter…but they… acknowledge [to the king] this assumption of the government without his majesty's order to be a presumption, and humbly submit themselves therein, and beg his majesty's most gracious pardon for it."[318]

Connecticut's petition was sent to the colony's agent in London, William Whiting. Whiting thought that this petition was unwise to submit to the king in its current form and so he did not. He wrote to Governor Treat: "There are several passages in it…that are pernicious both to yourselves and the rest of the country…but another address by word of mouth hath been made in your behalf which was well received." Whiting did not say how his oral presentation was worded. He did assure Treat however that "…in a plea before [the Council] it was asserted that there was neither record of surrender or judgment against your charter...so [I] suppose your charter to be good...."[319]

Treat sent a new petition in the name of the Council in January 1689. This petition was shorter and more direct and simply sought confirmation that their presuming to govern under the rules of the charter was permitted. It said, "... having a charter granted by King Charles the second... [and] by reason of our not so rightly understanding the methods used in reference to the procedure against charters under the late king, are brought under some uneasiness, though we neither resigned our charter, nor was it condemned. We do, therefore, humbly entreat your majesties favor, to confirm us...in our charter...."[320] Bulkeley knew about this second petition but did not actually see it. He said, "... we have no reason to think it any better than the first, for alas, we find no truth in their goings."

THE TEST OF ANY GOVERNMENT is the ability to collect taxes. Success is largely based on the voluntary cooperation of its citizens. During the year following the initial election of May 1689, the new government struggled because many of Connecticut's colonists did not pay their taxes. Therefore, it was ordered that "lists should be made of persons and estates rateable by law." The need for money was made more urgent by the decision to send an expedition to Albany to defend against the French and Indians attacking from Canada. Therefore, at a Special Court called by Governor Treat in August 1689, it had been enacted that "…if any person neglect to give in a true account of their persons and estates, it shall be in the power of the listers or General Court to rate them will and doom [i.e., at the discretion of the listers]."[321]

Still several towns refused to send in their lists. At the General Court of 9 October 1690, these towns were charged with resisting taxes and denying the legality of the government. It was not surprising that Bulkeley's home town of Wethersfield was one of these. Samuel Wolcott, Benjamin Gilbert, Nathaniel Foote and Samuel Smith were charged with failure to make the list for Wethersfield. Bulkeley said that these men had been selected to make the list, because it was known that they would refuse to do it. The court, he said, meant to make an example of them. Bulkeley had such detailed knowledge of these cases that it may be that he was somehow involved in this affair.[322]

A warrant was sworn out for the offenders:[323]

> Mr. Samuel Wolcott, Benjamin Gilbert, Nathaniel Foote, Samuel Smith, in their majesties name you are required to appear at the general court to be holden at Hartford tomorrow morning to answer for your neglect of making, gathering and perfecting the list of estate of your town to this court or your deputies. Hereof you may not fail. Hartford, Oct. 9th, 1690.

> To William Goodrich, constable of
> Wethersfield, to serve and return. And in case
> any of those summoned neglect or refuse to
> appear according to this summons, in his
> majesty's name you are required then to seize
> and in safe custody bring to said court, to
> answer the aforesaid complaint for their
> contempt. Hereof fail not. Per order, John
> Allyn, Secretary.

Bulkeley wrote, "With this rugged warrant" the constable
went to the home of Benjamin Gilbert, [who was
Bulkeley's brother-in-law]. Having read the warrant to
Gilbert, he asked whether Benjamin would go with him
tomorrow to Hartford. When Benjamin replied that he saw
no need to go, the constable stepped to the door and
signaled his waiting assistants to come. Then he rushed
over to Benjamin and pulled him out of his chair. Benjamin
put out his hand to ward him off and tore a piece from his
calico neck-cloth. They carried Benjamin off as a prisoner
and locked him up."

Next the constable went to the home of Samuel Wolcott
and demanded that he appear tomorrow in Hartford.
Wolcott replied that he might. The constable would have
treated him in the same rough manner used with Gilbert but
was persuaded by his companions to be more moderate.
Wolcott was left to appear on his own. When they went to
get Samuel Smith, he was not at home. However, when he
[Smith] heard that they [the constable] sought him, he
chose to go to Hartford to avoid more trouble.

The four accused all appeared before the court in Hartford and where asked why they had failed to prepare the tax list. Nathaniel Foote was dismissed when he could show that he had made some effort to make the list. Samuel Smith questioned their authority because, he said, he understood that they had received no orders from their majesties confirming their government. He said that he had heard that they had sent a petition to the king and begged pardon for having presumed to assume the government without consent. Furthermore, he said, he was not a member of their corporation and so was not obliged to them. This response [said Bulkeley] drew a heated reaction. The court demanded to know how Smith knew of the petition to the king. Governor Treat clapped his hand on his sword and said, "If I put on my harness I will subdue these rebellious fellows and make them pay their dues."

Smith was fined forty shillings and sentenced to post bond of forty or fifty pounds for his good behavior. The court ordered him sent to prison, but as he left the court room, a friend, who did not want to see him jailed, volunteered to post the bond. This was accepted, and Smith was released. Wolcott was fined forty shillings and released. Gilbert was fined forty shillings plus another fifteen shillings for affronting the constable. He was also sentenced to be locked up but was released after a day.

Passive resistance to tax collection was not the only opposition to the government. Others besides Bulkeley had harsh criticism of the legality of the government. In the

County Court held in Hartford on 28 November 1690, Ben
Crane of Wethersfield was charged with speaking against
the authority of the government. In *Will and Doom*
Bulkeley gave an account of the Crane affair. He wrote that
Crane had charged that those in the government had
perjured themselves by giving up the oaths they had taken
during the Andros administration, an argument that sounds
like an echo of Bulkeley. Bulkeley said that one would
have thought this might bring a suit for slander, but instead
a furious court issued a warrant for a band of armed men to
drag Crane into court. The party arrived at Crane's house
and broke in the door with a log. Crane was not at home,
but only his brother and Crane's pregnant wife were there.
Bulkeley said that she was so frightened that she nearly had
a miscarriage.

In court Ben Crane was alleged to have said that the
government was not of the King nor of God, but of the
Devil. Crane admitted that he had spoken these words in
passion. Crane was fined fifteen pounds and ordered to be
held in jail until it was paid. He was finally released when
his brother, John, posted a bond of fifty pounds for this
good behavior. Bulkeley said, these things "show what is to
be expected when enraged parties shall be our only
judges."[324]

GERSHOM HAD ALWAYS CHERISHED THE ROLE OF SAGE
ADVISOR. Even when he had become a controversial figure
due to his role in the Andros administration and to his
opposition to charter government, he still offered his

opinions on major issues whether they were wanted or not. Amid this political turmoil over the charter, there was a sensational murder case. On the morning of 23 June 1691, Mercy (Tuttle) Brown of Wallingford took an axe and began striking her seventeen-year-old son, Samuel Jr., in the head while he was sleeping. Her husband Samuel awakened and rushed to the upstairs bedchamber just as she delivered the third blow. He wrested the axe from her grip and turned to lift his son. Mercy, still in frenzy, snatched up the axe again and had to be subdued before she could attack the other three children. Samuel Jr. lingered six days before dying on June 29.[325]

This murder of a son by his own mother shocked the community. It was even more shocking because it was the second axe murder in this family. Fifteen years earlier, Mercy (Tuttle) Brown's brother, Benjamin Tuttle, had killed his older sister, Sarah, with an axe. Benjamin's crime, while stunning, seemed to have some understandable basis. He was an unmarried adult man living in the household of his married sister. Humiliated by her control over him, he became enraged and struck her down. No such easy explanation was available to understand a murderous assault by a mother on her sleeping son.[326]

Testimony in the case reconstructed the events of the morning of June 23.[327] Forty-one-year old Mercy had arisen early and tended to household chores. The fire had gone out and Mercy walked to a neighbor's house to get a burning brand to rekindle the fire. The flame faltered, and

132

she went back for another. She milked the cows, turned them out to pasture and began to prepare the family's breakfast. Mercy's oldest daughter, who was recently married, slept downstairs with her new husband. Mercy concealed the axe under her apron and went upstairs to where two of her three younger children were asleep. Then she attacked Samuel Jr.

Mercy was taken to the jail in Hartford. The authorities questioned her husband and the neighbors about Mercy's mental state on the morning of the murder. The neighbors said she seemed "somewhat crazed or under deep melancholy," but "seemed to have her reason." Samuel said that his wife appeared "as rational as he had known her any other time."

However, by the time the Court of Assistants had got around to having a trial,[328] Samuel had modified his view. He said that Mercy had "been at sundry times for many years past wholly deprived of the right use of her reason and understanding and always considerably disturbed." He pleaded that the court should acquit her because the murder was "wholly a fruit and effect of her distraction". Relatives and neighbors now began to give similar testimony in support of Samuel's plea. It was recalled that Mercy had made odd remarks about dreadful times that were coming and that she wanted her children to be buried in the barn. This had caused Samuel Jr. to ask his mother if she could kill him. She reportedly replied, "Yes, if I thought it would not hurt you."[329]

The jury could not reach a verdict and were given liberty to seek outside counsel. Surprisingly some of the jury turned to Gershom Bulkeley for his advice. Bulkeley himself was surprised that his opinion would be sought in the current political climate. He said, "I am very sensible that my opinion will be liable to a [biased] construction...." However, since it was a question of life or death, and because he saw larger issues for the country, he prepared a lengthy written opinion, dated 5 October 1691.[330]

Gershom framed four issues:

> Whether the court had jurisdiction in the case;
> Whether the indictment was sufficient;
> Whether Mercy was tried in the proper county;
> Whether Mercy was sane at the time of the murder.

Bulkeley said that, in considering this case, he put aside his doubts about the validity of the current, charter government. He examined the question of the court's jurisdiction based on the governing right granted by the charter. First, he said, there are no words in the charter granting the right to prosecute capital cases, but only lesser offenses. Second, he noted, that, the charter granted powers to act on these offenses in these words: "For the imposition of lawful fines, mulcts, imprisonment, or other punishment, upon offenders, etc., according to the course of other corporations within our realm of England." Thirdly, he said that by charter these courts can inflict no punishment that they cannot remit under their corporate seal.

Since only the king had the power to pardon felonies, Bulkeley concluded that no corporation, such as that created by Connecticut's charter, could pardon or punish felonies. He concluded that "consequently [they] have no jurisdiction of life or death." The fact that Connecticut had done so in the past was, he maintained, no justification to do it now that the king had sworn to govern the dominions as well as the realm of England.

Bulkeley did not deal with the question of the indictment, since he had not seen it. He turned to the question of whether Mercy was tried in the proper location. He asserted that it is a fundamental principle that offenders should be tried by a jury of their neighbors. Mercy, he argued, should have been imprisoned and tried in her county and town. She should not have been tried by a jury of strangers in Hartford. The law, he said, presumes that neighbors have more knowledge of the facts about one of their own community. Therefore, Bulkeley concluded that the current jury was not a proper jury and that they should therefore refuse to bring in a verdict He counseled them "not to meddle in" the case.

Finally, Gershom addressed the matter of whether Mercy was sane. If she was not sane, he stated, her act was not a "willful or malicious murder" and could not be prosecuted as a felony. He insisted that, even if she were known to be a lunatic with lucid intervals, there needed to be "very good and satisfying proof that she was *compos mentis* at the time of the act committed, for the law favors life." "...If I may freely speak my thought [I believe that] this matter [should] be deferred awhile, until their majesties have settled the government, which, in reason will not be long...where the life of man is concerned, no delay for due deliberation etc. is too long."

The jury did not know how to proceed. They asked the court to rule on the question of the defendant's mental competency at the time of the murder. The court refused and insisted that the jury must bring a verdict of either guilty or not guilty. The jury finally ruled that Mercy was guilty of murder.[331]

Now Gershom chose to act. He submitted a petition to the court outlining procedural violations that should nullify the verdict. Gershom's petition was not without effect. The court heard more witnesses about Mercy (Tuttle) Brown's mental state at the time of the crime. They decided to defer passing sentence on her and ordered her to be held in the Hartford jail until further notice. A month later her husband, Samuel, died. Mercy was held in jail for eighteen months before the court made a ruling. They ignored Gershom's arguments about trial irregularities.

It would not be until May 1693 they would finally decide that the trial evidence proved that Mercy "hath generally been in a crazed or distracted condition," and declined to sentence her to death. Instead, she was sentenced to be kept in custody until the magistrates of New Haven could find a way to prevent "her doing the like or other mischief for the future."[332]

AFTER THE GLORIOUS REVOLUTION had ousted King James, the government in the New York Colony fell to a popular uprising and militia captain, Jacob Leister, took control of the government. Connecticut was in sympathy with Leister's rebellion and sent Captain James Fitch and ten men to help Leister hold Fort James.[333] Bulkeley wrote, "… they [Connecticut's leaders] sent agents to New York, who promote the revolution there and help to keep out their majesties' Lieutenant Governor Nicholson and support Jacob Leister in his usurpation and intrusion, and (if we may believe their own report) engage this colony to maintain a certain number of men in this garrison."[334]

Late in 1690, King William and Queen Mary sent Colonel Henry Sloughter to New York to take control and be provincial governor. War with France had broken out and the need to unite the colonies against French and Indian attacks seemed urgent. Although Leister claimed that he had taken the government in the name of William and Mary, as did Connecticut, he was convicted of treason. He was executed in May 1691, having been sentenced to be hanged, drawn and quartered. Leister's fate must have concerned those in charge in Connecticut, because they still had not received an endorsement from England of their right to take up the government.

Bulkeley must have seen the dispatch of a royal governor in New York as the opening act of the reassertion of royal control over the New England colonies. Gershom, along with William Rosewell of New Haven and Edward Palmes of New London who had served as justices under Andros, began sending reports and complaints about the illegal government of Connecticut to Governor Sloughter in New York. Sloughter sent a letter to Governor Treat as early as 6 May 1691 saying that almost every day he received new complaints from several of their Majesties' good subjects of the Colony of Connecticut of great hardships and oppressions. Sloughter advised Treat to "use such methods that their Majesties subjects might be easy and have no cause of complaint".[335]

Sloughter drafted a letter (which may not have been sent) to Bulkeley and Palmes recommending that they send him a report of the wrongs and oppressions they had suffered since the revolution. He said he would use his influence on their behalf and forward the report to the King. Sloughter received a petition from them dated 20 April 1691. However, Sloughter died suddenly on 23 July 1691.[336] Bulkeley's hopes for a royal-approved government in Connecticut more directly under English law were, for the moment, disappointed.

IN MAY 1692 SIR WILLIAM PHIPS ARRIVED IN BOSTON as governor of Massachusetts. It was Sir William Phips, as Governor, who put an end to the Witch Panic in Salem. Phips ruled that most of the convictions rested on specter evidence and, hence, were invalid. He immediately released over fifty people being held in jail. Trials continued for a while but, without specter evidence, there were no more convictions.

Phips' commission from England did more than give him authority for the civil government of Massachusetts. It also included being "their Majesties Lieutenant and Commander-in-Chief of the militia and of all the forces by sea and land." This included the Colony of Connecticut. Bulkeley said. "They [Connecticut's General Court] knew that were he to put his commission of lieutenancy in force it would be likely to prove fatal to the government of Connecticut, as organized under the charter...."[337]

At Special Session of the General Court on 22 June 1692, the court prepared a letter in reply to Phips.[338] Connecticut's position was that the charter gave them the right to the militia, and they had received no direct orders from the King that this right was repealed. Therefore, until they did, they would not yield control of the militia. However, they would support Phips' actions against the French and Indians "to the furthest consistent with conservation of their charter privileges.[339]

Several letters were exchanged. Phips was concerned with the conflicts under way in upstate New York with New France and their Indian Allies. He was fully occupied and did not push acknowledgement of his commission. He apparently was satisfied to have Connecticut's active participation in the conflict. Bulkeley was disappointed by Phips' failure to press his claims to the Connecticut militia.

In August 1692 Colonel Benjamin Fletcher arrived to replace Sloughter as governor of New York. Fletcher's commission also gave him the Lieutenancy that had belonged to Phips, and, thus, apparent control over Connecticut's militia. It must have revived Bulkeley's hopes that the crown seemed committed to placing Connecticut and New England under more direct royal rule, as it had with Andros and the Dominion of New England.

Bulkeley, Palmes and Rosewell sent a communication to Fletcher to be forwarded to England, along with a petition. The communication, dated 16 September 1692, was called, "Address of the freeholders of Connecticut to the King and Queen." Bulkeley's group appears to request that Connecticut be brought under direct royal control: "…we accepted your coronation oath, which included all your dominions with gladness, promising as it did deliverance from our pressures." "We cannot orderly convene a general assembly…but, we beg the restoration of your own immediate government for the security of our lives, liberties and properties…."[340341]

The address was accompanied by a petition entitled, "Some Objections Against the Pretended Government of Connecticut." The petition presented the basic arguments against Connecticut's government that were expanded in Bulkeley's later publications. It mentions only in passing that the authors believe that the charter from Charles II was only a corporate charter and, thus, did not provide the basis for creating a government. Bulkeley had now abandoned the position that the charter of 1662 provided the basis for a government, although this was not a major theme in this particular petition.

The petition emphasized the fact that, even if the charter were good, the government in Connecticut had not been re-established in accordance with the rules of the charter, and hence was not legal. Bulkeley complained: "Yet they enforce their authority and government upon those who never consented...The greatest part of the people are not freemen of their company. This government in its exercise is an absolute arbitrary and despotic government regulated by no laws, but their own will & pleasure ...so that in effect we have no law but, as they term it, will & doom....We are disinherited of liberty, property, ye law and our King, all at once. We are English men as well as they & cannot bear to be thus basely dealt with. But, which is worst of all, the Throne is made a footstool and ye Crown ye football of an usurping corporation.... God Save King William and Queen Mary."[342]

Fletcher sent Bulkeley's petition to England to the court of William and Mary; although he may have edited it somewhat.[343] Fletcher asked Bulkeley and his associates to keep sending him reports and complaints against the government in Connecticut and promised that he would send them on to the King and Queen. The arguments presented in Bulkeley's brief petition to the King were later expanded and printed as a sixty-two-page pamphlet with the title *Some Seasonable Considerations for the Good People of Connecticut.* This publication was printed in New York and widely distributed. [344] The title page said that it was "licensed" by M. Clarkson, Secretary. Clarkson was Fletcher's secretary and Fletcher probably paid for production of the pamphlet. It was apparently intended to give Bulkeley's arguments a wider audience throughout New York and Connecticut to foment more support for Governor Fletcher to gain control of Connecticut. The pamphlet was more incendiary than the petition. Bulkeley waxed hot in the pamphlet, his anger rising to heated accusations. He wrote, "…Certainly Fire and Faggot or the Noose of an halter had been good enough for anyone that should offer to oppose it [Connecticut's new government] and refuse obedience to it." [345]

AMID THE POLITICAL TURMOIL over re-establishing charter government, a witch panic broke out in 1692. The trouble began in February and March in the small towns around Salem, Massachusetts. Before it ended in 1693, nineteen persons had been hanged, one pressed to death with rocks, hundreds accused and more than fifty imprisoned.

The main accusers were a group of young girls who cried out in unison that they were tormented by witches. The girls claimed to see invisible specters rise from the bodies of the accused and attack them. Reliance on spectre evidence had long been controversial. Sir William Phips arrived in Boston in May 1692 with a royal appointment as governor of Massachusetts. In February 1693, Phips banned conviction by spectre evidence and released most of those imprisoned. The trials continued until May, but there were no more executions.

The witch panic in Massachusetts had an echo in
Connecticut. Although Bulkeley's opinions were no longer
solicited, nevertheless he wrote: "In the Spring of the year
1692, there was a great noise of witchcraft in the
Massachusetts and a report that there are many witches
through the country. It is not long before some in the
county of Fairfield are accused of witchcraft."[346]

Several persons were accused. Charges against most were
dismissed, but Mercy Disborough (or Disbrow) and
Elizabeth Clawson of Fairfield were indicted for harming
several persons in a "preternatural way." The main accuser
was a young woman who was a servant in the home of
Daniel Wescott. She claimed that Mercy and Elizabeth
appeared to her as a spectre and tormented her.

Both women were searched and found to have possible
"witch marks" on their bodies. Both failed the controversial
"water test." Being bound and placed in a pond, they did
not sink, but floated on the water. After Elizabeth was
vigorously defended by her husband and her neighbors, she
was acquitted. Mercy's trial, however, ended with a hung
jury.

The chief magistrate, Samuel Wyllys, was reluctant to
proceed. There had not been an execution for witchcraft in
Connecticut for thirty years. All such trials since had ended
in acquittal except for the trial of Katherine Harrison of
Wethersfield in 1668 and 1669. Both Wyllys and Governor
John Winthrop Jr. had served as judges in the Harrison

case. The jury had found Harrison guilty, but Winthrop had engineered a reprieve. He had Gershom Bulkeley and a team of ministers review the evidence. They found the evidence insufficient for conviction and Winthrop overturned the verdict of the jury. Winthrop was now deceased, but Wyllys tried the same ploy in the Disborough case. He convened a panel of ministers to review the evidence.

This panel did not include Bulkeley who was no longer a minister and whose credibility was damaged by his opposition to Connecticut's government. The new panel concluded that: 1) The water test was "unlawful and sinful;" 2) Witch marks required certification by "some able physicians;" 3) The afflicted maid was suspected of faking and 4) The rest of the evidence was "upon slender and uncertain grounds."

Nevertheless, the jury again voted for conviction. Wyllys sent them back to reconsider, but they insisted on a guilty verdict. The three magistrates of Hartford, Wyllys, William Pitkin and Nathaniel Stanley then issued a reprieve and stay of execution, which then became a pardon. The basis of the reprieve was that one of the jurors who sat in the first trial was absent for the second trial and a substitute juror was used. This, they wrote, violated "due form of law." "Due form of law is that alone wherein the validity of verdicts and judgments in such cases stands, and if a real and apparent murderer be condemned and executed outside of due form of law, it is indictable against them that do it." Furthermore, the case lacked either of the two elements required for conviction: 1) a confession, or 2) the testimony of two good witnesses to exactly the same act of witchcraft.

For good measure, the magistrate criticized what was happening in Salem. "As for common things of spectral evidence, ill events after quarrels or threats, teats [witch marks], water trials, and the like, suspicious words, they are all discarded and some of them abominated by the most judicious as to be convictive of witchcraft, and the miserable toil they are in in the Bay for adhering to these last mentioned litigious things is warning enough. Those that will make witchcraft of such things will make hanging work apace and we are informed of no other but such as these brought against this woman."

Connecticut historian J. Hammond Trumbull has suggested a reason that Connecticut was spared from deadly results like those in Salem. "Had those who resumed the government in Connecticut received a confirmation of their authority from the crown, (as the magistrates in Massachusetts did by the King's letter of August 12th, 1689) so that they felt confident in the legality of their position and power, a like fearful and deplorable tragedy might have been enacted within our borders as in the neighboring province."[347]

However, there seems no reason to assume that Wyllys and the Magistrates were disingenuous in their belief in proper legal process. While the assertion of the primacy of "due form of law" was unusual, it was not without precedent. Strict adherence to the letter of the law was entirely consistent with the character of these men. Their behavior as magistrates throughout their terms in office reflected concern for proper legal procedure. Bulkeley's commented about the pardon: "[It] is the wisest act they have done since the revolution. For though I know no authority they have to condemn or reprieve, yet I think the reprieve is better than the judgment, because it prevents a mischief...."

VIII. *WILL and DOOM* (1692)

[Those governing Connecticut] are under great temptation to make their terror known...if they should presume, for any cause, to put any person to death, this they think would stop every mouth, and none would dare to deny or contradict their authority any more. No wonder then, if their fingers itch to be at that kind of work.

> ~*Gershom Bulkeley*

He claps a fool's coat on us and then derides us...to make us odious to the world...if the truth will not afford him the matter for it; lies must and shall.

> ~*Connecticut Governor Robert Treat*

GOVERNOR TREAT and his government had tried to respond against the mortal threat they perceived in Governor Phips' attempt to take control of the Connecticut militia, but they were handicapped by poor communications and the lack of a clear channel to the court of William and Mary. They attempted to send petitions to England in November 1692 protesting control of the militia by Phips, apparently not knowing that he had already been replaced by Fletcher in August. One petition, drafted by William Pitkin and dated November 25, 1692, was addressed by the Governor and Council of Connecticut to Captain Robert Fairfax, "Commander of one of his Majesties friggotts in Boston." The petition said, "Though we are strangers to you…such is the good character of your generous spirit…that we are in some more than ordinary confidence in succeeding with you…in our request…" The request, which was accompanied by a small gift of five pounds, was that should he come to Whitehall upon his return to England he present their petition "…to their gracious Majesties, praying only their pleasure therein."

They cautioned him not to make any of this known in New England. A second petition of the same date in a letter was prepared for Mr. James Porter, a merchant in London. It pleaded, "we have no better means than to send it to you with our request to use your endeavor that it be delivered and presented to their Majesties with all speed…." The petitions were entrusted to William Whiting to carry to Boston with instructions to first try to get Fairfax to carry the petition and, if that failed to send the letter directed to James Porter.[348]

BULKELEY GATHERED UP ALL HIS ARGUMENTS against the government of Connecticut in December 1692, and wrote a long, scathing indictment of the Connecticut government, which he entitled, *Will and Doom or The Miseries of Connecticut by and under an Usurped and Arbitrary Power, being a Narrative of the First Erection and Exercise, but especially of the late Changes and*

Administration of Government in their Majesties Colony of
Connecticut, in New England in America.[349]

While Bulkeley built on the arguments printed in *Some*
Objections to the Pretended Government of Connecticut, in
Will and Doom Bulkeley moved far beyond arguing the
legality of the resumption of charter government. In white-
hot anger he focused his argument on a claim that the
charter of 1662, granted by King Charles II, had never
actually allowed for the creation of a government in the
first place. The charter, he said, had been established to
make "the Governor and company" a corporate entity. This,
he maintained, was like the charters of many corporations
in England. There was nothing in the charter that could be
construed as a right to establish a government over the
people of the Connecticut Colony. Under a
misconstruction of this charter, he insisted, a small, self-
serving group of Puritan elites had created a tyrannical
government and deprived the majority of Connecticut's
population of its rights as subjects of the crown.

He accused the Connecticut government of imposing the
laws of their corporation on all the people of colony
whether or not they were freemen of the corporation. Thus,
he asserted, the majority of the people were deprived of
their rights under English law. He accused those in power
in Connecticut of being particularly eager to find a case in
which they could execute someone and, thus demonstrate
the complete power of their law.

Bulkeley said that those governing Connecticut reasoned
that, if they could actually execute someone under their

149

laws, the people would see that their authority was valid, because otherwise they would not dare to do it. "They are under great temptation to make their terror known...if they should presume, for any cause, to put any person to death, this they think would stop every mouth, and none would dare to deny or contradict their authority any more. No wonder then, if their fingers itch to be at that kind of work."[350]

Unlike his charge in *Some Seasonable Considerations* he did not refer to punishment by "Fire and Faggot" for disobedience to Connecticut's government. He did, however, say that their control was absolute so that they could, if they wished, "imprison or banish a man and even dismember him, cut off his nose or ears or hang him."[351]

Bulkeley denied that the government of Connecticut had the right to the ultimate power–the power to execute citizens. In *Will and Doom*, Bulkeley revisited several cases of capital prosecution to show that Connecticut's government had proceeded in an arbitrary and illegal manner. He insisted that they had no power to condemn anyone to death, since their charter did not allow for it and, in any event, the charter had been revoked. Gershom returned to the case of axe murderer, Mercy (Tuttle) Brown. Bulkeley charged that the court knew very well that Mercy was a "distracted woman *et non-compos mentis,*" but sought her execution for political reasons.[352] Gershom said "...she is still kept a prisoner at Hartford [as of Dec. 1692]."[353]

GERSHOM CITED THE MERCY DISBOROUGH witch trial[354] as
an example of Connecticut's pursuing a capital case for
which they had no judicial authority. Gershom criticized
the case, even though the guilty verdict was overturned by
a reprieve.

> Thereupon, about the middle of September
> last past, a Court of Assistants is called and
> held at Fairfield, wherein they proceed to inquire
> of it. Some of the persons accused were easily
> discharged by proclamation; upon what grounds,
> they know best who did it; but Mercy
> Disborough was indicted and tried upon her
> life for witchcraft (we must still understand it,
> by the laws of this colony). I cannot
> understand of anything brought in against her of
> any great weight to convict a person of
> witchcraft, yet some of the court were very
> zealous, others more moderate. The jury agreed,
> all but one, who could not be brought to agree
> to find her guilty.
>
> The court adjourns till after the General Court
> in October next purposing to take advice there. At
> the General Court in October, now last past
> they advise with them about it, showing them
> what was alleged against the prisoner. The
> ministers show their opinion, that those things
> were not sufficient to convict any person of
> witchcraft. Yet the General Court, as 'tis said,
> ordered them to hold another court at Fairfield
> about this matter. After the General Court, in the

latter end of October, now last past, another
Court of Assistants is held at Fairfield to
proceed in the trial of this woman. One of the
jury happened to be gone to New York,
whereupon they put in another in his room and
proceed.

I cannot hear of much more material brought
in against her. However, the jury find her
guilty and she is condemned to die, and it is
said a time was appointed for execution; but,
upon motion three of the Assistants of
Hartford send down a reprieve, whereby the
execution is suspended till next General
Court; which is the wisest act they have done
since the revolution. For, though I know no
authority they have to condemn or reprieve,
yet I think the reprieve is better than the
judgment, because it prevents a mischief....

Bulkeley concluded: "These two cases [Mercy (Tuttle)
Brown and Mercy Disborough] are enough to prove what is
aforesaid. That not only our estates and bodies, but our
lives also, are at the disposition, not of the King and his
laws, but of this pretending, usurping corporation, and in
what hazard they are. Our foundations being thus removed
and out of course, what can the righteous do? It is a great
scandal…."

THE DISTRIBUTION AND INTENDED AUDIENCE of Bulkeley's
Will & Doom treatise is uncertain. Gershom's," The

People's Right to Election", was sent a in 1689 as a letter to Robert Treat, and was clearly intended to dissuade Treat and his allies from resuming elections under the charter. His "Some Objections Against the Pretended Government of Connecticut", in September 1692 was written as a petition to the king and bolstered Governor Fletcher's attempts to bring Connecticut into his New York government. It also served as a rebuttal to the pro-charter pamphlets of James Fitch, written in 1691 and 1692. Fletcher sent the petition on to England. *Some Seasonable Considerations* was printed in New York as a book to give it a wider influence. The question is: What was the purpose of writing *Will & Doom*?

Since *Will & Doom*, completed in December 1692, repeated and elaborated on the arguments presented earlier, it may have been intended to provide Governor Fletcher with more material to send to England to enhance his claim to control the militia and government of Connecticut. Or Bulkeley may have felt the need to buttress his previous arguments. Clearly his anger had increased, and his denunciation of the Connecticut government was more vitriolic. However, there is no evidence that *Will & Doom* was distributed nor did a copy find its way to England until years later.

CAPTAIN JAMES FITCH OF NORWICH had been a major leader of the revolt against the Andros government. He was a leader of the "hot heads" who nearly kept Governor Treat and others from resuming their roles in the government. It has been argued that Fitch, as leader of the left-wing faction, was more dominant in the government after the revolution than Governor Treat, himself.[355]

In 1691 and 1692 Fitch published pamphlets attempting to refute Bulkeley and critics of the legality of Connecticut's new government. Fitch was the son of Reverend James Fitch, the first pastor of Saybrook and Norwich. Reverend Fitch was a venerated figure, who had served along with Bulkeley in Treat's War Council during the King Philip War. His son, James Fitch, was a much more controversial person and a ringleader among those insisting on resuming the government under the chart. Captain Fitch had always been a member of Connecticut's governing elite and had accepted a commission under Andros as Justice of the Peace in New London County.[356] Now, however he renounced the Andros government as illegal, and attempted to inflame the general population to resume government under the charter, but without Treat and the old guard, who had served Andros.

Captain Fitch wrote two pamphlets supporting arguments for Connecticut to resume charter government. One was called, *Plain Short Discourse,* published in 1691 and *Little of Much,* published in 1692. No copies of these publications survive, but we know their contents from Bulkeley's reply in *Will and Doom* to the arguments Fitch raised in his pamphlets.

Fitch expanded on the arguments sent to England and tried out different arguments in his pamphlets. One argument

was that the charter government had never ceased because
Connecticut had never yielded its charter to Governor
Andros. According to Bulkeley in *Will and Doom,* "The
charter [Fitch says] they preserved. (J. F. in his *Plain Short
Discourse*, p.1, triumphs and tells us it is safe at Hartford.)
But the charter government they deserted and extinguished,
and thereby disabled themselves from executing the powers
of the charter any more until restored and enabled by royal
power." Bulkeley asserted that Andros did not need to take
physical possession of the charter to take the government.
"We distinguish between the charter and the government,
and the question is not about the charter, whether it be
good, or void, or surrendered in law… The charter may be
good and yet this government be bad and void."[357]

Bulkeley heaped scorn on the idea that Sir Andros took the
government by surprise and force. "It is not true that they
were as they…represent…forcibly and by surprise put
under this [the Andros] government; for they put
themselves under it.…"[358] Bulkeley related: "Sir Edmund
Andros…came to Hartford with a company of gentlemen
and grenadiers, to the number of sixty. [I suppose] Sir
Edmund stormed and took Connecticut with sixty
grenadiers?" "…had they not their great council of war
sitting at Hartford…could they not command a hundred and
twenty or more stout musqueteers to face those sixty
grenadiers... could they not have commanded many more if
need had been?"[359]

Bulkeley wrote "the charter men are devious in their
arguments. Fitch acknowledged in one of his pamphlets

155

that the so-called election of May 1689 cannot properly be called an election because it was not held according to the rules of the charter. Instead of an election, he calls it a "resumption" of the charter government." Bulkeley said, "...we may observe how these men dodge and play fast and loose [with the truth so] that a man knows not where to have them. Sometimes they deny that Sir Edmund Andros has any commission from the king but was a cheat [then they affirm his commission]. Sometimes they will not own the action of May 9, 1689, to be an election [because it was not according to the rules of the charter], but deny it stiffly and call it … a resumption of their charter government... but, then it is said that they have chosen a governor and assistants according to the charter...."[360]

Another argument by Fitch was that there was no need for King William and Queen Mary to restore the charter since King James II, himself, had done so in 1688. When the Prince of Orange began his invasion of England, James had hastily, in a panic, issued a proclamation restoring the charters of towns and corporations which had been taken away.[361] Bulkeley marveled at how Fitch could argue that the charter was always in force because it was never taken away and then also argue that it is good because it was restored in 1688 by the proclamation of King James II. "Yea, but (says he, in his *Little of Much*, p. 11) we did not take anything till is was restored and given to us. Well then, it was not by virtue of the charter that you resumed [the government]." Bulkeley asserted that in any event the proclamation of King James II "...restores nothing to the corporation of Connecticut, neither charter nor government nor anything …the said proclamation did not extend to New England."[362]

Bulkeley noted that the proclamation restored corporations, cities, towns and boroughs "within the kingdom of England, dominion of Wales or town of Berwick upon Tweed." He invited Fitch to show to which of these the corporation Connecticut belongs. "Let him, with all his strength, shew which of 'em it is, if he can."[363]

Fitch also referred to the fact that no official judgement had been entered in England against the government of Connecticut. Bulkeley responded, "A man may die and be really and legally dead, tho' he be not condemned and hanged, and his death recorded. (It may be J.F. is not willing to die without the solemnity of such a ceremony.)"[364] While Bulkeley treated Governor Treat and the old guard with some respect, he was consumed with contempt for Captain Fitch. He wrote, "Indeed, I understand, that some of his brethren, who have more wit than he, cannot but laugh up their sleeves at the weakness and capriciousness of this Goat…yet they have been too ready to follow such unprofitable counsel, as would bring fish to their net and feathers to their nests."[365]

Fitch claimed, according to Bulkeley, that the meaning of the letter in 1686 to King James, which acquiesced to the combination of Connecticut with Massachusetts, was as follows: "If your majesty be resolved, contrary to all law and justice, to take away our charter privilege, as you have done with others, we must submit, etc." Bulkeley wrote that he never saw the letter and while. "…the rudeness of this language doth sort well enough with this rustic…we do believe the gentlemen to whom the writing of that letter was committed, to be men of better manners and … more discretion."[366]

Fitch had dire warnings for those like Bulkeley who oppose the resumption of government under the charter. He wrote, "Let those in authority… now draw forth the sword of justice to defend…[the] privileges of the Colony according to the charter; to screw up the ink-horns, still the tongues, empty the purses, and confine the persons of our objectors..." Bulkeley replied, "The man, we see, is for money in the first place and for amputation in the issue. These are his prescribed methods. The compulsion and force of prisons and fines are the cogent arguments of our conviction of the unlawfulness of their authority…."[367]

Bulkeley asked: "But by whom was the charter or its government restored? What! By James Fitch, Nathaniel Stanley and James Steel, and such like private men? Are these poor creatures become King James, that they can restore charters and erect governments by their own authority?"[368] "Who is it that sits upon the throne … King William and Queen Mary, or James Fitch and Nathaniel Stanley and their accomplices?…If then this power thus opposing the law of England be a lawful power, I must confess I want a better pair of spectacles."[369] The charter men know, said Bulkeley, that they do not have a right to govern. "No, they all (unless I may accept one ignorant dunce or two), do very well know that their government is unlawful and usurped, and therefore are necessitated to take indirect courses to uphold it." [370]

BULKELEY'S OPPOSITION to the government was not the only obstacle it faced. The government of Connecticut found it difficult to collect taxes. This was particularly vexing as they attempted to send troops north to fight New France and its Indian allies. At a Special Court held in Hartford on 21 February 1693, it was noted that "...some persons in several towns of this Colony, disaffected to the present government have opposed and threatened the constables and other officers in the discharge of their office and collecting Colony rates and other rates in contempt of the present government...." The court, therefore, ordered the local authority in each county to proceed against the offenders.[371]

A substantial number of people still refused to pay their taxes. At the Court of Elections on 11 May 1693, it was observed that "difficulties arise daily about persons imprisoned for non-payment of rates," as well as for failure to pay debts resulting from court judgments against them. The court ordered that, when such a person was arrested and imprisoned, whoever causes him to be imprisoned must pay for his daily maintenance... "at least to find him bread and water." The court also allowed that such prisoners could also add to their maintenance if they desired. All outstanding charges, the court noted, must be paid or security given before they are released from prison.[372]

Bulkeley was not a passive observer of these events and was likely active in promoting resistance to the government. He continued his appeals to Governor Fletcher. On 5 April 1693, he sent Fletcher a report of Connecticut's action which, he claimed, infringed on the liberty of the people and showed "contempt of their Majesties government". He urged Fletcher to send the report to their Majesties in England. He wrote, "As we rarely have ships passing from hence to England, I beg you forward it by first conveyance to their Majesties."

Bulkeley reported that five persons were imprisoned on the 8th of March 1693 for refusing to pay their country rate. They were arrested, he said, without a formal charge, but solely on a mandate of the constables given by the General Court. The prisoners sued for a writ of *habeas corpus* which the General Court refused. The five then complained to Bulkeley as justice of the peace, he then issued a warrant for their release subject to finding sureties to post bond for their appearance. The General Court issued a counter warrant. One of the prisoners bought his release, but, said Bulkeley, "The rest were very ill-treated, being shut up in a noisome place with felons and murderers until 24th March." The governor and council summoned Bulkeley to appear before them, but he refused. The court issued an order for him to be taken by force, but, Bulkeley said, the marshal did not dare do it. "So, the matter rests at present; but this suffices to show the resistance of this arbitrary government to your royal authority." Signed "Gershom Bulkeley."[373] This report did not reach England until 4 October 1693.

MEANWHILE CONNECTICUT RECEIVED a somewhat encouraging letter from King William. It did not seem to be a response to Connecticut's petitions, but rather to concerns from New York about the defense of Albany. It urged Connecticut to send troops in response to the "Governor or Commander in Chief of our said Province of New York." It did not say anything about giving up control of their militia. The letter dated 3 March 1692/3 at Whitehall was not addressed to Treat and/or the General Court. It was addressed; "To such as for the time being take care for preserving the peace and administering the laws in our Colony of Connecticut in our Territory and Dominion of New England in America."[374]

Bulkeley and Governor Fletcher maintained an active correspondence. On 15 September1693, a perplexed Bulkeley wrote to Fletcher that, "I received yours of the 11th and have seen the Queen's letter.[375]"He noted that the letter was vaguely addressed, not to a specific person, but to "such as for the time being take care of the preservation of the peace and the administration of law." Bulkeley feared that the letter would be taken by Connecticut as an endorsement of their current government. "The present rulers are resolved to crush those who comply not with their usurpation…" Gershom complains, "It is high time for their Majesties to settle a government, or it will be impossible for loyal subjects to serve them. So, we long for the frigates that we may see what they will do for us."[376]

Governor Fletcher decided that it was necessary for him to personally go to Hartford and assert his authority.[377] The

document certifying Fletcher's commission arrived from
England on 1 October 1693. He lost no time in pressing
Connecticut to acknowledge his control of their militia. He
hoped to raise forces in Hartford and to go directly to the
relief of Albany which was being assaulted by French and
Indian forces. He reached Hartford on October 23.
Governor Treat, Secretary Allyn and others came to the inn
where Fletcher stayed. He told them that he had come to
take control of the militia, as he had written them, and, for
that purpose desired to meet with the General Court. Treat
invited Fletcher to address the Court the next morning at 10
o'clock.

At the meeting on October 24, Fletcher asked that Treat
give a public reading of his commission, but Treat would
not do so. Fletcher's secretary read the commission and, to
avoid any misunderstanding, presented a written memorial
which Treat promised to answer in writing. Treat proposed
to present a reading of the charter, but Fletcher declined.
He said civil affairs were not his concern; only the militia.
One of the members shouted, "Let the charter be read, that
all the people may hear it." Fletcher later claimed that
members of the public were prevented from entering the
room to hear the reading, but forced their way in.

Several letters were exchanged, and conferences held. Treat
asked that Fletcher suspend execution of his commission
until Connecticut had received word from England.
Fletcher refused and warned Treat, that if Albany were lost
to the enemy due to Connecticut's refusal to comply with
his commission, "the consequences will be dangerous to
yourselves." The General Court gave their answer on

Wednesday October 25. They said that they found nothing in Fletcher's commission that superseded the control of the militia given to them in the charter. However, they offered 600 pounds for the relief of the garrison at Albany. Fletcher replied that he did not demand the militia from them because it belonged to the king. He did demand that they obey his commission or answer for the consequences.

On Friday morning, Fletcher went to see John Yale, one of the deputies to the General Court. Fletcher offered to restore Yale to his previous position as captain of militia for Wallingford. Yale refused. Fletcher emphasized the danger presented by Connecticut's obstinate refusal to obey his commission. Yale replied that he could not help it for they knew that if they gave up control of the militia, they would lose control of the civil government. Fletcher told him that these words were "fractious and seditious." Fletcher sent word to the General Court that he intended to execute his commission immediately. He offered a commission for Treat to command all the militia in Connecticut. The General Court replied that it stood by its answer of October 25th. At noon, a new offer came from the General Court. It said that rather than 600 pounds, Connecticut would raise fifty men to go to Albany and serve until spring, if that would be more useful.

That evening, a large group of men came to Fletcher, most offering to obey his commission. One man loudly proclaimed that he had his commission under the charter and did not need any other. Fletcher ordered him out of the room, but he continued his tirade. Fletcher took him by the arm and led him out of the room. When he continued his outburst, Fletcher threw him down the stairs.

On Saturday, October 28, Fletcher issued a proclamation declaring all existing commissions in the militia of Connecticut to be void and calling upon all loyal subjects to yield to his commission. This apparently caused a great commotion. Armed men circulated around the ordinary during the night and some threatened to shoot him if he published his proclamation in the streets. Secretary Allyn apologized to Fletcher for the affronts but said he could not help it because "the people were in great ferment."

Bulkeley sent a note from Wethersfield on Sunday and another on Monday, warning Fletcher that a mob was threatening to harm both of them. Bulkeley had been told that, if he dared to appear in Hartford, the mob would come to Wethersfield and pull down his house. He counseled Fletcher not to make a provocative public declaration or "the effect on the peoples' rage would be unaccountable". Gershom also reported that it was rumored that armed friends were coming from Wethersfield to guard him, and he feared a bloody fight.

Fletcher wrote to a friend, "I have been in this colony twenty days laboring to persuade a stubborn people to their duty...I never saw the like people...I have just now received a letter from a sure friend acquainting me that the mob have a design upon my life."[378]

On his return to New York, Fletcher wrote to the Lords of Trade and Plantations in England. He reported that Connecticut had contempt for royal authority and that he had been rudely treated. He said that he did see some positive signs. "Major Palmer [Palmes], Mr. Gershom Bulkeley, and the two Rosewells and Mr. Trowbridge are gentlemen of the best education, sense and estates among them. They and many other well-affected people have suffered very much from the arbitrary illegal proceedings there. If Connecticut be annexed to New York, these are the fittest men for Councilors."[379]

BULKELEY'S ATTACKS COULD NO LONGER BE IGNORED. Through Fletcher, he had access directly to England that Connecticut did not. Furthermore, his arguments had become more dangerous as he now asserted that the 1662 charter had never authorized the creation of a government. Connecticut felt the need to respond to Bulkeley's constant criticisms. With Bulkeley's petition having been sent to their Majesties in England and with the dissemination of a printed pamphlet in New England, Connecticut could no longer let Bulkeley's attacks go unanswered. An official response was needed. Rebuttals by private citizens like James Fitch were no longer sufficient.

Receiving no response from their attempts to petition the King and Queen of England, Treat and the General Court took two actions to shore up their position. First, they called for a vote of the freemen of Connecticut indicating their desire to continue the charter privileges and the control of the militia. At a session of the General Court held 1 September 1693 by special order of the Governor, that 2,182 persons voted in favor. The Court then voted "to send an address to their Majesties to procure the continuance of all our charter privileges." Secondly, the voted to appoint Major General Fitz-John Winthrop to go to England and to directly present their address to their Majesties.[380]

Fitz-John was given detailed instructions of the message he was to carry to England. He was to "…allege that of the three thousand men in the Colony about two thousand two hundred [approved of the government]. Furthermore, he was to say that there was a "papacy of malcontents …three or four persons…these appear possibly in the magnifying glass of some neighbors' representations in England for greater than they are." [381]

THE CHOICE OF FITZ-JOHN WINTHROP was an inspired move. He was well-known and well-liked both in New England and England. He was the son of the revered Governor John Winthrop, Jr. He served in the New Model Army under General George Monck in Scotland during the English Civil War and accompanied him into England. He had been with his father in England in 1661 when he successfully negotiated the charter for Connecticut. Even though he was a friend of Sir Edmund Andros and served in his administration, Fitz-John was chosen as a member of Connecticut's General Court after the fall of Andros's government. Fitz-John was two years younger than Gershom and the two seemed to have an amiable relationship, although Fitz-John was no scholar, flunking his entrance examination to Harvard. He preferred the outdoor life and was an important figure in several military capacities and campaigns.[382].

During September and October of 1693, Fitz-John attempted to reach an accommodation with the dissidents and gain the support of their prominent members for his mission. He reached out to long-time former assistant, Samuel Wyllys, and even to Bulkeley himself.[383] Wyllys, who was a hunting and fishing pal of Fitz-John[384] wrote to Fitz-John in September supporting his mission to England. He had talked with Bulkeley.[385] Wyllys told Fitz-John that, "It is the opinion of many prudent and considerable persons…that the best expedient to settle this Colony in peace and unity" would be to get King William to confirm and ratify the charter of 1662 or to endorse rule by some other legal means and containing certain provisions. These conditions, presumably, were also those required by Bulkeley for his support.[386]

These suggested provisions seemed mainly directed toward avoiding rule by democratic means or popular vote. The first requirement was that law should provide for a pious minister in every parish whose maintenance would not be dependent on "the arbitrary humors of the vulgar sort of people." The second requirement was that nothing should prevent the people of Connecticut from the enjoyment of their rights as Englishmen and subjects of the realm. Wyllys asserted that, "The wise men of this Colony will never bear it to have themselves enslaved and their posterity, to the arbitrary humors of their fellow-subjects and to be deprived of the English laws which our fathers esteemed the best in the world."

The third and final necessary requirement was that only persons of "quality" should be allowed to hold office. Wyllys pleaded, "That their Majesties please to declare that person of mean and low degree be not improved to the chiefest place[s]...to gratify some little humors...but that persons of good parentage, education, ability and integrity be settled in such offices..." "These things being obtained, it may be hoped that this part of the country may flourish under a peaceable and orderly establishment, and without which, it is feared, twill be like the waves of a troubled sea."

WITH THE HELP OF GOVERNOR FLETCHER Bulkeley's *Some Seasonable Considerations for the Good People of Connecticut* was finally published as a book in New York in 1694. Governor Treat and the Assistants met in Hartford on 23 April 1694 and agreed to publish a detailed response to the printing of Bulkeley's publication. Governor Robert Treat and Secretary John Allyn published *Their Majesties Colony of Connecticut in New England Vindicated from the abuses of a Pamphlet, Licensed and Printed in New York, 1694, Entitled, Some Seasonable Considerations for the Good People of Connecticut.*[387] In their response, Treat and Allyn did not mention Bulkeley by name, but obviously addressed him. They did not reference Bulkeley's expanded treatise, *Will and Doom*, and may not have seen it.

In their publication, Governor Treat and Secretary Allyn primarily concerned themselves with the charge that Connecticut disobeyed a royal order by refusing to honor the commissions of Governor Fletcher and Sir William Phips. Treat and Allyn made the case that these men, who sequentially held the position of their Majesties' lieutenant and commander in chief, were only in charge of the King's Militia. Treat argued that this was a different militia than the one that Connecticut had established under its charter.

In England, the King's Militia was erected by contributions from gentlemen of estate. By statute, the King's lieutenant could charge anyone with an estate of more than 6,000 pounds or annual revenue of 500 pounds with supplying a horse, horseman and arms for the militia. Anyone with estate of generating fifty pounds per year could be required to provide a foot soldier and arms.

Treat argued that Connecticut had no such militia, nor any standing militia. The militia of Connecticut, as constituted by the General Court by virtue of the charter, included all males from 16 to 60 years of age (with some exceptions) and without regard to ownership of estate. Treat and Allyn noted that neither Governor Fletcher nor Sir William Phips had tried to raise a militia according to the English statutes, even though they had been free to do so. However, they doubted that more than fifty to one hundred persons would have sufficient estate to qualify.[388]

Treat and Allyn did not name Bulkeley in their document, but they addressed his well-known complaint that his advice against holding an election in May 1689 had been ignored. They said that his advice - namely that the government should continue to be managed by the commissions given by Sir Edmund Andros, and that the resumption of charter government should not be attempted - had been considered but rejected. Nor, they noted, did any other New England colony follow this advice. Five years having passed since then, Treat and Allyn felt that there was, at least, an implicit acceptance of Connecticut's actions. They thought that this might have been reason to remove some of [Bulkeley's] fondness for his original advice. However, they said, "Some Counselors, if not attended, will be angry and seek revenge somewhere." Bulkeley had characterized his ignored advice as "casting pearls before swine". Treat and Allyn observed that "to compare a whole colony to swine, is hard".

They objected to the "misapplication of Holy Scripture". "What? Are his advices to be (made similar) with the truths of the Gospel?" They condemned his "excesses of this kind...cursing us by the mouth of the Scripture ...representing us to the world as ignorant and inconsiderate to an excess...."[389]

"He claps a fool's coat on us and then derides us."[390] "To make us odious to the world" seems to be the main intention and to stir factions....it seems to be of absolute necessity to the ends of the pamphlet, to charge (us) with rising in arms...opposing their Majesties, and so lay a foundation large enough to (support) all the reviling and menaces...He seems to be very sensible , that all his labor will be lost and his whole design of defaming Connecticut frustrated if he do not charge us with explicit resolves against their Majesties; and therefore if truth will not afford him matter for it; lies must and shall." [391],[392]

Under the circumstances, Treat and Allyn, were somewhat restrained in attacking Bulkeley. In the introduction to their pamphlet they said, "To those that have injured us by that book [*Some Considerations*], we would wish them no worse than repentance of it and pardon for it."[393]

On one issue, however, they made an unrestrained assault on Bulkeley's character and morality. That was because of Bulkeley's involvement in the Nathaniel Finch incest case. They said, "...however high his credit hath run abroad and formerly [here], we will tell him that it is no good principle for any to hold, that a man may lawfully marry with his deceased wife's natural sister, nor good practice to write a book to justify one that hath so done, which is said will be printed. This is contrary not only to the current of Protestant Divines, but even of Papists...."[394] If Bulkeley really did publish such a book, no copy survives.

Treat and Allyn denied that Connecticut had ever been in rebellion against the royal authority of England. They did not dispute the King's right to the militia, nor reject his authority by disputing the commissions of Phips and Fletcher. They argued the application of these commissions to Connecticut's militia and appealed to the King for a ruling.

They denied that Governor Fletcher had ever been in danger in Connecticut. "His Excellency was with all freedom and safety among us..." It is true, they said, that a boisterous crowd gathered about his lodging at the Public House and Inn and that there were loud disputes. "To raise such things to a hazard of his Excellency's life ...is a false inference …can he say that any man shouldered a gun, go on a sword, lift up so much as a hand in such a way?"[395]

They derided Bulkeley's hot rhetoric about brutal treatment of those opposed to their government. The general complaint, they said, was that Connecticut's government was too mild. As to his imagining punishment by "Fire and Faggot and the noose of the halter," they said, it would cause those who know Connecticut best to laugh.

IN ENGLAND, FITZ-JOHN WINTHROP'S EFFORTS finally bore fruit. At the court at Whitehall, the King and Council issued an order on the 19th of April 1694 in response to the petition presented by Fitz-John on behalf of Connecticut. The order explained New York Governor Fletcher's commission and restricted his control of Connecticut's militia. It confirmed that the 1662 charter from King Charles II had established the Connecticut Colony as a corporation under the name of the Governor and Company of the English Colony of Connecticut in New England in America. However, contrary to Bulkeley, the order acknowledged the charter provided governing powers in addition to those normally given to a corporation. It noted that this corporation had the power to "make laws, elect governors, deputy governors and assistants, erect judicatures and courts and chose officers for the civil government…and to assemble martial array…the charters and grants of those Colonies [Connecticut and Rhode Island] do give the ordinary power of the militia to the respective governments thereof…."[396]

Queen Mary sent a letter to the Colony of Connecticut on the first of June 1694 confirming all that had been agreed. It also included a welcome and encouraging passage: "And the said Major-General Fitz-John Winthrop will, upon his arrival, inform you and all our subjects of that our Colony, and particularly in what may relate to the preservation of the peace, welfare, and security of the same, and maintaining your just rights and privileges."[397]

After Queen Mary's tacit endorsement of Connecticut' government in 1694, Bulkeley gave up the fight. He no longer publicly campaigned against the legitimacy of the government. Others continued to use Bulkeley's treatise, *Will and Doom*, as fodder for political attacks against Connecticut. Several years later Joseph Dudley and Lord Cornwall, contending for control of Connecticut, sent Bulkeley's *Will and Doom* to England. The entry in the Public Records office in London reads, "Mr. Bulkley's book entitled *Will and Doom* relating to grievances and irregularities in the Province of Connecticut." It is marked as, "received with Lord Cornbury's of the 6th of November 1704." Historian Charles Hoadly said that he examined this document in 1879 and found that it was a copy and not in Bulkeley's handwriting, nor were the attesting signatures autographs.[398] The late arrival of this copy in England has raised questions about whether Bulkeley's arguments were ever known contemporaneously in England or Connecticut. However, as seen, the basic arguments used in *Will and Doom* were well known and were addressed by Governor Treat and Secretary Allyn in their rebuttal, *Connecticut Vindicated*.

Richard G. Tomlinson

IX. DIARIES AND CORRESPONDENCE (1696 – 1704)

...Redfin hath need to scratch his noodle and bethink himself; to beg forgiveness of ye God of truth ...and I have other fish to fry than to regard ye Tattle of malice.

I do not remember that I observed one indictment [for witchcraft] to be proved. I wish New England have not a great deal of innocent blood to answer for.

~Gershom Bulkeley

IN 1696 GERSHOM WROTE a letter in defense of Mercy Disborough. Mercy had been the last woman convicted of witchcraft, but her 1692 conviction had been overturned and she was reprieved. However, she was not left in peace. Four years later she was accused of giving birth to a child out of wedlock and, it was implied, murdering the child. In an apparent attempt to keep Bulkeley from interfering in the case, it was insinuated that Bulkeley took Mercy with him from New London to Wethersfield. The strong implication was that Bulkeley was the father of the murdered child. Bulkeley's nephew, Joseph Bulkeley, testified in Mercy's defense and traveled to Wethersfield to inform Gershom of what had happened. Not finding his uncle at home, he left a note. Bulkeley replied in an interesting letter that is preserved at the Connecticut Historical Society:[399]

> Loving Cousin,   Wethersfield,
> June 3, 1696
>
> Yesterday, when I was not at home, somebody (I know not who) left two loose papers at my house, one whereof was a copy of your and your wife's testimony, attested by Nathan Gold, Clerk, & relating to ye scandal cast upon Mercy Holbridge (now Disborough) by James Redfin whereby I perceive that ye matter hath been in court. I would wish it had been otherwise for though I am not insensible that ye scandal reflects upon me as well as upon her, yet had ye case been wholly my owne, I should not have troubled ye court with it: offering there is a sort of men whose tongues are to slander, also there is a time when such persons only can be heard, as innnocency must stop its mouth. There is a time to be silent as well as a time to speake. But being as it is, I shall for ye satisfaction of your fellows and any others that may be in any wise concerned about the matter, show you that this tale, so far as it concerns Mercy Holbridge, is a most malicious Lie from ye beginning to ye end of it. I cannot but wonder at the bloody malice of some men, who having by a good Providence missed their marke of taking away her life by one project

would now do it, if possible, by another, for I can make no construction of it, the thing being so wholly false, as to her, yet so falsely represented. I offer:

Whereas he saith that Mercy Holbridge was with child when she lived with me at New London: I say this. Viz. That it is true that she did live a while with me at New London, but that she was with child in that time, I heard nothing of it, nor had any reason to suspect any such thing by her. Her conversation while she was with me was, for ought I could observe or can remember, was as blameless and inoffensive as of any person (especially of her years) in all ye Colony.

Whereas he says, that she went to Wethersfield with me and was there delivered of a child: this is a very great lie. Mercy went not with me from New London to Wethersfield, but Elizabeth Walker (a Scotch wench whose time I bought in Boston & who afterward went for England, intending to go home) & she indeed was (to my grief) with child while she lived with me at New London & when with me at Wethersfield & was there delivered of a child. But what is this to Mercy? Redfin is in a great error, his certain knowledge notwithstanding.

Whereas he says that the child died & a great man being the father of it, it was smothered up. I answer 1. It is true that Elizabeth Walker's child born at Wethersfield did die, but that it was in any way smothered up is as false as ye other is true. After she was found to be with child, long before her travail, she was assisted by ye midwife & others in her travail. & after ye child was dead, before burial of it, because we had cause to suspect that she had not dealt so well by it as she ought, I desired a jury to be paneled, which was done by Capt. Wells his order (who was then a Commissioner in Wethersfield) & ye jury sat upon ye death of ye child & gave their verdict: & this much more I still remember of it, viz. that this was done on a Saturday night, ye case so requiring & that old Thomas Burhan of Hartford being then in town was taken to be one of ye jury, ye rest I do not remember. 2. It is possible James Redfin may know ye man whom she accepted to be the father of ye child. I shall spare his name, but he was then no very great man & was caused to appear at ye next County Court at New London to answer to her accusations, when (as I remember) he denied ye fact. (This, I suppose, ye Record of ye court at New London will testify to.) Now if this were a smothering of it up, then Redfin says true in that part, else not.

Whereas he says, that ye Country Marshall
was sent down about it, I do not believe it, nor
any part of it. It is true Capt. Allyn went down
to hold ye court there at that time, as well as
some other times, & tis probable ye Marshall
might go to attend upon him, as he used
sometime to do, but that he was sent down
upon that account is (I think.) a fiction. (But if
the Marshall had been sent down about it, he
is beside his mark still, for Mercy Holbridge
was not at all involved in it.)

Lastly, whereas he affirms ye thing upon his
certain knowledge be true, I am of the opinion
that he cannot but know he lies. For, did he
see Mercy go with me from New London to
Wethersfield, which she never did? Did he
see her delivered of a child there, which she
murders? Was he her mid-wife or other
assistant in her travail? Or how is it possible
that he living (I know not where) at ye sea
side, should have such certain knowledge of
things done at Wethersfield? In a word, how
could he come to know that to be true, that
never was at all? No, no, Redfin hath need to
scratch his noodle & bethink himself: to beg
forgiveness of ye God of truth & also of her
& to make good recompense for such a
heinous and willful wrong. As for my own
part, I value not a thousand such tongues. I
am so well privy to my own innocency in this

matter. And I have other; fish to fry than to regard ye Tattle of malice. For it behooves wise men, who not imbrue their hands in blood, to take heed how they give ear to such malicious liars lest they be partners in their sin.

This I thought good to write for ye satisfaction of friends & if it may be any ways beneficial, you may show it to whom you please: I shall stand by it to ye last, let Redfin muster up all the forces he can to the contrary. I have not to add but my love & respects to yourself and wife with other cousins and friends with you & so commending you all to God, I am your loving Uncle, Gershom Bulkeley

GERSHOM PURCHASED THE 1699 ALMANAC of John Tulley of Saybrook, Connecticut, which he used as his diary.[400] The almanac was interleaved with blank pages on which Gershom recorded his notes and observations. Tulley's sixteen-page booklet presented weather forecasts, information about the four eclipses expected that year, lists of roads and distances from Boston and New York, times for the daily rising and setting of the sun, scheduled court meetings and Anglican feast days. Tulley's calendar departed from earlier custom by designating January rather than March as the first month of the year.

Bulkeley must have routinely used almanacs as diaries, but the only other surviving one is a 1710 almanac. It is entitled, *An Ephemeris of the Celestial Motions, Aspects and Eclipses, etc. For the Year of the Christian Era MDCCX* by Thomas Robie, A. B., licensed by his Excellency the Governor, Boston, printed by Bartholomew Green for the booksellers and sold at their shops. 1710.[401] This almanac is in the Hoadly Collection of the Connecticut Historical Society.

Gershom was an active farmer. He farmed his land on the eastern side of the Connecticut River in the Nayaug section of Glastonbury. This is the land that caused the lawsuit with Lieutenant Hollister and resulted in the re-surveying of all the lots along the river. Despite being in poor health, Gershom often crossed the river to cultivate his land in Nayaug. Several entries in his 1699 diary were about his Nayaug farm and livestock and health:

> **Saturday, March 17**, Jno Rily cut [castrated] me 4 pigs, but 2 of them but half cut, ye other shoat could not be come at.
> **Saturday, April 7**, I had walked to Nayaug and had a small fit in ye meadow.
> **Wed, April 12**, I had a fit in dressing [cultivating] the Southwest field; was very heavy all day yet dressed 20 serpls [bundles].
> **Thursday, April 13**, I had another fit before dressing the Southwest field but was not
> so bad after as yesterday.

Thursday, April 19, The white faced black
heifer of 3-year-old, calved her first calf.
Friday, April 20, The red cow 4-year-old,
calved her 3rd calf
Sunday, April 22, The black cow's calf
(next Monday 3 weeks old) sent to son,
Thomas Treat.
Friday, May 25, The 2-year-old white
backed red heifer calved at ye pasture.

As a farmer, Gershom was keenly interested in the weather.
His 1710 diary is mostly filled with weather observations.
Some of his entries in his 1699 diary included:
March 14, As great a snow as any (that I
remember) we have had this winter; swift &
heavy.
June 26, This night [was] terrible for
lightening, & toward morning great thunder &
rain.
July 4, An extreme hot day, till in ye
afternoon a blustery northerly wind & a small
sprinkle of rain, but at Windsor a great
shower.
July 5, Hot early in ye morning, but by & by
a blustering northerly wind & a round thunder
shower, but no great thunder, after that a fine
cool day but little rain, till in ye night it rained
hard again.
July 27, A soaking rain in ye night & same
next day.

Nov. 20, Strange warm weather for ye most
part all this month till this day & and then
very cold.
Nov. 29, A freezing rain that glazed ye
ground so that a man could hardly go.

BULKELEY WAS VERY SICK in 1699. His diary is filled with
comments about his ills. In March, he tried one of the
recipes which he had copied from *Chymical secrets and
rare experiments in physick & philosophy* (written by Sir
Kenelm Digby, who died in 1655, and published in London
in 1683). The results were disastrous. Gershom wrote in his
diary, "It almost destroyed me." [402]

Next, he mixed some elixirs, one according to a recipe by
George Starkey, one of New England's most renowned
alchemical physicians. He does not comment on any effects
of the elixirs. Starkey had trained at Harvard, but removed
to England where he worked with Robert Boyle.

Gershom continued to experience what he called "fits,"
sometimes with vomiting. On March 15th, he wrote that he
was working at nailing fence boards in the fence around his
house when he was taken with a fit. It was so severe, he
said, that "I could scarce get into ye house." For a week, he
was ill almost every day.

While Gershom was ill, his wife Sarah was dying. She lost
the ability to speak and lay silent in her bed. On Sunday,
June 3rd she died. Gershom noted in his diary, "My wife

died about 2 of ye clock in ye afternoon having been speechless about a fortnight, & I think dying near all that time & yet died without groaning or [distress], but very still and quiet." He next day he wrote, "My wife was buried about sunset." Later in his will Gershom would ask that his burial in the crowded Wethersfield cemetery be placed "as near to my late dear wife as conveniently may be."[403]

Gershom was desperately ill and was seized with one fit after another. From June to October he recorded more than thirty fits, often with vomiting. He wrote that one on June 19 almost killed him. When he wrote his will in 1712, he would observe that, "having more than twenty years walked upon the mouth of ye grave, and under great infirmity that I can but wonder how I have all this while escaped falling into it." On July 25th Gershom wrote, "A tedious sick day all day, which almost took me off my legs & left me in such condition that for divers days I am yet scarce able to go, especially not to sleep & rise up without staggering ready to fall, yet have been able to write out Helmont & Segerus."[404] Although very ill, Gershom continued this work of copying the books of eminent alchemists. These were probably books that he had borrowed and needed to return.

Gershom continued to stay active despite his poor health. In January, he sent letters to England to his brother-in-law, Isaac Chauncy, and to Major Palmes. He ordered glassware for his laboratory from Isaac and on August 24th he was delighted when a hogshead of the glasses arrived in Wethersfield. Two days later, Major Palmes, freshly returned from pursuing his legal battles in England, paid

Gershom a visit and found him sick and in the middle of a vomiting fit.

Despite everything, Gershom stayed involved in the world around him. His diary contains entries on visitors and affairs of the day. He followed his children with interest. Gershom's twenty-year-old son, John, was in Boston where he was a member of the Harvard class of 1699. Gershom's twenty-two-year-old son, Edward, was a life-long resident and frequent official in Wethersfield. He recorded the comings and goings of his 35- year-old son, Peter.

Gershom depended on Peter for many things including, as noted, bringing his drugs and medicine from Boston. Peter has been written about as a simple seaman who sailed up and down the coast of New England and who drowned in a storm. Peter was clearly much more than this. Among Gershom's papers is a journal originally belonging to Peter. On the first page, Peter wrote his name and recorded his marriage to Rachel Talcott. Peter's handwriting, unlike Gershom's, was clear, flowing and beautiful. He had obviously received a good education.

> **Saturday, Jan. 6**, Son Peter came home from Boston, leaving his vessel at Saybrooke.

> **Thursday, Jan. 11**, I wrote to England again to my brother Isaac and also to M[ajor] P[almes].

> **Saturday, Mar. 3**, Peter went over ye river for New London.

Thursday, Mar. 15, Cousin Charles Chauncy came up to be married & was married to Mr. Wolcott's daughter.

Tuesday, Apr. 3, John went for Springfield toward Boston.

Friday, Apr. 13, This day my cousin C. Chauncy of Boston gave us a visit with Cousin Nathaniel.

Saturday, Apr. 28, Son Peter came home from Boston.

Friday, May 19, The Governor Winthrop called at my gate.

Tuesday, June 22, Son Peter went again down ye river toward Boston.

Tuesday, June 26, Edward went toward ye Bay for John.

Saturday, June 30, Peter came home from the sea.

Sunday, July 1,I & Peter walked over to Nayaug, very hot.

Saturday, June 14, Edward and John came home about noon from ye Bay & brought my Cousin Peter Bulkeley's daughter, Rebecca, with them.

Tuesday, July 31, Peter went down ye river again.

Saturday, Sept. 15, Peter came sick home from the sea.

Tuesday, Oct. 16, Peter went down ye river to Boston.

Saturday, Oct. 20, Edward, Catherine & Cousin Rebecca went to Saybrook.

Thursday, Oct. 25, The Governor's Honor was pleased to give me a short visit.

Sunday, Oct. 28, Cousin Jonathan Prescott Jr, came hither.

Tuesday, Oct. 30, I went over to Nayaug & Glastonbury & was at home again about ye middle of ye afternoon.

Thursday, Nov. 1, Public Thanksgiving.

Friday, Nov. 2, Cousin Rebecca Bulkeley & Cousin Jonathan Prescott went toward Concord.

Friday, Nov. 10, I went over (with John) to Nayaug to see little Thomas Treat. [He] being sick. This night Mrs. Mechs was taken with an apoplectic convulsion that they thought she would have died. I was called up thrice.

Friday, Nov.23, Son Peter came home again from the sea this evening.

BENJAMIN DAVIS, A BOSTON APOTHECARY, was the major source of drugs for Gershom and they carried on an extensive correspondence. Physicians like Gershom Bulkeley relied upon apothecaries who imported medicines and supplies from England and elsewhere. For thirty-three

years, from 1643 until his death in 1676, William Davis of
Boston dominated this drug trade in New England.[405] After
William's death, the apothecary business was carried on by
his son, Benjamin Davis. Gershom's brother, Peter
Bulkeley, and Benjamin Davis were the only two
apothecaries known to be operating in New England prior
to 1695.[406] After Peter's death in 1691, Gershom relied on
Benjamin Davis.

Davis was highly respected in the Boston community and
was elected captain of the Ancient & Honorable Artillery
Company in 1686. He was more than Bulkeley's medical
drug supplier. Bulkeley and Davis held many opinions and
interests in common. Gershom's letters ordering supplies
often contained comments on contemporary events. Davis
had been a member of Boston's Old South Church, founded
by the liberal and progressive element in First Church. He
left First Church to help found the aggressively liberal
"Church on Brattle Square." Gershom shared many of its
beliefs; particularly its advocacy of a more open policy for
church membership.[407]

Gershom's orders to Davis where accompanied by his
comments and opinions on matters of the day. Gershom
had given up actively opposing the government of
Connecticut. However, his fighting spirit was not
completely gone. His old comrade, Major Edward Palmes,
was still resisting the Connecticut authorities. Gershom
eagerly inquired whether Benjamin had any word from
Palmes. Palmes was Benjamin's step-father. He had
married Benjamin's mother, Sarah, as his second wife soon
after William Davis died. Palmes was in England pursuing

a legal ruling against Connecticut. Gershom wrote, "I shall be glad to receive good tidings, if any be, and, in particular concerning Major Palmes, who possibly may have written you."

Back in 1689, a wealthy New London merchant, John Liveen, had died and left the bulk of his two-thousand-pound estate "to the ministry of New London."[408] Liveen was an eccentric who had grown up as an orphan in Barbados, and had no known religious affiliation. He had married a widow, Alice Hallam, who had two grown sons, John and Nicholas. Palmes and Fitz-John Winthrop were appointed executors of the Liveen estate. Palmes had refused to submit the will for probate as he considered the then Connecticut government to be illegitimate. The New London County Court proceeded to settle the estate anyway. When Alice died, she willed the estate to her two sons, in direct violation of the original terms of Liveen's will.

The Hallam brothers went to court to enforce their mother's will. The town of New London was not willing to give up the Liveen legacy that paid for their minister. The brothers lost the fight in Connecticut courts, but demanded their right to appeal the verdict to the king and queen of England. Connecticut refused to allow the appeal.

Major Palmes was "at law" with Fitz-John and Wait-Still Winthrop. Palmes, who as joint executor with Fitz-John, originally defended the Liveen will, changed sides and supported the cause of the Hallam brothers. Fitz-John Winthrop, the remaining executor, continued to defend the original will. This legal dispute was not the only litigation then pending between Palmes and Winthrop.

Palmes' first wife was Lucy Winthrop, the daughter of Governor John Winthrop Jr. and Fitz-John's sister. Although Lucy had died in 1676, Palmes now claimed that she had never received her fair share of her father's estate. He sued his brothers-in-law, Fitz-John and Wait-Still Winthrop. When he lost in the Connecticut courts, he also demanded the right to appeal the verdict, which was denied. So, both cases were submitted to the crown and Palmes and Nicholas Hallam went to England to plead their case.

The case was heard by the Lord Commissioners of Trade & Plantations in Council. "In obedience to your Majesties' several orders in Council of the 23rd of February last, we have considered the petition of John and Nicholas Hallam and of Edward Palmes and John Hallam…relating to two particular cases, wherein they complain of obstruction of justice." Connecticut's agent, Sir Henry Ashurst, argued that Connecticut had, by its charter, the right to bring all controversies to a final conclusion with no appeal allowed elsewhere.[409] The Council did not agree, and sent their opinions to the king on 9 March 1689/90. They said that they did not have enough information to rule on the merits of the two cases, but that it was "the inherent right of your Majesty to receive and determine appeals from all your Majesties subjects in America."[410]

The king approved the right of appeal. On 24 April 1699, the Council sent a letter to "the Governor and Company" of

Connecticut, informing them of the king's order.
Connecticut's government was admonished not to obstruct
the course of justice nor deny the citizens' right to appeal to
the crown. The letter noted that the king "expects your
speedy and punctual obedience thereunto". The case was
sent back to Connecticut for retrial with the results and the
records of the proceedings were ordered to be sent to
England for a final hearing and determination.

IN A LETTER TO BENJAMIN DAVIS dated 18 May 1699,
Gershom appeared to have heard some rumors of how the
litigation in England was turning out. He wrote, "There is
a story here that our laws are all disallowed and your costs
thereupon shoot up. But how it comes, I know not, not what
truth there is in it. I am still of my old opinion that New
England had need to [heed] their dependence upon the
crown of England better than they do and not think
themselves an Empire and that it will still cost them a great
deal." Bulkeley offered his advice that a much better and
cheaper course for New England, instead of volumes of
litigation, would be to pass one brief Act of Recognition of
the laws of England. [411]

The Palmes case returned to Connecticut for retrial. In
October 1699, Major Palmes appeared before the
Connecticut General Assembly and complained strenuously
about their treatment of him. In a heated exchange, he
accused Governor Treat of showing contempt to the King's
attorney. Members of the General Assembly were outraged
by what they considered a disrespectful slander against

their governor. They demanded that Palmes be fined five pounds and immediately thrown into prison. The governor cooled the situation and remitted the fine.[412]

Magistrate Samuel Wyllys wrote to Wait-Still Winthrop on 13 December 1699 about the appearance of Major Palmes before the October court: "Major Palmes…carries it very disrespectfully to the Governor. But I hope the court will be careful that he may have justice according to law, and then there will be less danger of his complaints. I remember that when you were last in Hartford that in the Boston colony the judges and courts allowed the benefit of common law of England to the people there…if it were so also in this colony…it would be very much for the safety of our charter…though Major Palmes his case at New London was tried by the statute law of England."[413]

Palmes (and Bulkeley) finally won their point that the laws of the Connecticut colony were subordinate to those of England. Bulkeley must have been gratified that Connecticut had finally conceded that laws made under the charter could not take away the rights of citizens given to them as Englishmen. However, the ruling did not mean victory for Palmes and the Hallams in their lawsuits. In the retrials, they lost their cases based on the merits of the evidence.

In his letter of 24 June 1700, Bulkeley thanked Davis for sending a copy of "Stoddard's book". [414] This was probably the book by Solomon Stoddard, the minister of the Congregational Church at Northhampton, Massachusetts. His small tract, entitled *The Doctrine of Instituted*

Churches Explained and Proved from the Word of God,
was printed in London in 1700.[415]

Stoddard, like Bulkeley, was more Presbyterian than
Congregational in his views. He advocated more governing
power for the minister, open sacraments and less restrictive
membership requirements. Stoddard called for a national
church organization with centralized powers and was called
the most feared challenger to traditional Puritanism.
Bulkeley wrote that he thought Stoddard was "very right"
in many things. "Though I cannot run with him in all
things, yet it is a fair beginning." Bulkeley expressed the
desire that even those clergy that disliked Stoddard's ideas
should put them to the test. Thus, he thought, "the dross
being separated from ye truth will shine in its brightness
and more truth will break out than it may be they are aware
of." Bulkeley wrote to Davis: "Tis no strange thing that
some endeavor to undermine your Presbyterian church."

Many Congregationalists, emphasizing the preeminence of
the local congregation, took pride in following practices
that were pointedly at variance with that in other churches.
Bulkeley strongly opposed this stubborn independence. "It
is high time for us to leave off Independency, if we do not
mean that the Gospel shall take its leave of us. It has
almost paganized the country, and will do it in a little time
more, if it be not abandoned....There are some hopes that
Independency is dying, and very few die without pangs and
agony. Truth, holiness and peace are ye proper blessings of
ye church which Independency will never bless us with."

Gershom's son, John, who had recently graduated from Harvard, was the courier for this letter. John had begun preaching at Colchester, Connecticut. Davis sent his congratulations and good will for John's accomplishments. Bulkeley, however, was skeptical of the value of early preaching. "I thank God that he doth very well approve himself. Yet I could wish he had been longer spared from ye pulpit. There is a disadvantage in such early preaching in many ways."

ROBERT CALEF WROTE A BOOK entitled *More Wonders of the Invisible World: Or, the Wonders of the Invisible World, Displayed in Five Parts* which criticized the recent Salem witch trials. Davis sent Robert Calef's book to Bulkeley. While Bulkeley's opinions had been instrumental in overturning the witchcraft conviction of Katherine Harrison of Wethersfield in 1670 and while he approved of the pardon of Mercy Disbrow in 1692, it did not mean that he doubted that there could be witches. As he stated in *Will and Doom,* he thought that rebellion against the king was like the sin of witchcraft.

In his sensational book Calef sharply criticized Cotton Mather and Increase Mather and other leaders involved in the Salem events. His major point was that while the Scriptures promoted the execution of witches ("Thou shalt not suffer a witch to live." Exodus 22:18) they did not give guidance in defining the crime or in the means to detect it. Calef accused the leaders of making up their own definitions of crime and detection, and that these were not sanctioned in Scriptures.

The Mathers reacted with outrage. Increase Mather, the president of Harvard, had Calef's book burned in the college yard. They produced a book in rebuttal entitled: *Some Few Remarks Upon a Scandalous Book, Against the Government and Ministry of New England Written by One Robert Calef, Detecting the Unparalleled Malice & Falsehood, of the Said Book; and Defending the Names of Several Particular Gentlemen, by Him Therein Aspersed & Abused, Composed and Published by Several Persons Belonging to the Flock of Some of the Injured Pastors and Concerned for Their Just Vindication.* This seventy-one-page pamphlet was printed in Boston in 1701.

In his letter of 25 March 1701 Bulkeley thanked Davis for sending Calef's book. Of the witchcraft trials he wrote, "I do not remember that I observed one indictment to be proved. I wish New England have not a great deal of innocent blood to answer for, both of former and later time. The good Lord pardon his people & give them to see their error…Yet I cannot fully run along with him [Calef] in his notions about witchcraft."[416] Bulkeley said, however, that he could not cite specific objections since he did not have the book with him. He had sent it on, as Davis had requested, (probably to Reverend John Woodbridge of West Springfield) and had yet to get it back. Woodbridge would be interested since he and Benjamin Coleman, pastor of Davis's church, were engaged in a pamphlet war with the Mathers over religious dogma. Calef's criticisms of the

Mathers in his book would have been very satisfying to Woodbridge.

The Mathers defended their role in the recent witchcraft trials and they countered the religious ideas of Coleman. Reverend Benjamin Coleman's "Church in Brattle Square" in Boston was also known as "The Manifesto Church" due to its bold, unorthodox credo published by Coleman. Benjamin Davis was a founder and deacon of the "Church in Brattle Square," and Davis sent Bulkeley copies of Coleman's sermons.

In March 1700, Increase Mather had tried to refute the Manifesto with a treatise called, *The Order of the Gospel Professed and Practiced by the Churches of Christ of New England Justified.* The prefix included a point-by-point rebuttal of the Manifesto. Coleman immediately responded with the *Gospel Order Revived Being an Answer to a Book lately set forth by Reverend Increase Mather, President of Harvard, by Sundry Ministers of the Gospel of New England Being an Able Disquisition Upon Questions Proposed in the Former Work.* The publication was anonymous, but the authors were later identified as Coleman, Reverend Bradstreet of Charlestown and Reverend John Woodbridge of West Springfield. Due to the influence of the Mathers, no Boston printers had dared to print the book. It was finally published in New York later in the year.

The enraged Mathers responded with a twenty-four-page publication, *A Collection of Some of the Many Offensive Matters Contained in a Pamphlet entitled The Order of the*

Gospel Revived." This publication was filled with virulent invective and accused their unnamed opponent (Coleman) of "vilifying his Superiors unto whom he owes a Special Reverence."

In his letter of 25 March 1701, Bulkeley told Davis that he had recently received a copy of the *Gospel Revived* and the Mathers' *Collection of Offensive Matters* in answer to it. Bulkeley was unimpressed by the arguments of the Mathers. It seemed to him the Mathers were more interested in countering any damage to their reputations than in addressing the issues raised. Bulkeley wrote to Davis, "they had more reference to self than to ye cause, least of all to ye truth. I wish we were all of Christ's & Paul's mind that we came into this world to witness to ye truth…If we loved ye truth as we should, our reputation, or ye diminution of it, would be very little things to us…If their way be ye way of truth, why do they not prove it substantially? That is the best way to repair & secure their own honor."

Bulkeley was critical of the Mathers' failure to present arguments to support their views and to rely instead upon citing "authority" for their justification. "… [T]he pinning our faith upon other men's sleeves, believing this or that to be true or good & right because such and such men have said it, is & hath been one of the sins of New England. Yea taking the truth itself upon trust, is a large step toward Popery. And what profit is there in such a faith? Let us study Truth, Holiness and Peace. These will set us all at one."

There were many intellectual ties between Bulkeley and Cotton and Increase Mather. They held their Harvard backgrounds and on-going linkage to the college in common. Like Gershom, Cotton and Increase were active in alchemy and were members of Winthrop's informal network of alchemists.[417] While Gershom seemed annoyed with their failure to seriously address the arguments raised against them, he did not seem to disrespect them.

There were attempts within the churches to heal the breach between those in Coleman's camp and those supporting the views of the Mathers.[418] Bulkeley added as a postscript to his letter to Davis: "I have seen your letter to Mr. Woodbridge which gives hopes of accommodation and peace, which is good news if it proves true." Coleman's views would eventually prevail, and he was chosen to be president of Harvard College. He was so controversial, however, that his proposed appointment undermined attempts to obtain more adequate financial support for the office. To prevent that, Coleman declined to accept the position.[419]

TRAVEL BETWEEN WETHERSFIELD AND BOSTON was difficult. Bulkeley had to rely on someone traveling overland to Boston to take his letters to Davis and to bring back the supplies and medicines he ordered. Gershom used his sons, Peter and John, as his most reliable couriers. When he tried to use others, he was disappointed by their failure to promptly deliver. "The things you sent me by…Whitmore, I have not received. The oil of almonds was for my ears to see if that would do them any good, but he hath kept them all winter at Middletown. I suppose he means to bring them again to you shortly. If he do, I pray send them to me by some other person that will deliver them. He and John Smith will (I think) do me no good."

Bulkeley was clearly feeling his isolation. In his 1701 letter he wrote: "You may think it strange that you have received no line from me all ye while. I never knew so little traveling. I have had no opportunity of writing to you all ye winter and now this might come by sea. Indeed, I sent letters this winter to Boston for England, once by New London and afterward by Northhampton and have not yet heard whether any came to hand or not, but I was not willing to write to yourself or Mr. Coleman of such adventures." In November 1701, Gershom's son, Peter, was drowned in a storm at sea. The inventory of Peter's estate included parts of a broken sloop at Block Island.[420] In addition to losing a cherished son, Gershom lost his trusted courier and a vital link to the world at large.[421]

As an intellectual, Gershom was always hungry to have news about world affairs. In 1704, Gershom complained: "So many ships arriving last year and so lightly loaded. I thought they should have filled us with Gazettes [The London Gazette was official journal of the British government] and Mecuries that we should hardly found time to read them all. But I have seen but one all last year and that was of March, a month of little action. I would be glad to understand how things are in the world." Some of the news that Bulkeley sought would have included actions related to "Queen Anne's War." In 1702, England had declared war on France and Spain. There were repercussions for New England in fighting with the French and Indians, threats to sea lanes and economic hard times. Bulkeley sent Davis his thoughts about the recent (29 February 1704) raid by French and Indian forces on the town of Deerfield, Massachusetts. Forty-seven villagers were killed and 112 carried away captive to Canada. Bulkeley did not know that deep snow drifts helped the raiders scale the walls protecting the town. He wrote of the town "…they were too careless and secure for account is given that ye enemy entered into their fortifications, breaking into houses and killing them before any were discovered by the watch, which could hardly have been if a true watch had been kept. But tis too old a practice for watchmen, when tis late and they think it will not be taken notice of, to go to sleep. Nothing but calamity will teach us, and hardly that. God be gracious to the poor captives." [422]

GERSHOM WAS IN FINANCIAL DISTRESS. He had written to Davis on 18 May 1699 to thank him for continuing to fill his orders for medicines despite his not having paid for previous orders, and to place a new order.[423] Bulkeley's affairs were at a low ebb. His health was not good, and he no longer had his son, Peter, to carry his letters and orders to Davis in Boston. Gershom's wife, Sarah, was also in poor health. She would die the following month.

Gershom was trying to work his way out of debt. He complained that this was made more difficult because of the weak economy: "the money [hard currency] is gone…they say the merchants have sent it away to England." Drug suppliers in England demanded to be paid in hard currency and New England had very little.

Gershom carried out his duties as doctor with great dedication. Throughout 1699, he had been very ill and recorded continuing fits. On October 31th he wrote in his diary that, "I was very ill of a fever & cold, which held a week." Nevertheless, on November 10th he responded when called at night to treat a patient. "This night Mrs. Miches[424] was taken with an apoplectic convulsion that they thought she would have died. I was called up thrice."[425]

In his 1699 letter to Davis, Gershom had thanked Davis for continuing to fill his orders even though he had not paid his bill. By 1701, he had still not paid and so he wrote, "I should send you some money, but I am loath to send that by sea, but shall take the first opportunity I can send it by land.' When Gershom placed an order in September 1702, his bill was still unpaid. He wrote, "I hope I shall accomplish your satisfaction before or at least in ye Spring…." Bulkeley apparently did not pay up until 1704.

Bulkeley found a courier he trusted to go by sea, a twenty-four-year-old Wethersfield resident, Thomas Curtis. Curtis was a sea captain who sailed the New England coast. Although previously reluctant to send money by sea, Gershom now used Curtis to deliver his order and money to Davis. In a letter of 3 April 1704, Gershom wrote to Davis: "Your money hath waited for you a long time, but we have been buried in snow this winter, so that I have had no opportunity to send it to you." "[I] have ordered Thomas

Curtis (yea bearer hereof) to pay you sixteen or eighteen pounds. Please to give him your receipt."

The cost, quality and availability of medicinal drugs to New England became an issue during Queen Anne's War. Bulkeley had seldom complained to Davis about the quality of the drugs he provided. In his 1791 order, he had complained mildly about the aloe he had received. In his new order he said, "Let it not be Barbados Aloes…that hath a mixture of caffeine in it. It may be they think that would do ye world a kindness…but it is a mistake. It is an adulteration of ye Aloes and agrees not with many bodies." By 1704, Gershom and others had many serious complaints about the drugs they received from Davis. He said of one of the drugs that the first he received was very good, but "ye last was about half as rotten as dirt."

Drugs from England became expensive and sometimes unattainable. Saffron, a very expensive spice used for treating pain, was in great demand. In his 1702 order, Bulkeley wrote, "Please send these things by ye first good vessel that come thither, except ye saffron, which I would have brought by land, if it be possible." "We are so sick that I don't doubt that we shall want it before it will come by sea."

By 1704, Bulkeley was desperate for saffron and other drugs. "I am out of drugs and want supply, but I fear that things do grow so dear, that I am almost discouraged." Davis's suppliers in England demanded to be paid in hard currency, and Bulkeley said, "I can get very little by my practice …your Correspondents in England do take more advantage upon ye war than they have reason to do. There are, no doubt, crooks in old England, as well as new." Bulkeley was not alone in his complaints about the cost and quality of the drugs available from England as the war dragged on and new export duties were imposed.[426]

Bulkeley wrote that since Davis could not supply saffron, he had tried to get some in Hartford. "One man had a little and could spare me [some], but I had it for fourteen shillings…there is a great difference between fourteen and zero. I think no man will accuse our Connecticut merchants of selling too cheap. However, so long as I can do anything, people in their necessity will not suffer me to be quite idle and do nothing."

Bulkeley probably did not know how hard-pressed Davis was to supply New England's physicians nor the lengths he had to go to obtain quality drugs. Benjamin Davis's father had built a fortune as an apothecary, but Benjamin struggled. On 26 November 1704, only seven months after Bulkeley's last order, Benjamin Davis died. His estate was declared insolvent. He had extended credit to his customers, like Bulkeley, and many had not been able to pay their bills. [427]

Richard G. Tomlinson

X. SCIENTIST AND ALCHEMIST
(1694 – 1713)

[The elements are said to be] earth, air, fire and water. But do not go think that the body of man is compounded of these as its constituent parts, according to the vulgar opinion, for that is a mistake...

[The real juices of the body are] the vital spirit, the blood, the liver, the gall, the pancreatic juice, the humors of the eye, the nervous juice, the alimentary...humor and the marrow.

Be sure you never let your medicines carelessly about the house, as that children and fools may come at them, especially dangerous drugs such as mercury...[and] arsenic, whereby they may kill themselves...

~Gershom Bulkeley

FREE FROM POLITICS, Bulkeley returned to his interests in medicine, alchemy and scientific experiments. From the time of his ministry in New London and, perhaps, even earlier when at Harvard, Bulkeley had been interested in alchemy. Shortly after he left Harvard to take his first job as the minister in New London, he included a lengthy Latin copy of a paper on how to prepare the alkahest among his sermon notes.[428] The "alkahest" was a name attributed to the alchemist, Paracelsus,[429] for the hypothetical "universal solvent" which could dissolve any substance. The possibility of the creation of such a solvent was a constant preoccupation among alchemists.

Alchemists enthusiastically conducted experiments. For them, alchemy was an attempt to uncover the secrets of nature. As the renowned alchemist Paracelsus wrote:

> The great virtues that lie hidden in nature
> would never have been revealed if alchemy
> had not uncovered them and made them
> visible. Take a tree, for example, a man sees it
> in the winter, but he does not know what it is,
> he does not know what it conceals within
> itself, until summer comes and discloses the
> buds, flowers, the fruit…Similarly the virtues
> in things remain concealed to man, unless the
> alchemists disclose them, as the summer
> reveals the nature of the tree.[430]

Key figures in the emergence of a scientific alchemy based on experimental observation were Paracelsus (1493-1541) and Helmont (1580-1644). Bulkeley's library included works by both authors.[431] Paracelsus, born Philippus Aureolus Theophratus Bombastus von Hohenheim, was a Renaissance physician who laid the foundation for medical practice by insisting on using observations to deduce scientific conclusions, rather than citing ancient authors. Parcelsus demanded that the new alchemy science be firmly unified with medicine.[432] The inventory of Gershom's library includes *Paracelsus Chymistry*. As with the other books in the inventory, the listing lacks enough detail to make identification completely certain. According to Jodziewicz, this book is believed to be a posthumous translation by Gerhard Dorn with the full title, *Congeries Paracelsicae Chemiae de Transmutationibus Metallorum,* published in Frankfort in 1581.[433] Given its age, this book may have originally been in the library of Gershom's grandfather, Edward (1540-1621). Bulkeley commented that portions of his library were inherited from both this grandfather and his own father.

Jan Baptist van Helmont was the intellectual heir to Paracelsus. Gershom's library contained two books by Helmont, *Ortus Medicine. Id Est, Initia Physicae Inaudita,* published in Amsterdam in 1648 and *Dageraed aft Nieuwe Opkomst der Geneeskonst* published in 1659. Gershom mentions this second book in his will as the reason he also owned a book of Dutch grammar.

Gershom's library contained two books by Harvard-educated George Starkey (1628-1665) who went to England in 1650, and became a member of the alchemy network in London. These books were *Natures Explication and Helmont's Vindication* (1657), and *Liquor Alcahest; or a Discourse of that Immortal Dissolvent of Paracelsus & Helmont* (1665).

Bulkeley was a member of an informal network of New England alchemists established by John Winthrop Jr. Winthrop's network of alchemists and alchemical physicians in New England included Gershom and Gershom's father-in-law, Charles Chauncy, president of Harvard and his brother-in law, Isaac Chauncy. Many of the members of Winthrop's alchemist network came from the upper echelons of colonial society. Included in this informal membership were two colonial governors, two presidents of Harvard and one of Yale, twenty-two Puritan ministers and nineteen other men of great reputation.[434]

For the seventeenth century scientist, alchemy was a recognized as an important discipline. It primarily sought by experimental investigation to unlock the secrets of the transformation of things. In medieval times, the focus was on transforming base metals into precious metals, such as gold. It also invoked magic and spiritual forces. This evolved over time into the more modern pursuit of chemistry and physics, retaining experimental tests as the source of knowledge. John Winthrop Jr. and Gershom Bulkeley were particularly interested in "iatrochemistry" – the use of alchemy to develop solutions for diseases and medical aliments.[435] Gershom's library contained most of the essential books on alchemy.[436]

When Governor Winthrop went to England in September 1661 to negotiate the crucial charter recognizing Connecticut's right to conduct its own government, he had been inducted into the Royal Society on 1 January 1662. He was the first colonial member of the Society. This membership and the friendship of Society founder and leading scientist, Robert Boyle, were very important to the success of Winthrop's mission to obtain the charter.[437] Boyle had an intense interest in the settlement and development of New England. He served as governor of the Corporation for the Propagation of the Gospel in New England. Winthrop made presentations to this group and to the Royal Society and created a network of patronage that allowed him to aggressively pursue Connecticut's charter from King Charles II and later to defend it.[438]

Alchemists like Winthrop, Boyle and Bulkeley were interested in more than turning base metals into gold. They were laying the foundations of serious science in chemistry and physics. Rejecting the idea that answers to scientific questions were to be found by studying the writings of ancient authorities like Galen, they embraced disciplined research and experimental testing. They were still interested in precious metals; they looked for a universal solvent (the alkahest) which could dissolve rock and free the gold inside. But their interests were broader. They pursued iatrochemistry, the creation of medicines (phissick) that would have efficacy against specific diseases and ailments.[439] They attempted to understand the inner workings of every kind of phenomenon from the color of light to the growth of plants.

Although the transmutation of base metals into precious metals did not seem to be a focus of Bulkeley's alchemical research, he was not indifferent to the possibility of refining metal ore to extract gold or silver. One of the books that Gershom copied by hand was, *Chymical Search & Rare Experiments in Physick & Philosophy,* by Sir Kenelm Digby.[440] Digby was an influential English alchemist, who befriended Winthrop.[441] Digby died in 1665 and *Chymical Search* was published posthumously in London in 1683. Digby's book described a special furnace for refining metals and extracting gold and silver. Gershom made a detailed sketch of this furnace in his manuscript. He added the note: "I have made and used this furnace for coppelling [refining] as well as other uses without bellows ..."

The surviving books from Gershom's library include seven publications by Boyle on medicine, metals and alchemy. One of these books, *The Scepticall Chymist*,[442] which was published in Oxford in 1680, is considered to be the fundamental book in the establishment of modern chemistry. Perhaps the most intriguing book by Boyle in Gershom's library is *Some Receipts of Medicines for the Most Part Parable and Simple, Sent to a Friend in America*.[443] This book was published in London in 1688. It is not known how Gershom acquired this book or whether he ever corresponded with the alchemists of Boyle's network as Winthrop had done. However, it is clear that Gershom was conversant with the latest scientific developments in England and avidly followed them. He did correspond with his brother-in-law, Isaac Chauncy, who was living in England. Through Isaac, Gershom obtained laboratory equipment and newly published books.

One of Bulkeley's favorite authors was the German-Dutch alchemist and chemist, Johann Rudolph Glauber (1604-1670). Glauber was a prolific writer, producing over forty books. Gershom's library contained a dozen titles by Glauber and one book about Glauber. Gershom bequeathed all his books concerning medicine and chemistry to his grandson, Richard Treat. Gershom's will stated: "...among which I include Glauber's and Boyle's which I have whether in Latin or English...." The book about Glauber, published in London in 1689, was entitled, *The Works of the Highly Experienced and Famous Chymist, John*

Rudolph Glauber: Containing, Great Variety of Choice Secrets in Medicine and Alchemy.

Early in his ministry, Bulkeley had been content to gather local remedies for the benefit of his parishioners. With the political battles behind him, Gershom turned more of his attention to his medical practice and to the alchemical production of medicines and drugs. He studied the literature from abroad, and labored in his laboratory to test their recipes and to develop his own.

Bulkeley maintained a large library which included many medical books. Gershom sought to stay current with medical practice in England. The most popular author of the books inventoried in the probate of his estate was the English medical writer, William Salmon. The probate inventory did not include full descriptions of book titles. Jodziewicz has published an attempt to create as complete a description of the titles as circumstances allow, but the exact identification of these books represents a "best guess" by scholars.[444]

The books by Salmon were all published in London and are identified as:

> *A Compendium of Astrological, Galenical & Chemical Physick*, 1671
> *The London Dispensatory*, 1678
> *A Supplement to the New London Dispensatory*, 1683
> *Polygrahice or the Art of Drawing*, 1685
> *The Compleat English Physician*, 1693
> *Bates Dispensatory*, 1694

*The Family Dictionary or Household
Companion*, 1695
Chymrgiery (2 vols.), 1698-1699
*The Country Physician or a Choice
Collection of Physick*, 1703
The Practice of Physick, 1707
The Practical Physician, 1707
Synopsis Medicinae par Salmon, date
uncertain

Only a few of the books from Gershom's library have
survived, but many of his account books and manuscripts
are still extant. More than thirty volumes of his personal,
medical and account books, covering thousands of pages,
have been archived.[445] These are in the manuscript
collections of the Connecticut Historical Society, the
Watkinson Library at Trinity College and the Lyman
Maynard Stowe Library[446] at the University of Connecticut
Health Center Library. Gershom's account books, covering
various time periods between 1680 and 1713, show the
extent of his medical practice. It ranged over a wide area
that included all of Connecticut and reached north up the
Connecticut River into Massachusetts as well as south
down to Long Island.

Bulkeley's medical notebooks include recipes and cures,
some copied from medical publications and some collected
from local lore. In his notebooks, he quotes extensively
from the books of famous English doctors and from
scientists like Robert Boyle. Typical of Bulkeley's notes
are passages from Boyle's *Some Considerations Touching*

the Usefulness of Experimental Naturall Philosophy. In this publication Boyle gave a recipe for creating a powder which, when dissolved in hot water, produced a curing water for treatment "…of fistula & all manner of wounds & swellings or old ulcers, cankers, tattering, boiles or scabs in any place, or green wounds." [447] Gershom recorded that this "water" according to Boyle, will cure fistulas without surgery and solely with the external application of cloths soaked in it. Gershom noted that he had found the same recipe "almost word for word" in Bates (*Pharmacopoeia Bateana* translation by William Salmon, *Bate's Dispensatory,* London, 1694).[448] Gershom observed that whereas Bates recommended his water to dry up any old sore or heal any green wound; he "saith nothing in particular of fistulas."

Gershom was well versed in the work of Thomas Willis (1621-1675), a founding member of the Royal Society, and a major figure in the fields of anatomy, neurology and psychiatry. Two books by Willis appear in Bulkeley's library: *Cerebri Anatome: Cui Accessit Nervirym Descript et Usus* (1664) and *Pathologiae Cerebri et Nervosi Generis Specimen* (1667). In addition, Bulkeley made notes[449] from two other medical publications by Willis: *Diatribae duale medico-philosophicae* (1660) and *Pharmaceutics Rationalis* (1677).

While Bulkeley followed the latest medical science being produced in England, he did not automatically accept everything that was written. He compared authors and also performed his own experiments. In 1699, he copied from the book, *Arcana Philosophia or Chymical Secrets, containing the noted and useful chymical medicines of Drs. Witt and Rich Russel, chymists.*[450] The book was published in London by John Headrich in 1697, so Gershom had access to relatively recent English publications.

Headrich wrote in the introduction that he had worked for one of the doctors before their deaths and the reason for publishing their true medical recipes was to protect their memory from being debased by frauds and would-be imitators. Headrich wrote, "If anyone should be so obstinate as to proceed in any other manner of preparing them, under pretense of bettering them, I cannot but declare them Counterfeits." He asserted that one of Dr. William Russel's tinctures so pleased King Charles II that he declared it the Royal Tincture. Gershom inserted a comment in his copy: "Let it speak for itself. We must not believe all stories."

Bulkeley inserted many critical comments in his copies of English publications. At a later point in his copy of *Arcana Philosophia,* there was a recipe that used arsenic along with a warning that the fumes should not be inhaled during preparation. Gershom noted in his copy, "We think you give a dark, dubious Rx." Many alchemical recipes included arsenic. It was known to be a poison, but it was thought that it could be rendered safe in combination with other ingredients like vinegar. It was hoped that arsenic could draw out or kill the venom in ulcers, cancers and sores and thus cure them.

This manuscript also contains a copy of *Johannes Segerus Weidenfeld, Concerning ye Secrets of ye Adepts or ye Use*

of Lully's Spirits of Wine, A Practical Work[451] printed in
1685 also copied by Bulkeley 17 July 1699. Bulkeley was
nearly killed in his laboratory trying to follow one of
Weidenfeld's recipes for Philosophical Wine. Bulkeley
added a note in the manuscript in 1700. "For a caution to
any that may undertake ye preparation of ye Spirit of
Philosophical Wine, treated in ye following books of
Segerus. Let him observe what he says Cap. 1, pg. 28 viz
that it is ye most difficult and dangerous work of all the
Chymistry." Bulkeley also notes a word of caution from a
work of Paracelsus, "that it is ye most dangerous labor in
all alchemy." Bulkeley wrote that on May 24, 1700 he
began to work with Spirit of Vinegar made from honey.
The experiment, following the recipe, lasted several days.
One morning the mixture began to boil and froth and give
off white fumes. It caught fire and exploded with "a report
like a musket shot". The furnace was blown to pieces and
parts flung around the room. A heavy iron plate, which was
part of the apparatus, was bent double so that, when found,
Bulkeley was not certain what it was. "If I had been nearby
of it, especially looking into it, as I had done but a very
little before, it had certainly beaten me all to pieces and
killed me outright. But God preserved me, blessed be his
name,"[452]

GERSHOM'S MOST IMPORTANT SCIENTIFIC writing was
produced in 1704. He wrote a treatise of over 300 pages
which he called *Vade Mecum seu Fasciculus
Medicamentorum, a Packet of Medicines,* summarizing his

medical knowledge and presenting medical recipes. This treatise provides the most comprehensive presentation of the state of medical knowledge in Connecticut at the end of the seventeenth century. The purpose of this work was to instruct his 32-year-old daughter, Dorothy Treat and, perhaps, eventually, to instruct her 11-year-old son, Richard, should he decide to pursue medicine. The Latin, *Vade Mecum*, translates as, "Go With Me." This phrase was incorporated in the title of numerous handbooks which were meant to be carried around as a handy reference. Bulkeley probably did not mean this bulky manuscript to be carried as a portable reference. He probably meant "go with me" in the sense of "follow my teaching". He wrote, "Keep this in your cabinet and let it not be common for every eye to look into and read it whereby you would not do others so much good as you will do hurt to yourself. Therefore, keep this book close and secret to yourself."[453] Gershom finished the text of his manuscript and wrote "finis dated 6.5.1705". He soon gave it to Dorothy as her name appears on the inside cover of *Vade Mecum* along with the date, Dec. 17, 1705. Although Dorothy had no university training, it is clear from other notebooks of hers, particularly one written in 1721, that she did pursue laboratory work in alchemy and medicine.[454]

Medical education and practice at this time was a compromise and blend of the ancient theories of Galen (129-216) and the newer concepts of physicians like Jan Baptist van Helmont (1580-1644). Gershom's treatise quickly established that he rejected Galenism and largely embraced the theories of Helmont. Bulkeley's treatise was tutorial and instructive. He not only presented medical concepts and recipes for creating medicines, but he also quoted the sometimes-conflicting advice of multiple authors. These copies were not rote but contained his critiques. Gershom often inserted his own observations and conclusions. Even the revered Helmont did not escape criticism. Gershom wrote,[455] "That you may not wonder that I, who think much of Helmont's theory...take great exceptions at many things in his writings [though] granted now and then wondrous medicines [are based] upon his authority. I might have confessed to you once and for all that...I have not seen cause to disregard many things he delivers as matters of fact, provided they be rightly understood...."[456]

Bulkeley began *Vade Mecum* with a twenty-seven-page preface, covering the state of medical knowledge. Bulkeley presented a description of the "seven natl or natural things (usually so called)" relative to the body and health. He enumerated: 1. the elements; 2. the parts (members) of the body; 3. the humors; 4. the complexions; 5. the power of the faculties; 6. the operations and 7. the spirits. He wrote that in his view the humors, members and spirits should be collapsed into one and the complexions he rejected entirely. He then added one new category, "regions of the body," and said that there were five, not seven, natural things.

Bulkeley's rejection of the "complexions" is significant. Galenists believed that there were four humors and their imbalance (complexions) was the cause of disease. Bulkeley wrote, "The complexions are, sanguine, hot & moist, phlagaratick, cold & moist, choleric, hot & dry and melancholy, cold & dry. But these also built upon ye aforesaid fictitious grounds are a figment and vanish." By throwing out "complexions" Bulkeley was placing himself solidly in opposition to the Galenists.

Gershom wrote that the elements were earth, air, fire and water. "But", he cautioned, "do not go think that the body of man is compounded of these as its constituent principles, according to the vulgar opinion, for that is a mistake and in that sense, they are to be rejected from the number of things natural to the body."

As for the parts of the body, Gershom presented them as either solid or liquid, with the liquid being either contained or not. He noted that contained liquids were the called the humors or juices of the body and usually designated as blood, phlegm, yellow choler and melancholy. The last three of these, according to Bulkeley, were "figments." The real juices of the body, he wrote, were "the vital spirit, the blood, the liver, the gall, the pancreatic juice, the humors of the eye, the nervous juice, the alimentary (usually called the secondary) humor and the marrow."

Digestion was a major topic on which Helmont's ideas clashed with those of the Galenists,[457] and Bulkeley devoted a long section to its discussion. Galen had said that digestion occurred in three stages and thus he divided the body into three sections. Bulkeley said that this was still taught in the medical schools.

> The food taken in at the mouth is in the
> stomach turned into a clear transparent cream
> of liquid, called chyle, and from there

transmitted to the guts where the thinner and alimentary part is sucked in by ye mesenteric veins and by them transmitted to ye liver and ye gross excrementatious part, passing through ye belly or guts is cast out at ye fundament and so their first part of ye body extends from ye mouth to ye fundament on ye one hand and to ye hollow of ye liver on ye other hand. The second digestion (according to them) is sanguification performed in ye liver whereby ye thinner and the excrementatious part of the liquefaction aforesaid is separated for urine in the refines and ye bladder and ye thicker alimentary part is matured into blood and transmitted into ye vena cava and so ye second region (according to ye schools) contains ye liver and ye vena cava with all its branches, and (if I mistake not) ye urinary vessels and passages also and why not … The third digestion (according to them) is ye nourishment of all ye solid parts of ye body ... But Helmont, arguing this doctrine of ye schools defective and insufficient (and indeed it is) enumerates six digestions and distinguishes ye regions of ye body according to them

Bulkeley then presented Helmont's six-stage digestive process, largely based on the chemical actions of acids, alkalis, salts and ferments. While Bulkeley mostly agreed with Helmont's model, he was not above expressing some modest differences. "…I think his fourth and fifth digestions and regions are but one and ye same…how these can be two distinct digestions and regions, I cannot see."

IN HIS *VADE MECUM*, Bulkeley addressed the subject of astrology, and its supposed linkage to human health. He had read a popular book that had first been published in London in 1651, and went through multiple editions, the seventh edition being published in1689. His comments were:

> Thomas Brugis in his *Vade Mecum* or *Companion for a Chirurgion* gives this direction to know the danger of ye sick by ye age or days of ye moon as whereon he falls sick.Viz.1. He that falls sick on this day (i.e. the first day) of ye moon, if his sickness be wearie and tedious, he will quickly die. [He that falls sick on the 30th day] will hardly escape though he use many good medicines. (And I think so too; for when is ye moon 30 days old? But he says nothing of ye 31st day and tis possible that by moon he may mean month and reckon upon ye days of ye solar month. But then when shall we begin ye month? For some months have 31 days and one-month hath not 30 and ye odd days will put us out are account.) You may observe that I do not think you will find much in it. However, use good medicines at all times.

There is more in that than in ye days of falling
sick.

STANDARDS FOR MEASUREMENT and safety in medicinal
preparations were concerns for Bulkeley. He presented a
long account of the various weights and measures in use
and conversion between them. He complained of the
danger presented by poorly defined standards. "Thomas
Brugis in *his Vade Mecum* aforesaid says that avoirdupois
weight is now generally used among ye apothecaries. Yet
[he said] that a barley, wheat or peppercorn may be used
for a grain. But surely that will make very uncertain weight
and using of it may be dangerous...."

Nor did Bulkeley approve of recipes that called for
ingredients measured in coins, such as a sixpence. You
must determine, he said, whether the coins are English
money, and what the weight of them was then. Also, he
warned, money is often altered, and the weight changed.

Near the end of the preface in his treatise, Bulkeley wrote,
"Lastly some cautions." He warned that in distilling and
preparations the fumes, especially the mineral fumes of
mercury and arsenic, should not be inhaled "least you get
such a hurt by them as you can never heal." "Be sure you
never let your medicines carelessly about the house, as that
children and fools may come at them especially dangerous
drugs such as mercury, mercury sublimate ...arsenic,
whereby they may kill themselves presently. So always
keep them out of their way." "It will be good also always to
keep your medicines well distinguished by writing upon ye

papers, pots, boxes or glasses wherein they are that you may certainly know what they be and never be mistaken."

Following the preface, Bulkeley's *Vade Mecum* presents recipes for medicines covering a wide range of aliments. A selection of these follows.

One of the most extensive presentations, covering thirty-seven pages, is for Balsam Fuliginis or Balsam of Soot. This medicine was used for the treatment of cancers and ulcers. Gershom wrote, "This is called Balsam of Soot, not as if it were made of common soot, but because arsenic is by skillful [means] accounted ye smoke or soot of minerals...."[458]

Many colonial era medicines contained arsenic on the theory that the arsenic could kill the venom of some diseases, such as cancer. Bulkeley quoted Helmont as saying, "Arsenic, fixed by saltpeter and adulterated or mitigated extinguishes perhaps sixth diversities of ulcers, not because it corrodes and eats...but because it hath now a mild venom which is able to kill ye forger of ye ulcer and corrupter of ye blood which being once wholly dead ye flesh doth not cease afterward of its own accord to grow...." Bulkeley quoted Helmont's stories of hearing of curing cancers in women's breasts by the application of "indolent powder" and of curing ulcerated cancers of women's breasts without any considerable pain. Gershom commented, "Thus ye see what they say of it and no doubt but this Balsam Fulginis, duly prepared, is a very good medicine, transcending most, if not all others, for ulcers of ye worst kind. But yet know that arsenic is a dangerous drug to deal with."[459]

Most recipes involved processes to "correct" or "fix" the arsenic, and Bulkeley presented several of them. Some physicians had claimed that "fixed" arsenic was safe for internal use, but Bulkeley disagreed. After presenting the recipes of Angelus Sala and Johan Rudolph Glauber, Bulkeley criticized them. "Now though I do not at all approve of what either Sala or Glauber do say of the inward use of arsenic fixed by any of these ways, but think that Helmont's advice is much better. Arsenic, says he, however much fixed and adulterated is never to be taken inwardly, howsoever others do persuade to it."[460]

Throughout his discussion of Balsam Fulginis, Bulkeley interjected warnings against exposure to arsenic. "… in preparing of it you take good heed to yourself and that both in ye powdering and mixing of it, that none of the dusty powder get into your mouth or nostrils with your breath, so keep your mouth shut and slightly stop your nostrils with tow or wool and, especially in ye burning of it, take heed of ye fumes that they do not catch you before you are aware. For they soon may disable you and you shall not be able to help yourself or tell others what is the matter with you." Again, he invoked Helmont: "Take Helmont's advice and never, in any case, use this medicine internally, but only outwardly, sprinkling it lightly upon ye ulcers or some other convenient way."[461]

Some of the most exotic recipes involve the use of toads.[462] Medicines which included powders from grinding the dried skins of toads were considered efficacious in treating swollen lymph glands. These swellings, called bobes, could arise from venereal diseases such as gonorrhea and syphilis as well as from bubonic plague and tuberculosis.

As with arsenic, Bulkeley found that authors disagreed on whether these powders were for external application only or could be taken internally. Gershom quoted from the writings of Jacques Zwalfer, who recommended that this powder be taken internally. Zwalfer said that this these medicines "do exceedingly perfect in some most grievous diseases." Bulkeley was skeptical and wrote, "Zwalfer doth not tell us what those grievous diseases be wherein those [medicines] are so profitably taken inwardly, but, if he say true, I do think dropsy of urine is one of them." Gershom was intrigued by another author who claimed that a powder made from a strongly dried toad skin and put into wine would cure the dropsy of urine. Gershom wrote, "If ever I would use ye powder of toads inwardly, I would dry them thoroughly and with as much heat as is possible without burning them."

Bulkeley did not care for Helmont's method of killing the toad. "Helmont takes ye toad in June or July, sticks a sharp stick through ye very midst of his head (so he dies quickly), whereas if it be a little on one side, he is a long time dying, as I have seen, so that mere pity to ye poor creature hath found me to tie a string close about their necks to choke them."

However, he endorsed Helmont's preparation and use of the medicine. "Then he drys them in ye sun, and, when he uses them for pestilential buboes, etc. in any part of the body in man or woman, he only steeps them in a little warm water and applies them to the pained place...." "But he nowhere, that I remember, makes any inward use of them." Bulkeley did concede that Helmont advocated the use of a toad in treatment of a toothache "by touching ye [tooth] with ye shoulder bone of ye toad." But this, Bulkeley said, was external and not internal use.

LUNAR PILLS WERE OF INTEREST to Bulkeley. He devoted thirteen pages of *Vade Mecum* to the preparation and use of Lunar Pills or Pills of Silver.[463] These pills were considered "a most excellent medicine in all afflictions of ye brain". Gershom said they may be used for "men troubled with serositis [inflammation of the serious tissues of the body such as the lining of the lungs, heart, etc.], for distempers of ye head and of ye nervous kind and relieve an hereditary disposition to palsy". He also mentioned the use of these pills for "epilepsy, vertigo and other afflictions of ye brain."

According to Bulkeley the major issue in the preparation of Lunar Pills was the difficulty of obtaining refined silver of sufficient purity. He complained, "That which is commonly sold for refined silver is not pure enough. He presented a discussion of the means to refine crystals of silver and, to purge it of copper. "Here note. If ye silver be not very well refined from copper, that will produce vomiting otherwise decompose ye body. If ye crystals look considerably blue or green, there is copper still in them."

Bulkeley copied recipes from the famous physicians and scientists, Robert Boyle and Johann Glauber. He wrote of Glauber's crystals of silver that "They are profitable, says he, for madness, dropsy and fever and other things, for they are a purge which may safely be given to old and young."

Bulkeley reported that he had improved on the recipe given by Boyle, England's leading scientist. He said of his formulation: "These pills are affectual for all ye purposes aforesaid by Mr. Boyle and to be used in the same manner and are not so bitter and unpleasant as his. I find no difficulty in taking of them, but I think they are much better than his in all intents and purposes…." Bulkeley wrote that his Lunar Pills were "…excellent for stubborn hypochondrical maladies. I have divers times taken of them myself and have no reason to complain of them. Others, often taken of them, commend their use thanks to me, so that I need say no more."[464]

GERSHOM DID NOT BLINDLY ACCEPT everything he read. He was not hesitant to challenge the most enshrined recipes. His friend, Governor John Winthrop Jr., had a recipe which was claimed to be his favorite for measles, colics, headaches, sciatica and many other ailments.[465] He called it his "sovereign remedy" and named it "rubila".[466] It consisted primarily of nitre and antimony.[467] Among his recipes, Bulkeley recorded his own version. He wrote that this powder causes "vomits and purges" and "should not be given to weak bodies, unless it be in small doses". Gershom noted after his recipe, "I will not say that this is

Governor Winthrop's rubila, but this is that which I use for rubil and call, not rubila, but rubella and I will adventure to say that it is as good as his to all intents and purposes and to be used in ye same manner."[468]

At the end of his lengthy list of recipes, Bulkeley included an index to the entire manuscript. Following this index, he wrote, "Thus you will see that I have set down many things more than you may ever need to trouble yourself about." Then he referenced those recipes that seemed to him to be most important. "These I advise you especially to regard out of which you may pick and choose what will serve your turn and, as for all the rest, if you have need of any of them, here you have the directions for ye preparation and use of them. If you have not, yet possibly some of yours after you may need them...."[469]

Bulkeley ended his recommendations with an odd statement about the value of urine. "As for ye spirit of urine, as much as it is despised, it is a thing of more worth and use than ye would know, as well as believe. Use your wits well. And so, I conclude with that of Helmont: 'Wisdom despises those who refuse by ye fire to learn of matter, dispositions, contents and properties of urine.' Yet, I may add, Solomon would find great wisdom in little things."[470]

At the end of his medical treatise, Bulkeley wrote:
"Finis Dated 6.5.1705"-

BUT HE ADDED AN ADDENDUM to *Vade Mecum* later. It was a tender memorial to his eldest daughter, Catherine. Although Gershom had given *Vade Mecum* to his daughter, Dorothy Treat, five years previously, there was room at the end of the manuscript and the grieving Bulkeley inserted a memorial to Catherine[471]. He was particularly devastated by the thought that he could have saved Catherine if she had only trusted and confided in him.

Although Gershom was always absorbed with his books and his laboratory experiments, he was not an isolated recluse, but was very social. He was surrounded by a bustling household of family, friends and servants. He noted the comings and goings of his sons. He made an entry whenever Peter went down the Connecticut River to sail his trading sloop along the coast and noted when John and Peter went to Boston. He made a trip to Antigua with his son, John. His diary showed he enjoyed visits from friends and relatives, even while suffering poor health.

Gershom valued his daughters. His eldest daughter, Catherine, was born about 1674[472] in Wethersfield. She married Richard Treat in Wethersfield on 24 November 1704. Richard, then approximately 29, was the nephew of Governor Robert Treat, Gershom's old commander in the King Philip's War, and his later protagonist over the restoration of Charter government. Richard and Catherine had one child. On 26 August 1706, Catherine Treat gave birth to a daughter, Catherine, in Wethersfield. During childbirth, she was injured by the mid-wife. This injury would later claim her life despite Gershom's efforts to save her. She was somewhat rebellious and did not always cooperate with her father's attempts to treat her.

Gershom's daughter, Dorothy, was a few years younger than Catherine and, like her, she was headstrong. She too married a Treat. Her husband Thomas Treat, was also a nephew of Governor Robert Treat. They married in Wethersfield on 5 July 1693 and settled across the river from Gershom in Nayaug. Dorothy and Thomas had a large family. Their first son, Richard, was born 14 May 1694 in Nayaug. He suffered from some unspecified malady which made it unlikely that he would ever be able to attend college. Dorothy gave birth between 1691 and 1710 to a total of eight children: five boys and three girls.

Thomas Treat was an important man in his community, when Nayaug became part of the new town of Glastonbury, he served four terms as the town's deputy to the Legislature. Thomas served in Queen Anne's War and took part in the early phases of the successful campaign to capture Port Royal, Nova Scotia, from the French. The legislature awarded him "30 shillings for his extraordinary labor and service as interpreter in managing the Indians who served in the expedition to Wood Creek."[473] He was appointed lieutenant of the Glastonbury train band on 10 May 1710.[474]

Gershom made frequent trips across the river to be with his daughter, Dorothy Treat, and her family. A ferry across the river from the Rocky Hill section of Wethersfield to the Nayaug was begun as early as 1650, and, perhaps, sooner. When Gershom wrote of "walking to Nayaug", he probably meant that he left his horse at home and took the ferry across. Dorothy's house was a short walk up the lane from the ferry landing and Gershom's fields were in the meadows along the river.

At the time of Catherine's illness, Gershom was living, at least part time, with Dorothy Treat in Nayaug. As Catherine grew worse, she was invited to come to Dorothy's house so that Gershom could treat her. She came with her daughter and her servant; so, the little house in Nayaug was very crowded. On the morning of the 18th of April 1709, Catherine died there.

To Bulkeley's great sorrow his Catherine died despite his attempts to save her. Gershom wrote, "My loss is great, and ye circumstances of it very afflictive to me; which moves me to make this Memorial of them." He summarized her medical history. Soon after Catherine and Richard were married she had a false pregnancy. "…[S]he had a Mote or false conception, which proved very difficult, and was long before it was got away, notwithstanding much means (such as injections, etc.) used for that end; and seemed to grow fast to ye womb." Not for the last time, Catherine resisted her father's medical advice. "After it was come away, I advised to take the season to cleanse ye womb very well, to prevent further mischief; but young hearty persons are apt to be too negligent."

Catherine had a normal pregnancy in 1706 and gave an easy birth except that the afterbirth stuck fast to her womb. Bulkeley wrote, "Tis to be feared ye midwife was too rash and used too much violence in tearing of it away…."

Catherine complained of pain and soreness in her belly, which would continue until her death. Bulkeley again advised that the womb be cleansed and healed, but again his advice was ignored. He prepared medicines, but Catherine did not take them.

The following year, Catherine came down with a consumptive illness and was racked by a long and tedious cough. She also suffered occasional fevers with convulsions; Gershom wrote that, although he gave her medicines that were able to break these fits, they returned. She grew emaciated and seemed to be wasting away, but then recovered somewhat.

In the winter of 1708, Catherine grew worse, suffering ague fits and coughing and complaining of pain on the left side of her belly in the region of the uterus. Gershom treated her with injections and medicines, but, after her death, he found that she had not taken most of them, except for that that treated the ague fits. Gershom wrote that "the principal of them [were] never touched, but tis said she used Goodwife Clark's medicines." Gershom did not think that he could cure the consumption but thought that he could have cured the injury to her womb so that she would have lived for many more years.

Catherine's condition grew so bad that Thomas and Dorothy invited her to stay with them so that Gershom could more easily treat her. In January 1709, she came with her daughter Catherine and her maid servant and, Gershom noted, "...was yet pretty cheery". But that night the maid was seized with convulsions such that it was feared she would die, and a frightened Catherine also had convulsions. These passed.

Shortly after, Gershom learned, for the first time, that Catherine had suffered from diabetes for more than a year. Gershom lamented that his growing deafness may have interfered with his ability to communicate with his daughter. Gershom wrote, "…her diabetes had made her always thirsty and her manner was to have a cup of cold small beer stand by her bed in the night, to sip of when she would, which was a very mischievous thing, but I knew it not, till by chance I discovered it."

Toward the end of May, Catherine began to experience strange quivering in her belly, she said, "as if birds were fluttering there" This was accompanied by strong coughing fits and pain. Gershom wrote, "hitherto her strength and spirits held to admiration and her eye was lightsome still (and in good measure to ye last), but now her strength and spirits visibly decayed every day." Catherine would never allow her father to examine her body. Though he knew she had been injured by the midwife, he did not know the severity and status of the injury. "Poor heart, we little imagined the sore agonies that she underwent, did not feel what she felt, not knowing the cause of them, aforesaid, which appeared not to us until her death."

Gershom then prepared a Balsam medicine for her pain, which Catherine would only allow her sister, Dorothy, to administer. However, she often refused the Balsam because, she said, it made her faint. Gershom wrote,

"…that was her mistake, the true cause of her faintness, pains and other agonies was in that ulcer of her womb."

Catherine had not been a seriously religious person and may have been contemptuous of it. Gershom wrote, "Beside all this, poor soul, God hid his face from her and she was much in ye dark and under great despondency as to her spiritual state.…" Catherine confided in her sister that she had seen a figure in white sit on her bed and thought it was an angel. She asked Dorothy to tell no one about it. The night before Catherine died Dorothy asked her if she were renewed in Christ. She told her, "If anyone were in Christ, he were a new creature." Dorothy asked Catherine whether she loved the things that she once hated and hated the things she one loved? Gershom wrote that her reply was "Oh, if I were to live my time again, I would not do as I have done for all the world."

Gershom wrote, "I thank God that she had the present use of her reason and understanding in the midst of all her extremities to the very last." He expressed the hope that she was persuaded to put "…herself upon the sure grace of God in the mediation of Christ, who came to seek and save that which was lost." "A little before she died, she took my hand and put it to her belly, to feel the strange commotions and fluttering that was there…[S]he asked for her mother-in-law and her child, but they were not now here, then said she, I give up myself and my child to God, the Lord have mercy upon me, the Lord have mercy upon me and so died."

When she was dead, and they laid her out. Gershom could see for the first time the true cause of her misery. "She had a gangrene in the left side of her belly in region uteri, which was quite black for near ye breadth of ye hand and ye length of a good part of it, with some greenish and yellowish streaks and ye skin was hard and fast to ye little flesh left below it …"

Gershom bitterly reproached himself, "This without all doubt was the effect of the hurt she received by tearing off the afterbirth…." "Oh, that I had known this but 3 or 4 days before she died! For if we had had but so much time to have [operated upon] ye part to let out ye virulent matter and by application of proper means to correct and stop ye gangrene, I do not know but by God's help, she might yet have been recovered. But it was hidden from us, we were not aware of it, and ye will of God is done and we must with submission hold our peace."

Gershom also regretted belatedly that he had not done an autopsy. "It might also have been not altogether unprofitable, if she had been opened when she was dead, to see in what condition ye womb was within, but I knew nothing of all this before she was buried, and then it was too late. Otherwise, I doubt not but we should have with our eyes seen ye true cause of all her dolors."

XI. BULKELEY RESTORED (1701-1713)

...he was Eminent for his great Parts, both Natural and Acquired, being Universally acknowledged ...to be a Person of Great Penetration, and a sound Judgment, as well in Divinity as Politicks and Physick; having served his Country many years successively as Minister, a Judge and a Physician with great Honour to himself and advantage to others.

~ Boston News Letter, December 1713

GERSHOM SLOWLY REGAINED HIS PREVIOUS ROLE as a trusted counselor whose opinions were actively sought. When in 1701, a group of ministers began considering the establishment of a university in Connecticut, Bulkeley was one of those whose opinion they solicited. Gershom had responded with a letter dated 27 September 1701, and addressed, "To ye Reverend Elders deliberating of a Colledge, etc." Bulkeley understood there were still resentments against him. "Now my opinion in everything is so liable to objections, that it behooves me to be slow showing it, yet I am so willing to promote so good a work that I shall adventure to say thus much..." [475]

235

"Your design is so good that if I might & could [endorse it]" "…[y]ou must give me leave to tell you that I have made as much search in ye statutes & elsewhere, as my present incapacity will allow me, but cannot find that which satisfies me, or (I think) will satisfy you, in answer to your queries." Gershom cited many references in English law about how the formation of hospitals, institutions and schools of learning may be established. However, he noted that other statutes barred dissenters, etc., from teaching youth. However, he suggested that the "Act of Indulgence", then in force, might provide relief.

Bulkeley suggested that the General Court would probably not act favorably on the proposal "at present," and that they might be in some trouble if they did. "We all know that ye King and Parliament are above us, and so I should think that it will be much better to petition his Majesty to grant a liberty, ratified by act of Parliament, for ye founding of a College. …" "… I think this is ye most likely way to prevent a future defeat. …"

The ministers did not necessarily agree with Bulkeley about the need to establish the college under English law. One wrote, "… [A]ll his discourse is grounded upon the Statutes of the Realm of England …Yet I do no apprehend that the Resolution…be grounded upon the Statute Laws of England…since it has been declared in the Court of Assistants that the Statutes of England and acts of Parliament are not in force in the foreign Plantations…" The General Court concurred and, ignoring Bulkeley's advice, passed an act establishing a "Collegiate School,"[476] which became Yale College.

ABIGAIL THOMPSON WAS TRIED for the murder of her
husband in 1706. Bulkeley's advice was now readily
sought in this sensational murder case. Abigail Thompson
of Farmington was accused of murdering her husband by
throwing scissors at him during a fight. Once again
Bulkeley had an opportunity to involve himself in a high
profile and controversial case. Much had happened since
the days of Gershom's aggressive opposition to restoration
of government under the charter. England had
acknowledged the legitimacy of Connecticut's government.
Many of the principal players from those days were no
longer involved in the government. Fitz-John Winthrop
had returned in 1697 and was escorted in triumph from
Boston to Hartford and was chosen Governor in the May
election of 1698.[477] Governor Robert Treat stepped down to
Deputy Governor. Treat had died in 1702. The rancor had
dissipated and Bulkeley now seemed to have been restored
to his previous position as sage and wise counselor. He
would enjoy an easy relationship with Governor Fitz-John
Winthrop.

Abigail Thompson wounded her husband, Thomas, by
throwing a pair of tailor's shears at him during an
argument. The shears pierced his skull, but he did not, at
first, seem incapacitated. Then, after a few days, he
expired. Abigail was charged with murder. The records of
the legal proceedings in the Minutes of the Court of
Assistants are very extensive.[478]

The legal process in Connecticut had become quite formal.
There was an inquest, an indictment, a grand jury, and a
petit jury. In these proceedings Abigail was afforded the
opportunity to challenge the seating of each juror and, at
her request, was appointed a defense attorney. The case
was prosecuted by Richard Edwards, now the Queen's
Attorney, and Abigail was granted liberty to reply to the
testimony of each witness.

Richard Edwards was the same attorney that Gershom had
employed in his land lawsuit with Hollister. Edward's star
was rising. He had married into a leading family after a
lengthy and messy divorce from his first wife, Elizabeth
Tuttle. Ironically, Elizabeth was the sister of Mercy (Tuttle)
Brown, the subject of Gershom's previous involvement
with a murder trial.

Edwards had a relatively easy time with the prosecution, as
many witnesses came forward to testify that Abigail
Thompson had often assaulted her husband and threatened
to kill him. She had been seen to throw stones at him and
strike him; once with a chair and once with a pole. She was
quoted as saying she would kill him because he was "an old
rouge." She admitted that she had once taken a knife to bed
with her and said that she would kill him if he did not
change.

Abigail said that, on the day of the final event, they had had
a fight. Samuel, she said, hit her in the breast with a
broom, and so she threw the shears. She said that she did
not mean to kill him. One point of the shears pierced his hat
above his eye and penetrated into the brain. The injury was

not immediately fatal. Thomas remained active and working for several days, and then he died. The prosecution called Dr. Thomas Hooker, who testified that Thomas Thompson had died of the wound.

The jury brought in a verdict of guilty of murder on 20 May 1706. The chief judge pronounced a sentence of death and appointed June 19 as the date of execution. However, the Assistants delayed the execution and the Governor reprieved the sentence until the October General Court and then to the following May Court. Abigail was held in the jail in Hartford. Surprisingly, despite her stormy home life, Abigail was found to be pregnant and delivered her baby while in jail.

 In May 1707, the General Assembly heard the case and rejected further appeals. The governor was asked to advise the General Assembly on this difficult case. Gershom, unaware of the Assembly's action, wrote to Governor Fitz-John Winthrop, opposing the sentence of the Court of Assistants and arguing for a reduced sentence of manslaughter.

Gershom Bulkeley wrote to the governor again on 2 September 1707. He apologized for his earlier letter, which must have been harsh, and said that it was due to his lacking all the facts. Gershom indicated that since then William Pitkin, who served as prosecuting attorney, had visited and briefed him on the actions of the General Assembly. Bulkeley congratulated the governor for his continuing to stay the reprieve. He laid out his case for reducing the sentence to manslaughter.

"I find that the woman's act was in the nature of chance medley, done in a quarrel upon a sudden provocation." He noted that Thompson had lived and been active for eighteen days after the injury. Furthermore, he claimed that the wound might not have proved deadly, if properly treated, but "he was wholly left to the mercy, care & nursing of that bloody woman, who they knew had wounded him." Gershom asserted that "it is evident that he died of corruption, gangrene & suppuration of ye wound & brain through ye neglect…I cannot excuse her, any more than ye man or his friends. I think they are all to blame…."[479]

Governor Fitz-John Winthrop was convinced by Gershom's arguments and, though Winthrop was too ill to attend the meeting of the General Assembly, he sent them a letter recommending the reduction of the charge against Abigail to manslaughter. He further urged the Assembly to consult the Reverend Elders and with Gershom.

 It has been suggested that Abigail was ultimately executed. At the court held 28 May 1708 the court approved payment to Ichabod Welles, sheriff of the county of Hartford, for his "trouble and charge" [he] hath been at in order to the execution of Abigail Thompson, the prisoner…." [480] However, it is not clear whether Welles was being compensated for the execution of orders about Abigail or for her actual, physical execution.

LATE IN LIFE Gershom faced the issue of distribution of his possessions, especially his vast library, including his laboratory books and his manuscripts. Gershom's collection of books and manuscripts were very important to him; he wanted to ensure that they would be possessed by the people who could best make use of them. Some of these books had been handed down from his father and his grandfather. He had purchased many newer books from England, probably with the assistance of his brother-in-law, Dr. Isaac Chauncy.

Gershom frequently corresponded with Isaac, who practiced medicine in London. Isaac shared Gershom's interests in medicine and alchemy and often sent books and supplies to him, including glassware for his laboratory. A letter to Gershom from Isaac dated 14 April 1695 discussed the proper handling of chemical glassware, so both seem to have been involved in chemical and alchemical laboratory work. That this was a frequent occurrence is shown by the entries in Gershom's 1699 diary, Gershom received a hogshead of glassware in August of that year, and he also noted that he had written to Isaac in London on January 11. This arrangement continued for many years. In one of his laboratory notebooks Gershom recorded that he had received another hogshead of glasses from Isaac in London on 15 October 1706.[481]

It is probable that Isaac also helped Gershom with the acquisition of new publications in medicine and alchemy. In *The Works of the Highly Experienced and Famous Chymist, John Rudolph Glauber*, published in London by William Cooper in 1689 a catalogue was included giving the names of the subscribers. These entries included, "Isaac Chauncy, M.D." [482]

As Gershom prepared his will in May of 1712, his options were limited. All twelve of his brothers, half-brothers, sisters and half-sisters were deceased. Even his youngest brother, Peter, had died in 1691.[483] Peter's Harvard training and medical practice as a physician might have made him a logical candidate to receive some of Gershom's medical library. Of his nieces and nephews living in 1712, none seemed natural recipients of this library.

Even his kindred physician-alchemist and brother-in-law, Dr. Isaac Chauncy, had died in England that year. As for his own children, his eldest son, Dr. Charles Bulkeley of New London had died in 1692. His son, Peter, died at sea in 1701 and his daughter, Catherine, died in 1709, despite Gershom's desperate attempts to save her. That left only his daughter, Dorothy Treat, and his sons, Captain Edward Bulkeley of Wethersfield and Reverend John Bulkeley of Colchester.

While maintaining his home in Wethersfield, Gershom increasingly spent time across the river in Glastonbury at the home of Dorothy and Thomas Treat. On 27 January 1710, when Gershom filed a statement before the justice of the peace, he signed the document, "Mr., Gershom Bulkeley of Glastonbury." This document was to affirm that he had given his New London property to his son, Charles in 1688. Somehow this deed had not been recorded, and the original was destroyed in a fire.[484]

In April of 1712, Gershom gave his homestead in Wethersfield to his son, Edward, and lived with the Treats in Glastonbury. Gershom left some of his possessions behind in the Wethersfield house, because he wrote in his will, "To my son, Edward, I give and bequeath ye clock now standing in its case in his house, as also my seal ring, ye great gilt spoon, ye least of my two silver porringers...." However, he likely moved his laboratory equipment across the river to Dorothy's house where they both could use it. He left Edward the tools for operating the corn mill on Dividend Brook.

Edward Bulkeley was a prominent citizen of Wethersfield. He had frequently represented Wethersfield in the General Assembly. Edward also had an interest in law and would later serve as justice of the peace for Hartford County in 1714 and 1715 and from 1744 until his death in 1748.[485] Gershom willed him "all ye books and manuscripts that I have touching matter of law, except ye notes which I had sometime written out ... which notes I had formerly given to my son, John...."

Reverend John Bulkeley, now minister in Colchester, had been an outstanding scholar at Harvard; Gershom gave him the bulk of this library. "To my son, John, I have already given ye greatest part of my books and my silver pocket watch...I give and bequeath to him all ye rest of my books which I now have and also my manuscripts (written by my grandfather, my father and others). I say all such of my books...as concern Divinity or other learning except ye law (which books and manuscripts I have given to Edward), and except also medicine and chemistry and some few books which...I shall otherwise dispose of by and by."

Gershom gave eight pounds to Hannah Goodrich, the only child of his deceased son, Charles. He gave a golden ducat to Hannah Avery, the widow of Charles, and a golden ducat to Rachel Wolcott, the widow of his deceased son, Peter. To his son, Edward's wife, he gave a golden guinea and to this deceased brother, Peter's five children he gave each 10 shillings. To his daughter, Catherine's only child, Catherine, he gave several silver bowls, cups, etc., that he had intended for her mother, had she lived.

There remained the issue of his medical library. He fastened his hopes on his grandson. "To my grandson, Richard Treat, ye son of Thomas and Dorothy Treat I give and bequeath all my books and manuscripts which any way concern medicine and chemistry, among which I include all of Glauber's and Boyle's which I have, whether in Latin or English…also Littleton's Dictionary for the Latin Tongue and my Dutch Grammar…together with all my vessels and instruments useful, whether of glass, brass or copper, iron, stone or earth. All these I give him, provided he hold and pursue his inclination to that study."

Gershom named his son-in-law, Thomas Treat executor and bequeathed all the rest of his personal property to Dorothy Treat, including his Negro maid, Hannah, and all debts owed him by others. Except, he advised, that any poor widows or other truly poor persons be forgiven their debts at the discretion of the executor. "…by poor I mean such as are indeed poor- at least by Divine Providence and not by idleness, nor such as say they are poor and yet can find wherewith to drink, revel and swagger and make themselves poor and others too."

The will also contains further instructions about the Negro maid, Hannah. This section is left out of the Probate Records[486] printed by Charles William Manwaring for the Connecticut Historical Society in 1904. Hannah was clearly a slave (in the inventory she is valued at twenty-five pounds), and this discussion may have been considered too controversial. Gershom's will states; "And, to her, my said Dorothy Treat, I give and bequeath my Negro maid, Hannah. Willing and solemnly requiring that into whose hands soever she may happen to come, they use her well, and consider that she hath a soul to save as well as we, and is a Christian; and therefore, that they make conscience to promote her in her reading, catechism and all Christianity, that she may profit and grow in religion and godliness, and attain the end of baptism to the glory of God, and this I earnestly require on her behalf, as they will answer the neglect thereof to God."[487]

Gershom had always had domestic help. Mercy (Holbridge) Disborough, who was accused of being a witch, had been a servant in Gershom's New London household. Elizabeth Walker, whose baby had died under suspicious circumstances in Gershom's Wethersfield household, was an indentured servant. Gershom described her as a "Scotch wench whose time I bought in Boston & who afterward went for England, intending to go home." It was not uncommon in colonial records for slaves to be referred to as "servants" and in the case of Hannah; she was, without a doubt, a slave and not a servant.

Gershom made his will on 26 May 1712, designating himself, "Bulkeley, Gershom, Wethersfield, alias

Glastonbury, in ye Colony of Connecticut in New England, practitioner in Physick. Gershom's son-in-law, Thomas Treat, who was to be executor, died on 17 January 1712/13, so it was necessary to add a codicil to Gershom's will. On 24 November 1713, Dorothy Treat was named executrix. Gershom died on the second of December 1713.-

CONTROVERSY OVER THE OWNERSHIP of Gershom's books continued after his death. John Bulkeley sued his sister, Dorothy Treat, for withholding a book which, he thought, should be his. The book was Cotton Mather's *Magnalia Christi Americana*, valued at three pounds. This book included "The Lives of Sixty Famous Divines," one of which was the Reverend Peter Bulkeley, Gershom's father.

The case was before the County Court at Hartford in June 1715.[488] Litigation was continued to the September session of the Superior Court, and finally to the March 1716 session.[489] It was soon apparent that John's grievance against Dorothy was based on much more than one disputed book. John believed that Dorothy had gained, by trick and deception, a greater inheritance than was fair. He also claimed to have witnesses who heard Dorothy say she would prevent him from getting anything.

Testimony was submitted from Abijah Hollister, the wife of John Hollister of Glastonbury. Abijah said that Dorothy told her a story about her son, Richard, not wanting to pursue his grandfather's medical profession. According to this story, when Richard had been at his grandfather

Gershom's house in Wethersfield, his grandfather had asked whether he intended to follow the study of Physick. Gershom allegedly told Richard that, if he did he could have all the books and utensils related to that subject; if he did not Gershom would dispose of them otherwise. Richard's reply was that he would not study Physick and he did not love it [the study of medicine] because it made his head ache.[490] (Richard did eventually practice medicine since he left a manuscript showing medical accounts from1740-1755.)[491]

When Dorothy learned of this conversation, Abijah reported, she called her son a fool and ordered him to return his grandfather and write a promise that he would study Physick. She told Richard that whether he studied medicine or not, the things that his grandfather offered would be very valuable to him. When Richard resisted, his mother became very angry, and pushed him back into the room where his grandfather was and made him write his promise.

In the lawsuit with Dorothy over ownership of Gershom's books, John Bulkeley submitted a summary of the case to the Superior Court. His first point was that an inventory of the books left by Gershom must be taken. He said his sister had shown an extraordinary aversion to an inventory. Without an inventory, John said, it was not possible to tell what books had been left to him by his father's will. "I know not what books father had which fall under ye general head of those given me by will, nor is it possible I should, my father keeping many books in shelves which none but himself has opened (that I know of) for 20 years."

John claimed that many books that he knew his father had, and which he desired, were missing, and he believed that his sister had sold some of them. He said that he believed he would never receive what had been willed to him unless Dorothy was removed as executor.

He particularly wanted Mather's *Magnalia Christi Americana*, which she had kept because she said her father had given it to her. John disputed that Gershom had given it to her and produced witnesses. Edward Bulkeley and his wife testified to an incident at Dorothy's house in Glastonbury which occurred a week before Gershom's death. Gershom asked that a book be brought to him and asked that the witnesses note that he was giving it to Dorothy and told her to write her name in it. However, Edward said, they were not able to see the title of the book, which was in folio form. He said that he saw Dorothy write her name in the book. But Sarah Brooks, a neighbor who was also present, gave more confusing testimony. She testified that Gershom said it was John's book, but also said, *Magnalia* I give to Dorothy."

The case ended when John and Dorothy agreed to an out-of-court settlement. An inventory of the books was taken and included in the probate record. Although many books had been taken away, the inventory includes over three hundred books and a large number of manuscripts and demonstrates the extraordinary breadth of Gershom's library. The inventory record is frustratingly cryptic, but Thomas Jodziewicz has published a listing which attempts to identify the full titles and names of the authors.[492]

The books are gathered in three groups according to subject matter: chemical-alchemical-medical, theological and law. They were apparently intended for Richard Treat, John Bulkeley and Edward Bulkeley, respectively. Apparent publication dates range from 1537 to 1711. The oldest books probably are from Gershom's grandfather, Peter. Most of the books are in Latin or English with a few in Dutch or Greek. This list of books, as well as Bulkeley's surviving manuscripts, demonstrates the enormous reach and depth of Gershom Bulkeley's intellectual curiosity and vast knowledge.

GERSHOM WAS RESTORED to honor. By the time of his death on 2 December 1713, Gershom had been fully accepted back into Connecticut society. At his funeral, he was eulogized as one of the wisest and most intellectually gifted citizens that Connecticut had ever produced. On December 7, Reverend John James[493] of Brookfield, Massachusetts, delivered an epitaph, "On the death of the very learned, pious and excelling Gershom Bulkeley who had his mortality swallowed up of life, December the second, 1713, *AEtatis Suae 78*." The text, partially in Latin, was later printed in New London, Connecticut and included this:

> Gershom no more! Fatiques & Hazards past;
> He's safe arrived to the Promised Land at last.
> In Heavens Academy, he
> Adeptist; O how glad to be!

Where none do longer rack their Brains
In quest of Scientifick Gains.

The *Boston News Letter* for December 28, 1713 published the memorial opinion that "he was Eminent for his great Parts, both Natural and Acquired, being Universally acknowledged besides his good Religion and Vertue to be a Person of Great Penetration, and a sound Judgment, as well in Divinity as Politicks and Physick; having served his Country many years successively as Minister, a Judge and a Physician with great Honour to himself and advantage to others." [494]

 Gershom requested in his will that he be interred as near to his late wife as possible, and that he be "decently but obscurely buried, without much cost or ceremony." However, he was rather elaborately buried in the Wethersfield Village Cemetery with a "table top" gravestone carved with the Bulkeley family crest. The stone bears the inscription: "He was honorable in his descent, of rare abilities, extraordinary industry, excellent learning, master of many languages, exquisite in his skills in divinity, physic and law and of the most exemplary and Christian life. *In certam spem beate resurrections repositas.*"

ILLUSTRATIONS

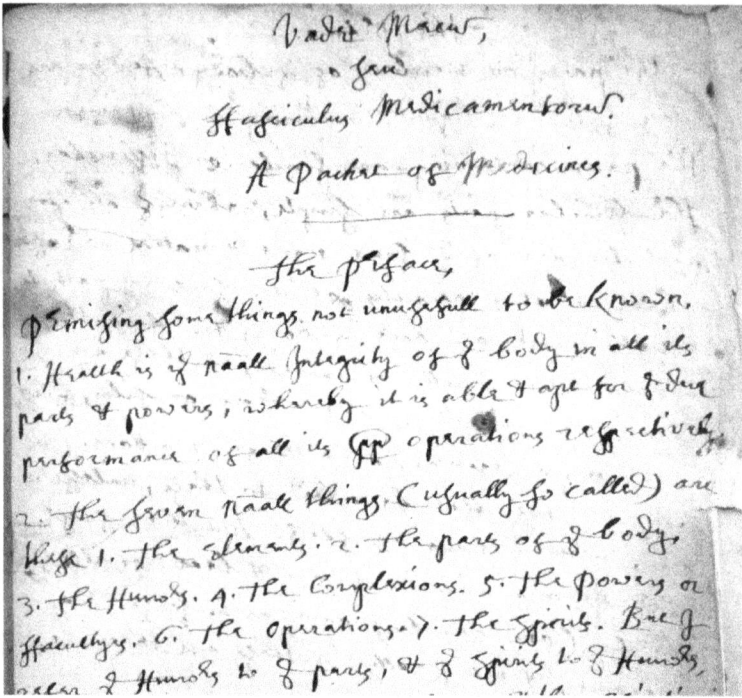

Title Page of Bulkeley's Medical Treatise, Vade Mecum, also known as "A Packet of Medicines"

Courtesy of the Watkinson Library, Trinity College, Hartford, Connecticut

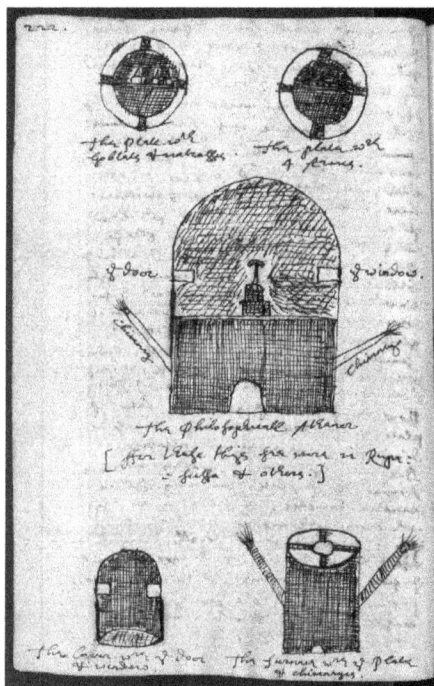

Alchemical Furnace Sketched by Bulkeley from Digby's
*Chemical Secrets & Rare Experiments in Physick and
Philosophy*

Courtesy of the Hartford Medical Society Historical
Library, University of Connecticut Health Center,
Farmington, CT

253

The Treat House in South Glastonbury where Gershom Bulkeley Died in 1713.

Courtesy of the Glastonbury Historical Society

Broadside Eulogy for Gershom Bulkeley

Courtesy of The Connecticut Historical Society

Gravestone of Gershom Bulkeley in the Wethersfield
Village Cemetery in Wethersfield, CT

Photo Credit: Richard Tomlinson

ABOUT THE AUTHOR

Richard G. Tomlinson lives in Boerne, Texas with his wife, Judith. After retiring from a varied career as research scientist, publisher and management consultant, he pursues his interests as a historian and genealogist.

He is a life member and former director of the Connecticut Historical Society. He is a life member, founder and director emeritus of the Connecticut Society of Genealogists. He is the creator of *Connecticut Genealogy News* magazine and of the Connecticut Society of Genealogists literary awards. In 2018 CSG named the Grand Prize in their annual Literary Award Contest, the "Richard G. Tomlinson Prize".

Tomlinson is a member and director of the Kendall County (Texas) Genealogy Society.

He is a member of the "Descendants of the Founders of Ancient Windsor" (CT) and traces his lineage to many early settlers of New England, including Henry Tomlinson of Milford, Connecticut.

Richard G. Tomlinson

RETROSPECTIVE

FAME IS FLEETING AND FICKLE. Few men can boast a longer list of accomplishments or of influential roles in the events of their time than could Gershom Bulkeley. And yet, his name is largely absent from histories of Connecticut. The Bulkeley name is still known in Hartford. There is Bulkeley High School and a major bridge spanning the Connecticut River is named, Bulkeley bridge. But these are not named for Gershom. They are meant to honor his great-great-great-great-grandson, the flamboyant Connecticut Governor, Morgan Gardner Bulkeley (1837 – 1922).[495]

Gershom, who was a central figure in all the events in Connecticut throughout the seventeenth century and into the early eighteenth century, has been passed over. Gershom along with Governor John Winthrop played a leading role in ending witchcraft executions in Connecticut. A fact that would be largely unknown where it not for the work of historian, Walter Woodward.[496] In the zeal of many histories to paint the judges and officials in witchcraft trials of the 17th and early 18th century as uniformly ignorant, misogynistic bigots, the role, or even the existence, of legal process in Connecticut has often been ignored or minimized. However, most Connecticut witchcraft trials ended in acquittal of the accused.[497] The legal process evolved in sophistication over the course of the seventeenth century to such an extent that the last person convicted and condemned was reprieved by the magistrates on a technicality. They declared the jury verdict

259

invalid because the trial failed to be conducted according "due form of law."

Bulkeley is not the only one to be slighted in Connecticut history. The ringing defense of due process by Hartford magistrates, Samuel Wyllys, Nathaniel Stanley and William Pitkin has never received the accolades it deserves. Their reprieve of Mercy Disborough (or Disbrow), who was convicted in 1692 in the era of Salem witch panic, should be one of the most honored documents in Connecticut history. The three magistrates wrote that, "Due form of law is that alone wherein the validity of verdicts and judgments in such cases stands and if a real and apparent murder be condemned and executed outside of due form of law, it is indictable against them that do it." For good measure, the three magistrates condemned the contemporaneous witchcraft trials associated with the Salem, Massachusetts witch panic. "As for the common things of spectral evidence, ill events after quarrels or threats, teats, water trials and the like, suspicious words, they are all discarded and some of them abominated by the most judicious as to be convictive of witchcraft and the miserable toil they are in in the Bay for adhering to these last mentioned litigious things is warning enough. Those that will make witchcraft of such things will make hanging work apace..."[498] Mercy was granted a reprieve, which later became a full pardon. After Mercy's reprieve, there were more witchcraft trials in Connecticut, but none resulted in a conviction.

During his lifetime, Gershom Bulkeley worked in his laboratory as an alchemist and scientist. Alchemy may seem to archaic to the modern eye, but in Bulkeley's time it was precursor to modern science. Even Robert Boyle, England's leading scientist, was proud to be called an alchemist. The important point is that the alchemists of this era had made a break with the past that had rested medical and scientific truth on the authority of ancient sages. They looked instead to experiment, personal observation and critical analysis to determine scientific truth. In his notebooks, even when copying from the texts of respected contemporary authors, Bulkeley would frequently interject his own critical comments and observations.

In his laboratory books, Gershom recorded his experiments and medicinal recipes, He also sometimes recorded local folk recipes, which could be bizarre, but there is no indication of whether he believed in the effectiveness of these folk prescriptions. Gershom's medical writings were extensive. In his *Vade Mecum,* he wrote what is probably the most comprehensive account of the state of medical knowledge in seventeenth century Connecticut. The value of this work has never been fully recognized.

Bulkeley has not been completely forgotten. In his hometown of Wethersfield, Connecticut he is still remembered in historic pageants, as a leading citizen and as the "good doctor." In Rocky Hill, Connecticut there is a community park and a state archaeologic preserve on Dividend Brook at the site of the mill pond used for Bulkeley's "corn mill." But when Gershom is recognized in Connecticut, it is usually with a negative connotation. In Glastonbury, Connecticut Bulkeley is noted as the person responsible for the town's loss of a slice of land to neighboring East Hartford in the Bulkeley-Hollister lawsuit.[499] Politically Gershom's opposition to Connecticut's self-appointed restoration of charter government is dismissed as the work of a Tory royalist.[500]

There is little doubt that Gershom Bulkeley could be opinionated, cranky and irascible, but he could also be humorous - as when he dismissed an accuser of Mercy Disborough with the comment, "Redfin hath need to scratch his noodle and bethink himself again…".[501]

 Like Samuel Wyllys he thought that only men of high education, breeding and moral character should hold public office. He did not believe in democratic rule. However, once laws were established, he was a stout defender of the rule of law over the rule of men. His defense of the unpopular and the outcast against the establishment would do credit to Clarence Darrow himself. He was a fierce defender of the rights of the accused no matter how unpopular the issue. He persistently argued that marriage to the sister of a deceased wife was not incest even though such as opinion was considered scandalous.[502]

Bulkeley's character and judicial temperament are well captured in his embrace of the assertion that everyone, even the Devil, himself, was worthy of a fair hearing. In his treatise on the office of Justice of the Peace, whether or not the quote was original, he included the statement; "If I were to condemn ye Devil …I would give him an hearing." For Bulkeley this was not empty rhetoric, but the core expression of his belief in the rule of law and impartiality.[503]

BULKELEY MANUSCRIPTS

GERSHOM BULKELEY'S LIBRARY included both books and manuscripts. The surviving manuscripts are found mainly in the Lyman Maynard Stowe Library at the University of Connecticut Health Center in Farmington, Connecticut, and in the Watkinson Library at Trinity College in Hartford, Connecticut. Books in colonial Connecticut were rare and precious. Many of these manuscripts include annotated notes from books that Bulkeley did not own but had borrowed and copied.

Lyman Maynard Stowe Library, Hartford Medical Society Historical Library, University of Connecticut Health Center, Farmington, CT

The collection in the Stowe Library originally belonged to the Hartford Medical Society. The Society was founded in Hartford in 1846, primarily to legitimize the profession and to regulate fees, but also as a venue for socializing and professional development. The Society met twice a month for lectures and discussion. They assembled a library of medicine of more than 27,000 volumes, A subsection of this collection included rare medical books from the sixteenth through the eighteenth century which were donated by members. Within this collection were twenty-four items relating to Bulkeley including his notes on contemporary, scientific, medical and alchemical works, as well as account books and laboratory experimental note books.

After the University of Connecticut opened a medical school in Farmington, Connecticut in the 1960s, its medical library evolved gradually to include a remarkable collection, especially of the history of medicine. The University of Connecticut acquired the library of the Hartford Medical Society in 2009 and moved it to Farmington that year.

The manuscripts associated with Bulkeley are as follows:

Manuscript #1
Most of this manuscript contains notes taken from the *Encyclopaedia Septem somis distinca* by the German author Johan Heinrich Alsted (Johannis-Henrici Alsted II). The book is in Latin and was published in 1630. The book is not listed in the probate inventory of Gershom Bulkeley's books and he probably did not own the book which is why he made the copy. In this manuscript, he has copied the scientific parts of the Encyclopaedia, covering 475 pages. Historian Perry Miller in his *New England Mind* said this about the Encyclopaedia:

> It was indeed nothing short of a summary, in sequential and numbered paragraphs, of everything that the mind of European man had yet conceived or discovered. The works of over five hundred authors, from Aristotle to James I, were digested and methodized, including those of Aquinas, Scotus, and medieval theology, as also those of medieval science such as *De Natura Rerum.*

On the last 88 pages of manuscript #1 the pages have been turned and Gershom Bulkeley's notes on the office of the justice of peace are recorded. This section is in English and contains references to the famous English legal authorities, Michael Dalton and John Bonds. There are two books by Dalton in the probate inventory of Gershom Bulkeley's books. One is identified as "probably: Michael Dalton's *The Country Justice, Containing the Practice of Justice of*

the Peace Out of Their Sessions, London, 1618 and
"perhaps" Daltons' *Officium Vicecomitum, The Office and
Authority of Sherifs,* London, 1623. The book by Bonds
could be one of the three editions of *A Compleat Guide for
Justices of the Peace* by J. Bonds, Esq. The first edition
was printed in London in 1685, and Gershom Bulkeley may
not have seen this. The second edition was printed in
London in 1696 and the third in 1706. In any event, it
likely that Gershom Bulkeley wrote his treatise well after
1688, when his service as justice of the peace for Hartford
County had ended. The office of justice of peace had not
existed in Connecticut prior to the Andros administration
and Gershom Bulkeley probably wrote his treatise to
instruct the restored Connecticut government on the proper
operation of the justice of the peace office, according to
English law.

Manuscript #2
This manuscript is not by Gershom, but belonged to his
grandson, Richard Treat (Yale 1719). The front and back
sections of this manuscript include medical accounts from
1740-1755. The center section contains notes from "An
Extract of Mr. Charles Morton's System of Philosophy" in
the *Compendium Physicae.* [Reprinted in *Publications of
the Colonial Society of Massachusetts*, Volume 33,
(Boston:1940).] Charles Morton (1627-1698) was an
English Puritan minister interested in alchemy and
astrology. He immigrated to New England in 1686. He was
a member of the corporation of Harvard. His textbooks on
logic and physics were used at Harvard and Yale. He was

the minister in Charlestown, Massachusetts, where he died in 1686, leaving a legacy and books to Harvard.

Manuscript #3
This medical and chemical notebook contains chemical observations taken from the *Philosophical Transactions of the Royal Society* of the 1660s. It includes a discussion of the general effects of wine (p. 21). It includes notes from a book by Andrew Yarranton "*On Clover*" (p 36). Yarranton (1616-1684) was an English engineer and agriculturist known for his work on making waterways navigable. He also wrote about blast furnaces and creating tin plate. He was one of the first to recognize the agricultural value of clover. Gershom Bulkeley's notes are dated 5 December 1663, so he could not have been reading Yarranton's best-known book, "*The Improvement improved by a second edition, or, The great improvement of lands by clover, or, The wonderful advantage by, and right management of clover*" which was printed in London in 1663. Gershom Bulkeley must have been reading one of Yarranton's earlier small pamphlets (circa 1677) on clover written when Yarranton was working as a salesman of glover seed. There are no publications by Yarranton in the inventory of Gershom Bulkeley's books. Gershom may have borrowed the book. The manuscript contains a "List of some universal and useful things" (p. 45). The manuscript includes notes from a book by Michael Bernhard Valentini (1657-1729), a German doctor and professor of medicine. There is a book by Valentini in Gershom Bulkeley's inventory. It was, perhaps, *Anamadversiones in Machiavellum Medicum de Ratione Status Medicorum*

published in 1711. If so, Gershom Bulkeley must have acquired it shortly before his death. However, Gershom may have taken notes from an early version of Valentini's most famous, multi-volume work, *Museum Museorum.* The second edition was published in 1714 after Gershom Bulkeley's death. Volume one contains descriptions of plants, animals, minerals and metals and their commercial and medical uses, which would have been of interest to Gershom Bulkeley. The final section of the manuscript contains a treatise, *Prolegomena de Arte in Genera,* which is not in Bulkeley's handwriting.

Manuscript #4
This manuscript contains laboratory notes and notes on agriculture. It also contains excerpts from chemistry books and is dated 1679. This manuscript has been digitized and is available on-line.

Manuscript #5
A laboratory book of chemical experiments contains notes from chemical books (1703-1706). It includes a note that, on October 15, 1706, Gershom had received a shipment of glasses (probably flasks) from his brother-in-law, Dr. Isaac Chauncy, who was living in London. Gershom Bulkeley maintained correspondence with Chauncy and others in England. This manuscript has been rebound.

Manuscript #6
This manuscript, *Vade Mecum,* includes many medical folk cures which Bulkeley gathered from local healers. It also includes recipes and medical excerpts. Many of these

recipes are quoted by Dr. Gurdon W. Russell in "Early Medicine and Early Medical Men in Connecticut" in the *Proceedings of the Connecticut Medical Society,* Hartford, 1892.

Manuscript #7
This manuscript includes a long treatise on Sal Alkali and other chemicals. Sal Alkali is alkaline carbonate which had many medical applications. The term, Sal Alkali, was used for both potassium and sodium salts.

Manuscript #8
This manuscript contains notes for sermons, chemical and medicinal matters and an index to chemistry books, mostly in Latin. The manuscript is the oldest in the collection. The first sermon is dated June 19, 1661, when Gershom was the minister in the church in New London, Connecticut. Interesting material includes the funeral sermons for Mr. Tinker, July 16, 1662 and Goodman Harris February 11, 1662/3.

Manuscript #9
This manuscript is a fragment in poor condition containing excerpts from chemical and medical literature. It contains an alchemical work on the nature of metals.

Manuscript #10
This contains multiple, small, non-descript notebooks.

Manuscript #11
This manuscript contains medical notes by Gershom's daughter, Dorothy Treat. The inscription on the flyleaf reads, "Dorothy Treat her booke, 1721". Dorothy had no

medical training but followed her father's footsteps including experimental lab work in alchemy and medicine. She battled with her brother, John, over the ownership of Bulkeley's books after his death in 1713.

Manuscript #12
This manuscript is a medical account covering the period of April 25, 1708 to March 9, 1714. The initial portion is in Bulkeley's handwriting, and the last three entries are in a different hand. The account records were apparently continued after Bulkeley's death in 1713.

Manuscript #13
This manuscript has varied content. It includes an index for *Praedicamentum Substantia,* a philosophical-scientific treatise by John Fox taken over by Gershom. It includes Gershom's notes on medical and alchemical books by Thomas Willis and Richard Mathew. It contains notes on *Transubstantiation* by John Hooper.

Manuscript #14
This manuscript is by Peter Bulkeley (either Gershom's brother or son). It contains many pages of poetry as well as medical and chemical notes, some of which are in Gershom's hand. It contains the "short-hand" code sometimes used by Gershom.

Manuscript #15
This manuscript contains an invoice of goods bought of Thomas Bulkeley on July 3, 1684. It also includes some

notes on chemistry books and expense accounts. This manuscript has been digitized and is available online.

Manuscript #16
This manuscript contains notes dated January 8, 1673 on *Praxeis Medica.*

Manuscript #17
This manuscript contains notes dated April 1687 on *Chemica Rationaoli Collecta.* It also contains the description of diseases and medical recipes and includes a 1695 letter from Gershom's brother-in-law, Isaac Chauncy, from London.

Manuscript #18
This manuscript dates to 1672 and contains medical pharmacopeia and experiments. It cites *Chymicall Secrets and Rare Experiments in Physicke and Philosophy* by Sir Kenelm Digby (1603-1665), which was published by George Hartman after Digby's death. This manuscript has been digitized and is available online.

Manuscript #19
This manuscript contains notes from the *Encyclopedia of Medicine* written by German theologian and educator, Johann Heinrich Alsted. It contains notes from the history of the Royal Society of London, the history of making gun powder and Sir William Petty's history of common practices of dying. It contains several chapters of clinical observations.

Manuscript #20

This manuscript includes notes from *Medicine for Poor People*.

Manuscript #21

This is a small certificate signed by Gershom and certifying that he will pay Goodman Curtis of Wethersfield three pounds and five shillings in wheat and Indian corn on April 12, 1680.

Manuscript #22

This manuscript on pharmacopeia is in Latin.

Manuscript #23

This manuscript contains medical excerpts from multiple sources.

Manuscript #24

This manuscript is not in Gershom's hand and contains notes from *The Family Physician* by George Hartman.

Watkinson Library, Trinity College, Hartford, Connecticut

The Watkinson Library serves as a public research library and houses the rare book and special collections of the Trinity College Library and the repository of the College's archives. The Bulkeley manuscript collection in the Watkinson library consists of several book-length manuscripts in two boxes.

Box 1: Contains Five Documents

1.) This manuscript (sometimes referenced as #6) contains Bulkeley's most important surviving work, *Vade Mecum*. In a treatise of more than three hundred pages Gershom summarized his medical knowledge and presented a long list of medical preparations. The flyleaf is inscribed, "Dorothy Treat, Dec. 7, 1795." *Vade Mecum* was written to instruct Gershom's daughter, Dorothy Treat, and his grandson, Richard Treat. It is the best and most comprehensive presentation of the leading edge of medical knowledge in Connecticut at the end of the seventeenth century. At the end of the manuscript Gershom appended a poignant memorial to his youngest daughter, Catherine.

2.) This small manuscript contains notes in Latin from *Regula Universales in Curatione Morbarum Observed*. It is not in Gershom's hand.

3.) This manuscript contains notes in Latin from a book by Dr. Thomas Willis (1621-1675) on fermentation and flavors. Willis was a founding member of the Royal Society, and a major figure in the fields of anatomy, neurology and psychiatry. The book was printed in London in 1660. Bulkeley's notes were completed on March 2, 1692.

4.) This is a large book in Latin. The first 233 pages are notes on *Observations que data ex Bicheri Minerva Arnaria, Duumvirate, Alphabeto Mineral*i. The later portions of the manuscript are notes from *The Complete Chymist or a New Treatise of Chymistry* by Christopher Glaser, printed in London, 1677.

5.) This manuscript (sometimes referenced as #7) contains notes from *Arcana Philosophia or Chymical Secrets, containing the noted and useful chymical medicines of Drs. Witt and Rich Russel, chymists.* The book was published in London by John Headrich in 1697. Gershom's notes are dated July 17, 1699, so he seems to have had access to relatively recent English publications. This manuscript also contains notes from; Johannes Segerus Weidenfeld, *Concerning ye Secrets of ye Adepts or ye Use of Lully's Spirits of Wine, A Practical Work*, printed in 1685 and copied by Bulkeley 17 July 1699. Bulkeley inserted notes in this section, saying he was nearly killed in his laboratory trying to follow one of Weidenfeld's recipes for Philosophical Wine. This manuscript also includes a copy of a letter from Robert Boyle to

"J.S.W." Gershom also refers to a letter dated May 26, 1701 that he received from Dr. James Oliver in London in answer to one of his own.

Box 2: Contains Four Documents

1.) This manuscript contains records originally kept by Gershom's son, Peter. It is inscribed by Peter, in a beautiful script. On the title page, he made a record of his marriage to Rachel Talcott, the daughter of Captain Samuel Talcott, on March 21, 1699/1700. Peter's script indicates that he must have had more education than previously noted. After he was drowned at sea in 1701, Gershom took over this manuscript to record his accounts.

2.) There are two small books with metal hinges, containing notes in Latin in this box.

3.) This item is a fragment containing four pages of a medical log, 1688-1704.

4.) Miscellaneous papers.

Connecticut Historical Society Library, Hartford, Connecticut

The Waterman Resource Center at the Connecticut Historical Society Library in Hartford, Connecticut holds the following Bulkeley material:

> Manuscript 64768: A letter from Gershom Bulkeley letter, to his nephew, Joseph Bulkeley, dated June 3, 1696 June 3. This letter defends Mercy (Holbridge) Disborough from charges that she had a baby out of wedlock and murdered it. The accuser had implied that Gershom might have been the father.
>
> Manuscript in Hoadley Autograph Collection, Box 7, Folder 7. A 1710 Ephemeris used by Gershom Bulkeley as a diary 1710.
>
> Manuscripts 64769: Gershom, John and Joseph Bulkeley Papers, 1674 -1743/4, including the 1713 will of Gershom Bulkeley.
>
> Broadsides 1714 J27o. "On the death of the very learned, pious and excelling Gershom Bulkeley, Esq. M.D.: who had his mortality swallowed up of life, December the second 1713", by John James.
>
> Account Book. Peter Bulkeley, merchant accounts 1680-1681.
>
> Account Book. Gershom Bulkeley, medical accounts 1682-1697.

Richard G. Tomlinson

ACKNOWLEDGMENTS

Fɪʀsᴛ ᴀᴄᴋɴᴏᴡʟᴇᴅɢᴍᴇɴᴛs ᴍᴜsᴛ ɢᴏ ᴛᴏ Cᴀʀᴏʟ Wʜɪᴛᴍᴇʀ. She was the indispensable person in this project. She accompanied me on trips to the Trinity University, Watkinson Library and the University of Connecticut, Lyman-Stowe Library. She photographed page after page of Bulkeley manuscripts and transferred them to CDs for easy reference. She was a great help in deciphering Bulkeley's crabbed hand writing. Bulkeley was truly a doctor in every sense of the word. She is very knowledgeable about colonial Connecticut history. She read the original manuscript and offered many useful suggestions and was very useful in keeping my feet on the ground when it came to excessive praise of Bulkeley.

I am deeply indebted to Judith Bowen, who is a very tough task master. I think she despairs of ever teaching me the Chicago Style Manual…especially when it comes to footnote citations. Judith is meticulous and not only checks and corrects the form of your footnotes but does some original research to be sure you are correct. The scope of her knowledge is astounding.

A Stranger in the Land, Gershom Bulkeley of Connecticut, a 1988 publication of Professor Thomas W. Jodziewicz of the University of Dallas, Texas, was a constant source of information and inspiration. This scholarly work is the best thing ever published about Gershom Bulkeley. One of its most valuable contributions is the attribution of the titles and authors of the books in Gershom's library. The books were listed in Bulkeley's probate records, but translation of these sometimes sketchy and/or illegible records is an exercise in frustration and cannot be done without a great deal of auxiliary research.

I am indebted to Connecticut State Historian, Walter Woodward, for his encouragement to go forward with this project when it almost seemed to be too daunting. His work in *Prospero's America,* and the illumination it showed of the interaction between Gershom Bulkeley and John Winthrop, Jr. was eye opening.

Finally, it is a pleasure to acknowledge the librarians of the Watkinson, Lyman-Stowe, Connecticut State Library, Connecticut Historical Society and Massachusetts Historical Society libraries. Without them the road would be much steeper and rockier and some references never uncovered.

INDEX

CITATIONS

Chaper I: Introduction

[1] Bulkeley, Gershom, *Will and Doom, or The Miseries of Connecticut by and under and usurped and arbitrary power*, repr in *Collections of the Connecticut Historical Society,* vol. 3, (Hartford, Conn: Connecticut Historical Society, 1895), 69-269. Hereinafter *Will and Doom.*

[2] Perry Miller, *The New England Mind: from Colony to Province* (Cambridge, Mass.: Belknap Press of Harvard University Press, 1939), 152.

[3] Samuel Eliot Morison, *The Intellectual Life of Colonial New England* (New York: New York University Press, 1956), 203.

[4] J. Hammond Trumbull, ed., *The Trumbull, Public Records of the Colony of Connecticut, from 1665 to 1678; with the Journal of the Council of War, 1675 to 1678*, vol. 2 (Hartford, Conn.: F. A. Brown, 1852), 388-389. Hereinafter Trumbull, *Public Records 1665-1678*).

[5] John Gorham Palfrey, *History of New England*, 5 vols. (Boston, Mass.: Little, Brown& Co., 1870), 3:544.

[6] The detailed citations that support the following paragraphs of the Introduction are to be found in the body of this work.

[7] Donald Lines Jacobus, comp., *The Bulkeley Genealogy, Reverend Peter Bulkeley, Being an account of his career, his ancestry, the ancestry of his two wives, and his relatives in England and New England, together with a genealogy of his descendants through the seventh American generation* (New Haven, Conn.: [Tuttle, c1933]), 105.

[8] Lemuel Shattuck, *History of the Town of Concord; Middlesex County, Massachusetts, from its Earliest Settlement to 1832 and the Adjoining Town, Bedford, Acton, Lincoln, and Carlisle* (Boston, Mass.: Russell, Odiorne, and Co., 1835), 241.

[9] Trumbull, *Public Records (1665 to 1678)*, 84.

---

[10] Sherman W. Adams and Henry R. Stiles, *The History of Ancient Wethersfield,* 2 vols., a facsimile of the 1904 edition (Somersworth, N.H.: 1974), 1:639. Hereinafter *History of Ancient Wethersfield.*

[11] Walter W. Woodward, *Prospero's America, John Winthrop Jr., Alchemy, and the Creation of New England Culture, 1606-1676* (Chapel Hill, N.C.: University of North Carolina Press, 2010), 202.

[12] Connecticut *Court of Assistants, Colony of Connecticut Minutes of the Court of Assistants, 1669-1711,* transcribed by Helen Schatvet Ullmann, (Boston, Mass: New England Historic Genealogical Society, 2009), 7. Hereinafter *Court of Assistants.*

[13] Richard G. Tomlinson, *Witchcraft Prosecution; Chasing the Devil in Connecticut* (Rockland, Maine: Picton Press, 2012), 123-137.

[14] Trumbull, *Public Records 1665-1678,* 271.

[15] Trumbull, *Public Records 1665-1678,* 580-584.

[16] George Madison Bodge, *Soldiers in King Philip's War,* 3rd ed. (Boston, Mass.: George Madison Bodge, 1906; repr. Boston, Mass.: New England Historic Genealogical Society, 2014), 83-87.

[17] Annie Eliot Trumbull, *Records of the Particular Court of Connecticut, Administration of Sir Edmund Andros, Royal Governor, 1687-1688* (Hartford, Conn.: Case, Lockwood & Brainard Co., 1935), 3.

[18] Bulkeley, *Will and Doom,* 93.

[19] Franklin Bowditch Dexter, ed., *Documentary History of Yale University, Under the Original Charter of the Collegiate School of Connecticut 1701 – 1745* (New Haven, Conn.: Yale University Press, 1916), 9-12.

[20] *Court of Assistants,* 163-164.

[21] Connecticut Archives, *Crimes & Misdemeanors,* series 1, 1662/3-1789, 6 vols., 1:167, 172,173,175,178. Hereinafter *Crimes & Misdemeanors.*

[22] *Court of Assistants,* 389-396.

[23] Bulkeley Papers, Connecticut Historical Society.

[24] Thomas W. Jodziewicz, "A Stranger in the Land: Gershom Bulkeley of Connecticut", Transactions of the American Philosophical Society, Vol. 28, Part 2 (Philadelphia, Pa.: American Philosophical Society, 1988), 73-92.

[25] Gurdon W. Russell, M.D., "Early Medicine and Early Medical Men," Proceedings of the Connecticut Medical Society, 25 May 1892, New Haven, CT, 32-3.

[26] *Vade Mecum*, MS6, Gershom Bulkeley Manuscripts 1661-1721, Lyman Maynard Stowe Library, University of Connecticut, 313-319.

[27] Will of Gershom Bulkeley in Charles William Manwaring, comp., *A Digest of the Early Connecticut Probate Records*, 3 vols. (Hartford, Conn.: R. S. Peck & Co., 1904-1906), 2: 165-167.

[28] John Langdon Sibley, *Sibley's Harvard Graduates: Biographical Sketches of Graduates of Those Who Attended Harvard College...with biographical and other notes, 3 vols.*, (Boston: Massachusetts Historical Society, 1873), 1:397.

Chapter II. England to New England

[29] Cotton Mather, *Magnalia Christi Americana: or the Ecclesiastical History of New England from its First Planting in the Year 1620 unto the Year of our Lord 1698*, (London: Thomas Parkhurst, 1702, 3 vols. (London: Thomas Parkhurst, 1702), 3: 96-98. Hereinafter *Magnalia.* Also reproduced in full in two Bulkeley genealogies

[30] Mather, *Magnalia* 3: 95. This profile is also reproduced in Rev. F. W. Chapman, *The Bulkeley Family or Descendants of Rev, Peter Bulkeley, who settled at Concord, Mass., in 1636* (Hartford, Conn.: Case, Lockwood & Brainard Co, 1875), 247-253, and in Jacobus, *The Bulkeley Genealogy*, 93-99.

Chapman, *The Bulkeley*, 2-2

[32] Jacobus, *The Bulkeley Genealogy*,14-15.

[33] Jacobus, *The Bulkeley Genealogy*, 888-890.

[34] Jacobus, *The Bulkeley Genealogy*, 99-100.

[35] Jacobus, *The Bulkeley Genealogy*, 39-43.

[36] Jacobus, *The Bulkeley Genealogy*, 111.

[37] Jacobus, *The Bulkeley Genealogy*, 100.

[38] Robert Charles Anderson, *The Great Migration Directory, Immigrants to New England, 1620-1640* (Boston, Mass.: New England Historic and Genealogical Society, 2014), 1.

[39] Donald Lines Jacobus, comp. and ed., *History and Genealogy of the Families of Old Fairfield,* 2 vols, (New Haven, Conn.: The Tuttle,

Morehouse & Taylor Company, 1930), 1:109; also, Jacobus, The *Bulkeley Genealogy,* 101-104.

[40] Jacobus, *The Bulkeley Genealogy*, 102.

[41] Francis Manwaring Caulkins, *History of New London from the first survey of the coast in 1612 to 1860* (New London, Conn.: H. D. Utley, 1895). Pg.132. Caulkins says that "this story has often been related." It is likely that Captain Charles Bulkeley, the great grandson of Gershom (Gershom[1], Edward[2], Major Charles Bulkeley[3], and Capt. Charles Bulkeley[4]) was still living when Caulkins began gathering material for her 1852 publication. Therefore, the oral tradition of Gershom's unusual birth would be reasonably fresh and probably substantially true.

[42] Wethersfield Vital Record, 1:38, says "Dr. Gershom Bulkeley, d. Dec.2, 1713, age 77 y7, 11 mo." Jacobus in *The Bulkeley Genealogy,* 111 puts Gershom's birth date at Jan. 1635/6. In *History and Genealogy of the Families of Old Fairfield,* 1:110, Jacobus says Dec. 1635, Caulkins says Dec. 26, 1635 while Chapman in *The Bulkeley Family* 38 and 78, says Dec. 6, 1636, Sibley in *Sibley's Harvard Graduates*, 1:389, says "2 December 1636 or 2 January 1637, or it may have been a year earlier."

[43] Chapman, *The Bulkeley Family*, 36.

[44] Mather, *Magnalia,* in Jacobus, *The Bulkeley Genealogy,* 92-98 and in Chapman, *The Bulkeley Family*, 247-253.

[45] Jacobus, *The Bulkeley Genealogy*, 116 fn., Cambridge or perhaps Concord.

[46] Jacobus, *The Bulkeley Genealogy*, 105.

[47] Chapman, *The Bulkeley Family*, 27 fn.

[48] Jacobus, *The Bulkeley Genealogy*, 106.

[49] Jacobus, *The Bulkeley Genealogy*, 105-6

[50] Chapman, *The Bulkeley Family*, 29.

[51] Jodziewicz, "A Stranger in the Land", vi.

[52] Jacobus, *The Bulkeley Genealogy*, 94.

[53] Jacobus, *The Bulkeley Genealogy*, 114.

[54] Sibley, *Sibley's Harvard Graduates*, 1:52.

[55] Jacobus, *The Bulkeley Genealogy*, 114.

[56] Sibley, *Sibley's Harvard Graduates, 1*: 30.

[57] Sibley, *Sibley's Harvard Graduates, 1*: 52-54.

[58] Sibley, *Sibley's Harvard Graduates, 1*: 389-90.

[59] Jodziewicz, "A Stranger in the Land", 6-7.

[60] Sibley, *Sibley's Harvard Graduates, 1:*572.

[61] Jacobus, *The Bulkeley Genealogy*, 111, 127.

[62] Sibley, *Sibley's Harvard Graduates* 2:68-71.

[63] Jacobus, *The Bulkeley Genealogy*, 92.

[64] Chapman, *The Bulkeley Family*, 30, 32.

[65] Anna Maria Fay, "Some Account of the Life and Times of the Reverend Peter Bulkeley", *Register* 31 (1877), 153-59.

[66] Shattuck, *History of the Town of Concord*, 161.

[67] Shattuck, *History of the Town of Concord*. 241.

[68] Jodziewicz, "A Stranger in the Land," 10, fn 9.

[69] Jacobus, *The Bulkeley Genealogy,* 127, 136-140.

Chapter III: Minister

[70] Caulkins, *History of New London*, 115-117.

[71] Manwaring, New London County Court Records, I; 20, 22.

[72] Caulkins, *History of New London,* 131.

[73] Jodziewicz, "A Stranger in the Land", 10-11.

[74] Caulkins, *History of New London,* 131.

[75] Jacobus, *The Bulkeley Genealogy*, 136.

[76] Caulkins, *History of New London,* 148-149.

[77] Jacobus, *The Bulkeley Genealogy,* 119.

[78] Caulkins, *History of New London,* 150.

[79] Homer W. Brainard, "The Reverend Henry Smith of Wethersfield," TAG, July 1933, 12. In Adams and Stiles' *History of Ancient Wethersfield*, 2:647, she is erroneously identified as Rev. Smith's youngest daughter, Elizabeth.

[80] Crimes & Misdemeanors, Connecticut State Library, 3: 296.

[81] Caulkins, *History of New London,* 150-1.

[82] Adams and Stiles, *History of Ancient Wethersfield,* 1:166.

[83] On 14 April 1653, the whole water-course of Alewife Brook had been granted to John Winthrop with privileges for making dams and erecting mills. Caulkins, *History of New London*, 96.

[84] Douglas Richardson, "John Tinker of Boston and Lancaster, Massachusetts and Windsor and New London, NEHGS Register, 1995, V, 149, 401-425.

---

[85] Caulkins, *History of New London*, 280.

[86] Caulkins, *History of New London*, 151.

[87] Caulkins, *History of New London*, 96.

[88] Crimes & Misdemeanors, 3: 198.

[89] Caulkins, *History of New London*, 248.

[90] Crimes & Misdemeanors, 3: 296.

[91] Crimes & Misdemeanors, 3: 207-8.

[92] The letter does not survive, but is referenced by Smith in his letter.

[93] Crimes & Misdemeanors, 3: 198-205.

[94] County Court Minutes, 71.

[95] Adams and Stiles, *History of Ancient Wethersfield* ,1: 153.

[96] Adams and Stiles, *History of Ancient Wethersfield*, 2: 647

[97] Adams and Stiles, *History of Ancient Wethersfield,* 1: 320.

[98] New London Town Records, 1D: 6.

[99] Jodziewicz, "A Stranger in the Land", 10.

[100] Jodziewicz, "A Stranger in the Land", 12.

[101] Caulkins, *History of New London*, 137.

[102] Caulkins, *History of New London*, 137-140.,

[103] Chapman, *The Bulkeley Family*, 88-90.

[104] John Dean & Dean Dudley, "Descendants of Gov. Bradstreet", *Register*, 9 (April 1855), 117-118.

[105] Adams and Stiles, *History of Ancient Wethersfield*, 1: 23-24 and 1: 320-323.

[106] The authority for the votes cited here and throughout this section is "Wethersfield Town Votes" a multi-volume set containing the record of the proceedings of the proprietors and inhabitants of the town at their annual and special meetings. The first volume of this set covers 1647 to 1717. The original volumes are kept in the Town Clerk's office along with a copy of the first volumes of the Town Votes and the Land Records made by 19th century Wethersfield historian, Judge Sherman Adams. (also on microfilm, reel#2, Wethersfield Town Records, CSL.) These votes are frequently referenced and quoted in Adams and Stiles, *History of Ancient Wethersfield*.

[107] Wethersfield Town Votes, 1:94.

[108] Wethersfield Town Votes, 1:96. Also quoted in Adams and Stiles, *History of Ancient Wethersfield,* 1: 324-325 fn.

[109] Jacobus, *The Bulkeley Genealogy*, 120.

---

[110] Sibley, *Sibley's Harvard Graduates*, 1:396.

[111] Adams and Stiles, *History of Ancient Wethersfield*, 1:324.

[112] Alfred Sereno Hudson, *The History of Concord, Massachusetts*, vol. 1 (Concord, Mass.: The Erudite Press, 1904), 155-156.

[113] Trumbull, *Public Records* (1665 to 1678), 84.

[114] It has been suggested that Bulkeley's view lay between that of Congregationalists and Presbyterians, advocating more inclusive membership, but strict requirements regarding communion and more reliance on control by the elders than by synods. See Jodziewicz, "A Stranger in the Land" 10 fn.

[115] Woodward, *Prospero's America*, 243.

[116] Trumbull, *Public Records 1665-1678*, 99.

[117] Notebook, MS 3, Gershom Bulkeley Manuscripts, 1661-1721, Lyman Maynard Stowe Library, University of Connecticut.

[118] Enoch Buck received a land grant in Wethersfield in 1649. There is confusion as the records sometimes refer to Emanuel Buck as alias Enoch Buck. See Adams and Stiles, *History of Ancient Wethersfield*, 2: 137-138.

[119] Russell, "Early Medicine and Early Medical Men," 42-43.

[120] Judith Varlet, a sister-in-law of Gov. Peter Stuyvesant, was accused of witchcraft in the Hartford Witch Panic of 1662 and was rescued by a letter from him attesting to her good character.

[121] Russell, "Early Medicine and Early Medical Men," 39.

[122] Probably Dr. Thomas Pell (1613-1669) of Fairfield.

[123] Richard Ely (1656-1698).

[124] Rev. James Fitch (1622-1702).

[125] Hugh Caulkins (1600-1690).

[126] John Caulkins (1634-1702).

[127] MS 3, Gershom Bulkeley Manuscripts, University of Connecticut, [46]. Also see Russell, "Early Medicine", 41.

[128] Notebook, MS 4, Gershom Bulkeley Manuscripts, University of Connecticut, 565.

[129] Notebook, MS 4, Gershom Bulkeley Manuscripts, University of Connecticut, 14.

[130] Tomlinson, Witchcraft Prosecution, 32-37.

[131] Mather, *Magnalia*, 2: 456.

[132] Tomlinson, Witchcraft Prosecution, 39-47.

[133] Woodward, *Prospero's America* 224.

[134] Tomlinson, Witchcraft Prosecution, 92-103.

[135] Peter R. Christoph, Florence A. Christoph, Kenneth Scott, eds, *New York, Historical Manuscripts, English*, 5 vols. (repr. Baltimore: Genealogical Pub. Co.,1980)

[136] Tomlinson, Witchcraft Prosecution, 123-137.

[137] Many of the records of Harrison's trial are found in the Samuel Wyllys Papers: depositions on cases of witchcraft in Connecticut 1662-1693, (Hartford: Connecticut State Library, 1930). 6-15 and Wyllys Papers Supplement 46-53. A complete set of the Wyllys Papers is also held in the John Hay Library, Brown University, and Providence, Rhode Island. Both libraries hold a mix of original documents and copies.

[138] Wyllys Papers Connecticut State Library, 6-12, Supplement 46-53.

[139] Carolyn S. Langdon, "A Complaint Against Katherine Harrison, 1669," *The Connecticut Historical Society Bulletin*, 34 (January 1969), 19.

[140] *Court of Assistants*, 3.

[141] *Court of Assistants*, 3.

[142] Langdon, "A Complaint Against Katherine Harrison, 1669," 19-21.

[143] *Court of Assistants*, 7.

[144] Winthrop Family Papers, Massachusetts Historical Society, Boston, (microfilm P-350, 53 reels), reel 9, letter from Gershom Bulkeley to John Winthrop on 19 February 1669. When Gershom's wife Sarah was ill, he was comfortable in writing to Winthrop urging him to "speedily come over to my house" to attend his wife. In Winthrop. See also Woodward, *Prospero's America,* 243 fn.

[145] Samuel Wyllys Papers Supplement: 52.

[146] *Court of Assistants*, 11

[147] James Savage ed., *The History of New England from 1630-1649 by John Winthrop, Esq. First Governor of the Colony of the Massachusetts Bay, From his Original Manuscripts with Notes*, two vols., (Boston, Mass: Little, Brown and Co., 1853), 56-57. See also [147] Francis J. Bremer, *Building a Better Jerusalem John Davenport, a Puritan in Two Worlds* (New London, Conn & London, England: Yale University Press, 2012), 212.

---

[148] Bremer, *Building a Better Jerusalem,* 230. According to Bremer, they mean rape.

[149] Charles J. Hoadly, ed., *Records of the Colony or Jurisdiction of New Haven from May 1653, to the Union* (Hartford, Conn: Case, Lockwood and Co., 1858), 572, quoting *New Haven's Settling in New England and some Lawes for Government* (London: Livewell Chapman, 1656).

[150] Hoadly, *Records of the Colony or Jurisdiction of New Haven,* 557.

[151] Samuel Wyllys Papers Supplement, Connecticut State Library, Hartford, CT: 1-2.

[152] William Perkins, *A Discourse of the Damned Art of Witchcraft, So Farre forth as it is revealed in the Scriptures, and manifest by true experience, Framed and Delivered by M. William Perkins, in his ordinarie course of Preaching,* published by Thomas Picketing, Bachelor of Divinity and Minister of Finchingfield in Essex ([Cambridge]: Cantrell Legge, 1618). Perkins died in 1602 and these sermons were likely preached in the period from 1581 to 1594.

[153] Perkins, *A Discourse of the Damned Art of Witchcraft,* 644.

[154] Trumbull, *Public Records 1665-1678,* 184.

[155] Trumbull, *Public Records 1665-1678,* 260-262.

[156] *Court of Assistants,* 20-21, 23-24.

[157] *Court of Assistants,* 29.

[158] Trumbull, *Public Records 1665-1678,* 189.

[159] *Court of Assistants,* 163-164.

[160] *Their Majesties Colony of Connecticut in New England Vindicated from the Abuses of a Pamphlet, Licensed and Printed at New York 1694, entitled Some Seasonable Considerations for the Good People of Connecticut by an Answer Thereunto,* Collections of the Connecticut Historical Society 1 (Boston: Bartholomew Green ,1694); repr. Hartford, Conn.:1: 57-75., 1860), 112. Hereinafter *Connecticut Vindicated.*

Chapter IV: Army Surgeon

[161]. Trumbull, *Public Records 1665-1678,* 569.

[162] William Hubbard, *A Narrative of the Indian Wars in New England, from the first planting thereof in the year 1607, of the year 1677, containing a relation of the occasion, rise and progress of the war with the Indians in Southern, Western, Eastern and Northern parts of said*

country (Stockbridge, Mass.: Herman Willard, 1803). A contemporaneous history of the war written by William Hubbard, the minister of Ipswich, MA and originally published at Boston by authority of the Governor and Council of Massachusetts on 29 March 1677. It is considered to contain the most authoritative history of the King Philip War, 58-250.

[163] Trumbull, *Public Records 1665-1678*, 331.

[164] Memorandum of Sir Edmund as quoted in Trumbull, *Public Records 1665-1678*, 582 fn.

[165] *Trumbull, Public Records 1665-1678*, 579.

[166] *Trumbull, Public Records 1665-1678*, 582.

[167] Trumbull, *Public Records 1665-1678*, 580, where the letter of Robert Chapman to Gov. Winthrop, dated 8 July 1675, Saybrooke, is quoted.

[168] Trumbull, *Public Records 1665-1678, 585-586*, where letter of Reverend Thomas Buckingham is quoted, original in "Colonial Boundaries": Connecticut State Archives. Colonial and State Boundaries, 2nd Series, 1662-1820, 40.

[169] Trumbull, *Public Records 1665-1678*, 582-585.

[170] Trumbull, *Public Records 1665-1678*, 583-584.

[171]Trumbull, *Public Records 1665-1678*, 583-4

[172] Jacobus, *The Bulkeley Genealogy*, 120.

[173] Thomas Hutchinson, *The History of Massachusetts from the first settlement thereof in 1628, until the year 1750*, 3rd ed., 2 vols. (Salem, Mass.: Thomas C. Cushing, 1795), 1:255-259. Hereinafter, *The History of Massachusetts.*

[174] Hubbard, *A Narrative of the Indian Wars,* 71-75.

[175] Trumbull, *Public Records 1665-1678*, 336.

[176] "War 1675-1775" (Hartford: Connecticut State Library), 10 vols. 1:4a. Hereinafter, *War.* Letter dated 1 July 1675 also reproduced in Trumbull, *Public Records 1665-1678,* 332.

[177] Hubbard, *A Narrative of the Indian Wars*, 100.

[178] Trumbull, *Public Records 1665-1678*, 585.

[179] Trumbull, *Public Records 1665-1678*, 338.

[180] *War,* 1: 11e.

[181] *War,* 1: 11f.

[182] Hubbard, *A Narrative of the Indian Wars*, 111.

[183] Hubbard, *A Narrative of the Indian Wars*, 67.

[184] Hubbard, *A Narrative of the Indian Wars*. 112-115.

[185] Hubbard, *A Narrative of the Indian Wars*, 118-119.

[186] Trumbull, *Public Records 1665-1678*, 383.

[187] Hubbard, *A Narrative of the Indian Wars*, 122-123.

[188] Trumbull, *Public Records 1665-1678*, 266-267.

[189] Samuel Deane, *History of Situate, Massachusetts, from its first settlement to 1831* (Boston: James Loring, 1831), 177-178.

[190] Trumbull, *Public Records 1665-1678*, 271.

[191] Trumbull, *Public Records 1665-1678*, 382-383.

[192] Hubbard, *A Narrative of the Indian Wars*, 128-129.

[193] Trumbull, *Public Records 1665-1678*, 373-374.

[194] Trumbull, *Public Records 1665-1678*, 384-387.

[195] Bodge, *Soldiers of King Philip's War*, 136.

[196] Trumbull, *Public Records 1665-1678*, 388.

[197] Bodge, *Soldiers of King Philip's War*, 135.

[198] Benjamin Church, *The Entertaining History of King Philip's War, which began in the month of June 1675, also of the Expeditions more lately made against the common enemy, and Indian rebels, in the eastern parts of New England; with some accounts of Divine Providence towards Col. Benjamin Church*: by his son, 2nd edition (Boston: Printed 1716), 57. Hereinafter, *The Entertaining History.*

[199] Many of the Massachusetts officers distrusted all Indians and, unlike the Connecticut forces, did not even use them as scouts. This may partially account for the frequent ambushes of Massachusetts expeditions which Connecticut avoided.

[200] Bodge, *Soldiers of King Philip's War* 182-187.

[201] Hubbard, *A Narrative of the Indian Wars*, 136.

[202] Church, *The Entertaining History*, 28.

[203] Hubbard, *A Narrative of the Indian Wars*, 135.

[204] Bodge, *Soldiers of King Philip's War,* 187.

[205] Hubbard, *A Narrative of the Indian Wars*, 136-138.

[206] Bodge, *Soldiers of King Philip's War,* 194.

[207] Capt. Oliver's letter in Hubbard, 273.

[208] There were two surgeons with the MA forces and one with the Plymouth forces.

[209] Church, *The Entertaining History*, 28-29.

303

[210] Bodge, *Soldiers of King Philip's War,* 83-87.

[211] Hutchinson, 272.

[212] Bodge, *Soldiers of King Philip's War,* 197.

[213] Trumbull, *Public Records 1665-1678,* 392-395, On 10 Jan. 1675, the Council in Hartford passed a thirty-point set of rules to be read to Treat's army for "keeping their soldiers to their duty".

[214] Trumbull, *Public Records 1665-1678,* 399-400.

[215] Trumbull, *Public Records 1665-1678,* 405-409.

[216] Eric B. Schultz, Michael Tougias, King *Philip's War, The History and Legacy of America's Forgotten Conflict,* (Woodstock, VT: The Country Press, 200), 143

[217] Bodge, *Soldiers of King Philip's War,* 34-35.

[218] Hubbard, *A Narrative of the Indian Wars,* 186.

[219] Trumbull, *Public Records 1665-1678,* 416.

[220] *War,* 1:51 and Trumbull, *Public Records 1665-1678,* 424,

[221] Schultz and Tougias, 55-59.

[222] Trumbull, *Public Records 1665-1678,* 433.

[223] Trumbull, *Public Records 1665-1678,* 277.

[224] *War,* 1: 73.

[225] Trumbull, *Public Records 1665-1678,* 451.

[226] Trumbull, *Public Records 1665-1678,* 444.

[227] Trumbull, *Public Records 1665-1678,* 450-451, ltr from Major Talcott, May 31.

[228] Trumbull, *Public Records 1665-1678,* 453, ltr from Major Talcott, June 8.

[229] Caulkins, *History of New London,* 185.

[230] Trumbull, *Public Records 1665-1678,* 456.

[231] Caulkins, *History of New London,* 186.

[232] Schultz and Tougias, *King Philip's War,* 66.

[233] Church, *The Entertaining History,* 72-73.

[234] Trumbull, *Public Records 1665-1678,* 483.

Chapter V: Miller, Doctor, Lawyer, Farmer
[235] Wethersfield Town Votes, 1:71.

[236] Adams and Stiles, *The History of Ancient Wethersfield,* 1.116.

[237] Adams and Stiles, *The History of Ancient Wethersfield,* 1: 103. A later chapter (1: 922) says that the claim was transferred in February 1677, but this appears to be in error.

[238] Adams and Stiles, *The History of Ancient Wethersfield,* 1: 639.

[239] Wethersfield Town Votes, 1:71 and Adams and Stiles, *The History of Ancient Wethersfield,* 1: 155, 639.

[240] Wethersfield Town Votes, 102 and Adams and Stiles, *The History of Ancient Wethersfield,* 1: 324-325.

[241] Adams and Stiles, *The History of Ancient Wethersfield,* 1: 103, 255, 639.

[242] Adams and Stiles, *The History of Ancient Wethersfield,* 1: 325.

[243] Hartford County, *Connecticut, County Court Minutes, vols. 3 and 4, 1663-1687, 1697,* transcribed by Helen Schatvet Ullmann (Boson: New England Historic Genealogical Society, 2005), 247. Hereinafter *County Court Minutes.*

[244] *County Court Minutes,* 293.

[245] *County Court Minutes,* 275-276.

[246] *County Court Minutes,* 350.

[247] *County Court Minutes,* 398-399.

[248] *County Court Minutes,* 405.

[249] Thomas W. Jodziewicz, "The 1699 Diary of Gershom Bulkeley of Wethersfield, Connecticut", *Proceedings of the American Philosophical Society* (Philadelphia Pa: American Philosophical Society, 1987) 131. The original is in the Rare Book and Special Collections Division of the Library of Congress.

[250] Adams and Stiles, *History of Ancient Wethersfield,* 1: 921-922.

[251] Rocky Hill Historical Society pamphlet by June Cooke.

[252] Bulkeley Notebook, MS 3, University of Connecticut, 36.

[253] Bulkeley Notebook, MS 3, University of Connecticut.

[254] Bulkeley, *Will and Doom,* 71, preface by Charles J. Hoadly.

[255] Adams and Stiles, *History of Ancient Wethersfield,* 1:326.

[256] Rev. John Williams, *The Redeemed Captive Returning to Zion or the Captivity and Deliverance of Rev. John Williams* (repr. from 6th edition, Springfield, Mass.: H.R. Huntington Co. 1908), 202-207. (Springfield, MA: 1908), 202-207. The first edition was printed in Boston in 1707.

---

[257] Probably Hannah Allyn, wife of Colonel John Allyn, secretary of the Connecticut Colony. Wells was apparently also boarded at the home of Jonathan Gilbert whose widow, Mary, unsuccessfully sued Wells for room and board given, "during his lameness." See *Court of Assistants,* 340-341.

[258] George Sheldon, *A History of Deerfield, Massachusetts: the times when and the people by whom it was settled, unsettled, resettled, with a special study of the Indian Wars in the Connecticut Valley,* 2 vols. (Deerfield, Mass.: Press of E.A. Hall & Co., [Greenfield, MA] 1895), vol. 1:166.

[259] *County Court Minutes,* 287.

[260] J. Hammond Trumbull, ed., *The Public Records of the Colony of Connecticut, May 1678 – June 1689; with Notes and Appendix Comprising such documents from the State archives and other sources, as illustrate the history of the Colony during, The Administration of Sir Edmund Andros,* vol.3 (Hartford, Conn: Case, Lockwood & Co.,1859), 510. Hereinafter *Public Records 1678-1689*)

[261] J.H. Trumbull, *Public Records* 1678-1689, 218.

[262] Russell, *Early Medicine and Early Medical Men,* 33.

[263] Trumbull, *Public Records* 1678-1689, 98-99.

[264] Trumbull, *Public Records* 1678-1689, 149-150.

[265] Trumbull, *Public Records* 1678-1689, 202.

[266] Wethersfield Town Votes, taken on 10 October 1673.

[267] Adams and Stiles, *History of Ancient Wethersfield,* 1: 104.

[268] Adams and Stiles, *History of Ancient Wethersfield,* 1: 106.

[269] Adams and Stiles, *History of Ancient Wethersfield,* 1: 918-919.

[270] *County Court Minutes,* 375.

[271] *Court of Assistants,* 102.

[272] Trumbull, *Public Records* 1678-1689, 163.

[273] Trumbull, *Public Records* 1678-1689, 167.

[274]For details of the trial see: Private Controversies, Connecticut State Library, 3: 114-134 or Adams and Stiles, *History of Ancient Wethersfield,* 1: 899-902.

[275] Ava Chamberlain, *The Notorious Elizabeth Tuttle, Marriage, Murder, and Madness in the Family of Jonathan Edwards,* New York University Press, (New York: New York University Press, 2012), 144.

[276] Almost 400 years later the main channel of the Connecticut River has moved so far west that Pewter Pot Brook no longer flows into the main channel, but into Keeney Cove a mile to the east.

[277] Alonzo B. Chapin, *Glastenbury for Two Hundred Years,* facsimile of the 1853 edition (Hartford, Conn: Finlay Brothers, 1976), 182.

[278] Almost 400 years later the main channel of the Connecticut River has moved so far west that Pewter Pot Brook no longer flows into the main channel, but into Keeney Cove a mile to the east.

[279] Marjorie Grant McNulty, *Glastonbury: From Settlement to Suburb,* ([Glastonbury, Conn.]: Woman's Club of Glastonbury, 1970), 17.

Chapter VI: Justice of the Peace

[280] For correspondence on the issue of the Quo Warrantos, see Trumbull, *Public Records 1678-1689,* 347-367.

[281] Trumbull, *Public Records 1678-1689,* 368-381.

[282] Charles J. Hoadly, *The Hiding of the Charter,* Publication 2 (Hartford: Case, Lockwood & Brainard, 1900, 12-13.

[283] Bulkeley, *Will and Doom,* 137.

[284] Trumbull, *Public Records 1678-1689,* 248.

[285] Roger Wolcott, "A Memoir for the History of Connecticut," *Collections of the Connecticut Historical Society,* vol. 3: (Hartford: 1860), 3: 321-336.

[286] Benjamin Trumbull, *A Complete History of Connecticut, Civil and Ecclesiastical, from the Emigration of its First Planters from England, in the Year 1630, to the Year 1764; and to the Close of the Indian Wars,* 2 vols. (New Haven, Conn.: Maltby, Goldsmith and Co. and Samuel Wadsworth, 1818), 1: 371-372.

[287] Trumbull, *Public Records 1678-1689,* 402-405, 411-415.

[288] Trumbull, *Public Records 1678-1689,* 424.

[289] Annie Eliot Trumbull, *Records of the Particular Court of the Colony of Connecticut. Administration of Sir Edmund Andros, Royal Governor, 1687-1688* (Hartford, Conn: privately printed,1935) 3.

[290] No one of this name has been identified. The closest match seems to be Joseph Mallerie of New Haven who was convicted of rape in 1706. (*Court of Assistants, 406-7.)*

[291] A. E. Trumbull, *Records of the Particular Court of the Colony of Connecticut. Administration of Sir Edmund Andros,* 3.

[292] A. E. Trumbull, *Records of the Particular Court of the Colony of Connecticut. Administration of Sir Edmund Andros*, 27-28.

[293] A. E. Trumbull, *Records of the Particular Court of the Colony of Connecticut. Administration of Sir Edmund Andros*, 16.

[294] MS 1, Gershom Bulkeley Manuscripts, 1661-1721, Lyman Stowe Library, University of Connecticut.

[295] Jodziewicz, "A Stranger in the Land", 27, 91.

[296] MS 1, Gershom Bulkeley Manuscripts, 1661-1721, Lyman Stowe Library, University of Connecticut.

[297] Trumbull, *Public Records 1665-1678*, 33.

[298] Trumbull, *Public Records 1665-1678*, 111.

[299] Trumbull, *Public Records* 1678-1689, 26.

Chapter VII: Opponent of Connecticut's Government

[300] John Gorham Palfrey, *History of New England*, vol. 3 (Boston: Little, Brown & Co., 1879), 574.

[301] Gershom Bulkeley, "The People's Right to Election or Alteration of Government in Connecticut Argued in a Letter," repr in *Collections of the Connecticut Historical Society*, vol.1, (Hartford: 1860 1:58-81, orig. (Philadelphia Assignees of William Bradford,1689). Hereinafter "The People's Right."

[302] *Bulkeley, Will and Doom*, 150-151.

[303] *Bulkeley, Will and Doom*, 152-160.

[304] Trumbull, *Public Records 1665-1678*, 456 fn.

[305] Bulkeley, *Will and Doom*, 237.

[306] Bulkeley, "The People's Right", 59-75

[307] Bulkeley, "The People's Right", 59.

[308] Adams and Stiles, *History of Ancient Wethersfield*, 2:153.

[309] Bulkeley, "The People's Right", 59-75.

[310] Bulkeley, *Will and Doom*, 157-159.

[311] Bulkeley, *Will and Doom*, 162.

[312] *Bulkeley, Will and Doom*, 198-1199.

[313] Trumbull, *Public Records* 1678-1689, 252.

[314] Bulkeley, "The People's Right", 1.

[315] Richard S. Dunn, *Puritans and Yankees, the Winthrop Dynasty of New England, 1630-1717* (Princeton, N.J.: Princeton University Press, 1962), 289. (citing Winthrop Mss. XI, 89.)

[316] Bulkeley, *Will and Doom*, 167-8.

[317] Bulkeley, *Will and Doom*, 168.

[318] Bulkeley, *Will and Doom*, 163.

[319] Charles J. Hoadly, ed., *Hoadly Memorial: Early Letters and Documents Relating to Connecticut, 1643-1709, gathered by Charles J. Hoadly* [*Connecticut Historical Society Collections*, vol. 24] (Hartford: Connecticut Historical Society, 1932), 37-39.

[320] Bulkeley, *Will and Doom*, 164-5.

[321] Charles J. Hoadly, ed., *The Public Records of the Colony of Connecticut, 1689-1706*, vol. 4 (Hartford, Conn.: Case, Lockwood and Brainard, vol., ,6. Hereinafter *Public Records 1689-1706*.

[322] Bulkeley, *Will and Doom*, 205-209.

[323] Bulkeley, *Will and Doom*, 205-206.

[324] Bulkeley, *Will and Doom*, 209-211.

[325] *Crimes & Misdemeanors*, Connecticut State Library, 1:165-166, 168.

[326] Chamberlain, *The Notorious Elizabeth* Tuttle, 68, 90.

[327] *Crimes & Misdemeanors*, 1:167, 172,173,175,178.

[328] See *Court of Assistants*, 135-136.

[329] *Crimes & Misdemeanors*, 1: 170-178, 181.

[330] The original document in *Crimes & Misdemeanors*, 1:182, has faded and is barely legible, but the full text was published in 1895 as a footnote in *Will and Doom*, 232-233.

[331] *Crimes & Misdemeanors*, Connecticut State Library, 1: 180.

[332] *Court of Assistants*, 152.

[333] Trumbull, *Public Records 1678-1689*, 255.

[334] Bulkeley, *Will and Doom*, 291.

[335] Bulkeley, *Will and Doom*, 74.

[336] Bulkeley, *Will and Doom*, 73.

[337] Bulkeley, *Will and Doom*, 74.

[338] Trumbull, *The Public Records of the Colony of Connecticut, 1678-1689*, 389.

[339] *War*, 2: 159.

[340] Hoadly., *Hoadly Memorial*, 49-52.

[341] J. W. Fortescue, ed., *Calendar of State Papers Colonial, America and West Indies, 1689-1692* (London: Her Majesty's Stationery Office, 1901), 13: 704-5.

---

[342] John Romeyn Brodhead, ed., *Documents relative to the Colonial History of the State of New York: procured in Holland, England and France,* 10 vols. (Albany: Weed, Parsons 1853-1887), 3:849-854.
[343] The copy of the petition found in *Calendar of State Papers* is somewhat altered, particularly in the final paragraph which is made less passionate.
[344] Gershom Bulkeley, *Some Seasonable Considerations for the Good People of Connecticut,* (New York: William Bradford, 1694), 1-63.
[345] Bulkeley, *Some Seasonable Considerations,* 31.
[346] Bulkeley, *Will and Doom,* 233-234.
[347] Bulkeley, *Will and Doom,* 235 fn by Charles J. Hoadly.

Chapter VIII: *Will & Doom*
[348]Hoadly, *Hoadly Memorial,* 55-56
[349] Bulkeley, *Will and Doom,* 99-269.
[350] Bulkeley, *Will and Doom,* 229.
[351] Bulkeley, *Will and Doom,* 227.
[352] *Crimes & Misdemeanors,* 2:182.
[353] Bulkeley, *Will and Doom,* 233.
[354] Bulkeley, *Will and Doom,* 233-234.
[355] Dunn, *Puritans and Yankees,* 315-319.
[356] Bulkeley, *Will and Doom,* 140.
[357] Bulkeley, *Will and Doom,* 182.
[358] Bulkeley, *Will and Doom,* 173.
[359] Bulkeley, *Will and Doom,* 177-8
[360] Bulkeley, *Will and Doom,* 145.
[361] Henry Alworth Merewether and Archibald John Stephens, *"The History of Boroughs and Municipal Corporations of the United Kingdom from the earliest to the present time: with Examination of Records, Charters, and Other Documents Illustrative of Their Constitution and Powers* in three volumes (London: Stevens and Pardon, 1835), 3:1836-1839.
[362] Bulkeley, *Will and Doom,* 182-183.
[363] Bulkeley, *Will and Doom,* 184.
[364] Bulkeley, *Will and Doom,* 183.
[365] Bulkeley, *Will and Doom,* 84.
[366] Bulkeley, *Will and Doom,* 135.

[367] Bulkeley, *Will and Doom*, 84.

[368] Bulkeley, *Will and Doom*, 181.

[369] Bulkeley, *Will and Doom*, 257.

[370] Bulkeley, *Will and Doom*, 190.

[371] Hoadly, *Public Records*1689-1706, 88.

[372] Hoadly, *Public Records*1689-1706, 100.

[373] *Colonial State Papers*, 14:73.

[374] Hoadly, *Hoadly Memorial*,56-57.

[375] It is not clear why Fletcher called this the Queens's letter.

[376] *Colonial State Papers*, 14:173-174.

[377] J.W. Fortescue, ed., *Calendar of State Papers, Colonial Series, America and west Indies, January 1693 – 14 May 1696, (London:* Mackie & Co. Ltd., 1908),172-179, 194-199. Hereinafter, *Calendar of State Papers.*

[378] Brodhead, *Documents Relative to the Colonial History of the State of New York,* 4:71-72.

[379] *Calendar of State Papers*, 205-206.

[380] Hoadly, *Public Records*, 192.

[381] Hoadly, *Hoadly Memorial*, 59.

[382] See the website of the Connecticut State Library, https://ctstatelibrary.org/governors, for details of Fitz-John Winthrop's life.

[383] Jodziewicz, *A Stranger in the Land*, 58-59.

[384] Dunn, *Puritans and Yankees*, 235.

[385] Dunn, *Puritans and Yankees*, 301.

[386] MHS Collections 6th series, vol.3, 398-400.

[387] Treat and Allyn, *Connecticut Vindicated*, 83-130.

[388] CHS Collections, Vol. 1, 102-104.

[389] Treat and Allyn, *Connecticut Vindicated*, 88-89.

[390] Treat and Allyn, *Connecticut Vindicated*,126.

[391] Treat and Allyn, *Connecticut Vindicated*, 95.

[392] Treat and Allyn, *Connecticut Vindicated*, 91.

[393] Treat and Allyn, *Connecticut Vindicated*, 86.

[394] Treat and Allyn, *Connecticut Vindicated*, 112

[395] Treat and Allyn, *Connecticut Vindicated*, 121.

[396] Hoadly, *Hoadly Memorial*, 89-95.

[397] Hoadly, *Hoadly Memorial*, 95-97.

398 Bulkeley, *Will and Doom*, preface, 77-79.

Chapter IX: Dairies & Correspondence
399 Bulkeley spelled the name Disborough, but court records often use Desborough. Mercy's husband spelled his name as Disbrow and the surviving family name is Disbrow.

400 Thomas W. Jodziewicz, "The 1699 Diary of Gershom Bulkeley of Wethersfield, Connecticut"", Transactions of the American Philosophical Society, Vol. 131, No. 4 (Philadelphia, Pa.: American Philosophical Society, 1987), 425-441.

401 Hoadly Autograph Collection, Box 7, Folder 7, Connecticut Historical Society, Hartford Connecticut.

402 Jodziewicz, "The 1699 Diary of Gershom Bulkeley", 434.

403 Manwaring, *A Digest of the Early Connecticut Probate Records*, 2: 165.

404 Jodziewicz, "The 1699 Diary of Gershom Bulkeley", 438, probably Johannes Segerus von Weidenfeld.

405 Norman Gevitz, "Apothecaries and the Drug Trade: Essays in Celebration of the Work of David L. Cowen", *American Institute of the History of Pharmacy 19* (new series) (Madison, Wisc.: University of Wisconsin, 2001), 10.

406 Gevitz, "Apothecaries and the Drug Trade", 18.

407 [Henry H. Edes?], "Note on Benjamin Davis, the Loyalist" Publications of the Colonial Society of Massachusetts", Transactions 1899, 1900 (Boston: The Colonial Society of Massachusetts, 1904), 124-125.

408 Caulkins, *History of New London*, 222-228.

409 Caulkins, *History of New London*, 226

410 R.R. Hinman, comp., *Letters from the English Kings and Queens, Charles II, James II, William and Mary, Anne, George II, Etc. to the Governors of the Colony of Connecticut Together with the Answers Thereto, from 1635 to 1749* (Hartford: John B. Eldridge Printer, 1836), 274-278.

411 Jefferies Family Papers, Massachusetts Historical Society, "Papers of David Jefferies III, 1652-1713, box 5, vol. 5 (also microfilm, P493, reel 1), Letter of Gershom Bulkeley to Capt. Benjamin Davis at Boston, dated Wethersfield, 18 May 1699.

[412] Hoadly, *Public Records 1689-1706*, 303-305.

[413] Collections of the Massachusetts Historical Society, 6th Ser., vol. 5, (Cambridge, Mass.: University Press; John Wilson & Son, 1892), 51-52.

[414] Jefferies Family Papers, Letter of Gershom Bulkeley to Capt. Benjamin Davis at Boston, dated Wethersfield, 24 June 1700.

[415] Jodziewicz, "A Stranger in the Land", 8-10.

[416] Jefferies Family Papers, Letter of Gershom Bulkeley to Capt. Benjamin Davis at Boston, dated Wethersfield, 25 March 1701, also, in Jodziewicz, "A Stranger in the Land", 53.

[417] Woodward, *Prospero's America*, 202.

[418] "Memoir of Rev. Benjamin Davis, D.D.", Register, 3 (April 1849), 119-122.

[419] "Memoir of Rev. Benjamin Davis, D.D.", Register, 3 (July 1849), 222-223.

[420] Manwaring, *A Digest of the Early Connecticut Probate Records*, 2:29.

[421] Jacobus, *The Bulkeley Genealogy,* 136.

[422] Jefferies Family Papers, Letter of Gershom Bulkeley to Capt. Benjamin Davis at Boston, dated Wethersfield, 3 April 1704.

[423] Jefferies Family Papers, Letter of Gershom Bulkeley to Capt. Benjamin Davis at Boston, dated Wethersfield, 18 May 1699.

[424] It is not clear who was meant here.

[425] Jodziewicz, "1699 Diary of Gershom Bulkeley," 441.

[426] Gevitz, "Apothecaries and the Drug Trade," 18, 20.

[427] Gevitz, "Apothecaries and the Drug Trade," 18.

Chapter X: Scientist & Alchemist

[428] Woodward, *Prospero's America*, 243.

[429] Paracelsus (1493-1541) was a Swiss German scientist of the Renaissance who published widely on alchemy. He believed that alchemy was not just for making precious metal, but had great power in medicine for curing disease.

[430] Allen G. Debus, *The Chemical Philosophy: Paracelsian Science and Medicine in the Sixteenth and Seventeenth Centuries,* 2 vols. bound as 1 (New York: Watson Academic Publications, 1977; repr Minneola, New

York: Dover Publications, 2002), 1, citing Paracelsus, *Paragranum* (1530). Hereinafter, *The Chemical Philosophy*.
[431] Jan Baptist van Helmont (1580-1644), a Dutch alchemist and physician, carried the work of Paracelsus to a higher level.
[432] Debus, *The Chemical Philosophy* 46.
[433] Jodziewicz, "A Stranger in the Land", 78.
[434] Woodward, *Prospero's America*, 200 - 202.
[435] Alan G. Debus, *The Chemical Philosophy*, 19.
[436] Woodward, *Prospero's America*, 204.
[437] Woodward, *Prospero's America*, 255, 262.
[438] See Woodward, *Prospero's America*, Chapter 8, for a full discussion of Winthrop's developing and sustaining links to a supporting network of English alchemists which were critical to winning and retaining Connecticut's charter rights.
[439] Debus, *The Chemical Philosophy,* 46.
[440] MS 18, Gershom Bulkeley Manuscripts, University of Connecticut, 129.
[441] Woodward, *Prospero's America*, 264-265.
[442] Jodziewicz, "A Stranger in the Land", 79.
[443] Jodziewicz, "A Stranger in the Land", 83.
[444] Jodziewicz, "A Stranger in the Land", 73-94
[445] Jodziewicz, "A Stranger in the Land", 73-92.
[446] These come from the former holdings of the Hartford Medical Society Historical Library.
[447] Notebook 1679, MS 4, Gershom Bulkeley Manuscripts University of Connecticut, entry 45.
[448] Jodziewicz, "A Stranger in the Land", 78.
[449] MS 13, Gershom Bulkeley Manuscripts, University of Connecticut.
[450] Gershom Bulkeley, Account Book and Medical Notes, 2 boxes, Watkinson Library, Trinity College, Hartford, Conn., Medical MS 7.
[451] Johannes Segerus Weidenfeld, *Concerning ye Secrets of ye Adepts or ye Use of Lully's Spirits of Wine, A Practical Work With a Very Great Study Collected Out of the Ancient, as well as Modern, Fathers of Adept Philosophy, Reconciled Together,* printed by Will Bonny for Tho. Hawkins in George-Yard in Lombard Street, London,1685. See Medical Notebook, MS 7.
[452] Medical Notebook, MS 7, Watkinson Library, 10.

[453] *Vade Mecum,* MS 6, Gershom Bulkeley Manuscripts, University of Connecticut, preface 27.

[454] MS 11, Gershom Bulkeley Manuscripts, University of Connecticut.

[455] It is possible that Bulkeley was quoting Boyle.

[456] Notebook 1679, MS 4, Gershom Bulkeley Manuscripts University of Connecticut, 138.

[457] Allen G. Debus, *Chemistry and Medical Debate, van Helmont to Boerhaave* (Canton, MA: Science History Publications, 2001), 46-47.

[458] *Vade Mecum*, MS 6, Gershom Bulkeley Manuscripts. University of Connecticut, 52.

[459] *Vade Mecum*, MS 6, Gershom Bulkeley Manuscripts. University of Connecticut, 47-49.

[460] *Vade Mecum*, MS 6, Gershom Bulkeley Manuscripts. University of Connecticut, 42-43.

[461] *Vade Mecum*, MS 6, Gershom Bulkeley Manuscripts. University of Connecticut, 49.

[462] *Vade Mecum*, MS 6, Gershom Bulkeley Manuscripts. University of Connecticut, 275-278.

[463] *Vade Mecum*, MS 6, Gershom Bulkeley Manuscripts. University of Connecticut, 160-173.

[464] *Vade Mecum*, MS 6, Gershom Bulkeley Manuscripts. University of Connecticut, 168-169.

[465] Woodward, *Prospero's America*, 195 where Woodward noted, "Rubila was not John Winthrop's most frequently prescribed medication, or even nearly so, but, because it was widely distributed by his sons after his death, many historians incorrectly assumed that is was Winthrop's primary prescription."

[466] Howard Pearson, "Colonial Pediatrics in the 1600s: Governor John Winthrop the Younger of Connecticut," *Pediatrics* 126 (September 2010), 405-407.

[467] Oliver Wendell Holmes, *Medical Essays, 1842-1882* (Boston: Houghton, Mifflin & Co., 1883) 335.

[468] *Vade Mecum*, MS 6, Gershom Bulkeley Manuscripts. University of Connecticut, 223.

[469] *Vade Mecum*, MS 6, Gershom Bulkeley Manuscripts. University of Connecticut, 311.

[470] *Vade Mecum*, MS 6, Gershom Bulkeley Manuscripts. University of Connecticut, [312]

[471] *Vade Mecum*, MS 6, Gershom Bulkeley Manuscripts, University of Connecticut, 313-319.

[472] Several sources say she was born in 1668, but this seems unlikely. Gershom Bulkeley did not leave New London until 1668. Also, her husband Richard Treat was born about 1675 and they were married in 1704.

[473] Charles W. Hoadly, ed, *The Public Records of the Colony of Connecticut from October 1706 to October 1716 with Council Journal from October 1710 to February 1717*, vol. 5 (Hartford, Conn.: Case Lockwood & Brainard, 1870), 153-154. Hereinafter *Public Records 1706-1716*.

[474] Trumbull, *Public Records* 1678-1689, 218.

Chapter XI: Bulkeley Restored

[475] Dexter, *Documentary History of Yale University*, 9-12.

[476] Hoadly, *Public Records 1706-1716*, 363-365.

[477] Hoadly, *Public Records 1689-1706*, 234.

[478] *Court of Assistants*, 389-396.

[479] *Winthrop Papers*, vol. 3, (Boston: Massachusetts Historical Society, 1889), 399, 403.

[480] Hoadly, *Public Records*, 1706-1716, 28,62,65.

[481] MS 5, Gershom Bulkeley Manuscripts, University of Connecticut.

[482] Frederick Kyle Satterstrom, "Alchemy and Alchemical Knowledge in Seventeenth-Century New England", (Bachelor's degree thesis, Harvard University, 2004), 67.

[483] Jacobus, *The Bulkeley Genealogy*, 111-128.

[484] Chapman, *The Bulkeley Family*, 90.

[485] Jacobus, *The Bulkeley Genealogy*, 138.

[486] Manwaring, *A Digest of the Early Connecticut Probate Records*, 2:165-167.

[487] Chapman, *The Bulkeley Family*, 85.

[488] Hartford County, County Court Records 1706-1881, Connecticut State Library, March 1706/7 – November 1717 (Executions) 1716 – 1756, vols. 1&2, 403.

[489] Hartford County, Superior Court Files, 1711-1899, Connecticut State Library, container box 2, 1715-1718, vol. 64; 95, 142.

[490] Court Records 1706-1881, Testimony of Abijah Hollister, 19 April 1714.

[491] MS 2, Gershom Bulkeley Manuscripts, University of Connecticut

[492] Jodziewicz, "Stranger in the Land," 73-92.

[493] J.H. Temple, *History of North Brookfield, Massachusetts* (Boston: Town of North Brookfield, 1887). Reverend James was in the process of becoming the minister at Wethersfield.

[494] Sibley, *Sibley's Harvard Graduates,* 1:397.

Retrospective

[495] Kevin Murphy, *Crowbar Governor: The Life and Times of Morgan Gardner Bulkeley* (Middletown, Conn: Wesleyan Press, 2011).

[496] Woodward, *Prospero's America*, 210-213.

[497] Richard Tomlinson, *Witchcraft Prosecution: Chasing the Devil in Connecticut* (Rockland, ME: Picton Press, 2012), 173-175.

[498] Wyllys Papers Supplement, 35-6.

[499] McNulty, 17.

[500] Trumbull, Public Records (1665-1678), 388-389.

[501] Letter of Gershom Bulkeley to Joseph Bulkeley, Bulkeley Papers, Connecticut Historical Society.

[502] Treat and Allyn, *Connecticut Vindicated*, 112.

[503] MS-1, Gershom Bulkeley Manuscripts, Lyman-Stowe Library, University of Connecticut.

* 9 7 8 0 5 7 8 4 1 5 0 9 3 *